The Long Weekend

THE LONG WEEKEND

LIFE IN THE ENGLISH COUNTRY HOUSE,
1918–1939

Adrian Tinniswood

BASIC BOOKS
A Member of the Perseus Books Group
New York

357 0845

Books published by Basic Books are available at special discounts for bulk purchases in the United States by corporations, institutions, and other organizations. For more information, please contact the Special Markets Department at the Perseus Books Group, 2300 Chestnut Street, Suite 200, Philadelphia, PA 19103, or call (800) 810-4145, ext. 5000, or e-mail special.markets@perseusbooks.com.

Designed by Jack Lenzo

Library of Congress Cataloging-in-Publication Data
Names: Tinniswood, Adrian.
Title: The long weekend : life in the English country house, 1918-1939 /
  Adrian Tinniswood.
Description: New York : Basic Books, a member of the Perseus Books Group,
  2016. | Includes bibliographical references and index.
Identifiers: LCCN 2015049302 (print) | LCCN 2015049573 (ebook) | ISBN
  9780465048984 (hardback) | ISBN 9780465098651 (ebook) | ISBN 9780465098651
  (e-book)
Subjects: LCSH: England--Social life and customs--20th century. | Country
  homes--England--History--20th century. | Mansions--England--History--20th
  century. | Country life--England--History--20th century. | Aristocracy
  (Social class)--England--History--20th century. | Aristocracy (Social
  class)--England--Biography. | Landowners--England--History--20th century.
  | Social change--England--History--20th century. | England--Social
  conditions--20th century. | BISAC: HISTORY / Europe / Great Britain. |
  HISTORY / Modern / 20th Century. | HISTORY / Military / World War I. |
  HISTORY / Military / World War II.
Classification: LCC DA566.4 .T56 2016 (print) | LCC DA566.4 (ebook) | DDC
  305.5/2094209042--dc23
LC record available at http://lccn.loc.gov/2015049302

10 9 8 7 6 5 4 3 2 1

For my friend
Godfrey Napthine
1954–2015

People who formerly lived in very large houses are now getting out of them. As to who goes in is another matter.

COUNTRY LIFE (OCTOBER 25, 1919)

"It's rather sad," she said one day, "to belong, as we do, to a lost generation. I'm sure in history the two wars will count as one war and that we shall be squashed out of it altogether, and people will forget that we ever existed. We might just as well never have lived at all, I do think it's a shame."

NANCY MITFORD, *THE PURSUIT OF LOVE* (1945)

CONTENTS

FOREWORD

THERE IS NOTHING QUITE AS beautiful as an English country house in summer.

And there has never been a summer quite like that Indian summer between the two world wars, a period of gentle decline in which the sun set slowly on the British Empire and the shadows lengthened on the lawns of a thousand stately homes across the nation.

At least, that is the conventional view of a period that has always been seen as witnessing the end of the country house. One by one, so the story goes, the stately homes of England were deserted and dismantled and demolished, their estates broken up, their oaks felled, and their parks given over to suburban sprawl.

There's certainly truth in that. But it masks an alternative narrative that exists side by side with the familiar tale of woe. A narrative that saw new families buying, borrowing, and sometimes building themselves a country house, which introduced new aesthetics, new social structures, new meanings to an old tradition. A narrative, in fact, that saw new life in the country house. That is what *The Long Weekend* is all about.

1

THE HOUSE PARTY

In 1931 John Galsworthy, the gentle chronicler of a passing age, captured the essence of a certain type of interwar house party, in all its lovely, lazy, languorous tedium. "One day is very like another," he wrote:

> The men put on the same kind of variegated tie and the same plus fours, eat the same breakfast, tap the same barometer, smoke the same pipes and kill the same birds. The dogs wag the same tails, lurk in the same unexpected spots, utter the same agonised yelps, and chase the same pigeons on the same lawns. The ladies have the same breakfast in bed or not, put the same salts in the same bath, straggle in the same garden, say of the same friends with the same spice of animosity, 'I'm frightfully fond of them, of course'; pore over the same rock borders with the same passion for *Portulaca* [moss roses]; play the same croquet or tennis with the same squeaks; write the same letters to contradict the same rumours, or match the same antiques.[1]

Perfect. Yet in defining the house party, in pinning down the sameness, Galsworthy allowed something of its infinite variety to escape. Country-house parties were not all the same.

Some were small, intimate affairs involving half a dozen old friends. Others were big and formal and packed with dignitaries. In November 1934, for example, the Duke and Duchess of Devonshire entertained twenty guests at Chatsworth for one of their grandest parties. Guests of honor were the Princess Royal and the Earl of Harewood, who hadn't visited since 1921 when the earl, then Viscount Lascelles, proposed to his princess. Shooting parties were laid on for the Saturday and the Monday, and the Devonshires invited a glittering gaggle of acquaintances for the weekend to meet the royal couple, including the Duke and Duchess of Portland from Welbeck Abbey, the Marquess and Marchioness of Londonderry, art historian Kenneth Clark, and Conservative politician Lord Hugh Cecil.

Some house parties lasted no more than forty-eight hours. Others went on for an awfully long time: in Scotland, a long train ride from London, an invitation to shoot often meant a visit of three weeks. Besides meeting royalty and shooting, many parties were convened for a particular purpose. In January 1935, Chips Channon and his wife drove up to Lincolnshire to stay with Lord Brownlow, better known as Peregrine Cust, the courtier who the following year would take Wallis Simpson to France while her lover renounced his throne. Fellow guests at Brownlow's seventeenth-century Belton House were Duff and Diana Cooper, Viscount and Viscountess Weymouth, and Lieutenant-Colonel the Hon. Piers Legh and his American wife. Channon was a little overwhelmed by Belton; it was "almost overful of treasures," he thought. And his fellow guests were "frankly bores."[2] (Being rude about the company was part of the fun: Harold Nicolson, who stayed with the Channons in Austria in September 1936, thought them "a trifle vulgar."[3]) The real purpose of the gathering lay elsewhere. After dinner, the party set out in cars for an invitation ball the Duke and Duchess of Rutland were holding for their two teenage daughters at Belvoir Castle, ten miles away.

Channon was altogether more impressed with Belvoir. The ducal daughters both looked beautiful; colored lights in the trees lit the way up to the house; and the ball, with music by Emilio Colombo and his orchestra, was "a glorious Disraelian festival, and the castle illuminations could be seen for miles."[4] Violet, the seventy-eight-year-old dowager duchess of Rutland (and mother of Diana Cooper), cut a particularly imposing figure in white, surrounded by her descendants, thirty of them, including a gaggle of small grandsons in black suits.

A fortnight after the Belvoir ball, the Rutlands hosted a small house party for guests who were going to a charity ball in aid of nearby Grantham Hospital. It was common, usual even, to host a house party for events like this: a trip to the races, a ball, a political gathering. The Earl of Harewood hosted one every year at Harewood House for the Doncaster Races; the Duke of Westminster did the same for Aintree. In April 1932 Lady Warwick hosted a small party at Warwick Castle for Prime Minister Baldwin, Lady Warwick's brother-in-law Anthony Eden, then the undersecretary for foreign affairs, and their wives. They were also there for a purpose: to attend the opening by the Prince of Wales of the new Shakespeare Memorial Theatre at Stratford-on-Avon, which took place on Shakespeare's birthday, Saturday, April 23.

Like the Channons' visit to Belton and the Warwick Castle party, most country-house parties were weekend affairs. Born out of a burgeoning railway network—there was after all no point in going away for a weekend if you spent the entire weekend traveling to where you wanted to be—and helped along by the rise in car ownership, the very word "weekend" had only just joined the lexicon of leisure. A contributor to *Notes & Queries* at the end of the nineteenth century wrote that in Staffordshire "if a person leaves home at the end of his week's work . . . to spend the evening of Saturday and the following Sunday with friends at a distance, he is said to be spending his *week-end* at So-and-so."[5] Was this usage confined to Staffordshire?, he asked.

By the 1920s the country-house weekend was an institution, although in polite circles it still wasn't actually *called* a weekend. The accepted phrase was "Saturday-to-Monday." The Duchess of Buccleuch recalled that it was "awfully non-U to call them weekends. I remember being surprised that anyone should use the term."[6] The phrase also distinguished the leisured classes from those who had to be at work first thing on Monday morning, and for whom a weekend began on Saturday afternoon and ended on Sunday evening. People invited you "for a Saturday to Monday and that was precisely what they meant," said Loelia Ponsonby. "It would have been very rude to leave on Sunday night."[7]

How did it work? Whether a Saturday-to-Monday or a more extended stay, the country-house party began with invitations given and received.

Turn-of-the-century etiquette manuals were full of fiendishly complicated instructions on the theory and practice of invitations, how they must be worded, when they must be sent, and how they should be responded to, along with dire warnings of the catastrophic social consequences of transgressing them. "To widely depart from any of these received canons of etiquette," cautioned Maud C. Cooke in the classic *Manners and Customs of Polite Society*, "is to commit a decided solecism and to discover an utter unfitness for the desired social rank."[8] But the interwar years were changing times: by the early 1940s Stephen Tennant could ask Sibyl Colefax down to his Wiltshire country house for the weekend by simply writing "Sybil dearest, do come to Wilsford soon. Suggest a day. I will meet you at the station."[9]

To be sure, there were plenty of people who would regard *that* degree of informality as a decided solecism, if not a signal that civilization was teetering on the edge of extinction, but the times were changing. Laura, Lady Troubridge, a baronet's wife whose books on etiquette and entertaining were best sellers in the 1920s and 1930s, announced in 1939 that "the new etiquette is informal":

> Remember you are of your day, and of your time, and therefore you will not be doing the wrong thing if you accept this new spirit, and waive any petty, cramping little rules which were intended for another, and far more formal, age.[10]

What did it matter if you felt sleepy and got up to go to your room at a house party before your hostess had authorized your departure from the drawing room, or invited friends to stay over by telephone

"THE NEW ETIQUETTE IS INFORMAL": CECIL BEATON HOSTING A
WEEKEND PARTY AT ASHCOMBE WITH, FROM LEFT, ADELE ASTAIRE,
PRINCESS POLNY, TALLULAH BANKHEAD, AND TILLY LOSCH. (Copy-
right: Sasha/Getty Images)

rather than by letter, or used someone's Christian name when you had
only just been introduced? "Simplicity—that's the key-word for social
demeanour nowadays."[11]

Having accepted an invitation to spend a few days in the country,
the next hurdle was deciding what clothes to take. "One's clothes were
a worry," said Lady Marjorie Stirling, daughter of the Earl of Dun-
more. Even for a seven-day shooting party, a woman was expected to
dress for every day of the week. "There were very rich people who had
marvellous clothes, but on the whole one just scraped through."[12]

Loelia Ponsonby suffered agonies on her first visit to the Duke
of Westminster's Eaton Hall, going down to meet the rest of the
guests in the library that evening in a recently bought chiffon dress,
"a singularly inappropriate choice for December," she remembered
with a shiver, and appearing the following morning in a "reach-me-
down green tweed suit."[13] (The Ponsonbys were always hard up. When

Loelia came out, she had to re-cover her worn-out dancing shoes, dipping the heels in red ink and stitching black satin above the soles.)

Here again, Laura Troubridge was on hand with words of advice. Avoid anything too smart. Otherwise, when you get into a muddy lane, "you will wish you had chosen a classically plain tweed coat and skirt, the skirt wide enough to walk in, and the colour a soft tone to melt into the landscape."[14]

Once the invitation had been accepted and the right clothes were packed, the next step was to get to one's weekend destination. If that destination weren't too far from town, and sometimes even if it was, a leisurely drive was the usual option. In the summer of 1935 (and on a Friday—Saturday-to-Monday seems to have been a movable feast), the Channons motored down from London to Longleat in Wiltshire. It was quite a long journey, well over a hundred miles, and they took their time, stopping off on the way to picnic and have a snooze in a field. Everything was quite relaxed, as was their reception. "We found the splendid domain lying in the full heat of a June day," Chips wrote in his diary, "with its amber-stone, gardens, dogs and almost overpowering beauty."[15]

Loelia Ponsonby's arrival at the Earl of Lonsdale's Lowther Castle in the 1920s was anything but relaxed. She and her mother traveled up to the earl's Westmorland house by train, and they were greeted on the platform at Penrith Station by a groom clad in buckskin breeches, high boots, a cloth coat in the Lonsdale yellow, and a beaver hat. He conducted them to a coachman waiting in an open, yellow landau drawn by a pair of cream-colored horses, and when the two women were safely ensconced, the groom leapt up beside the liveried coachman, and the landau set off on a stately progress through the town, leaving the Ponsonbys' luggage to follow in a yellow van.

When Marmaduke Furness invited Thelma Converse up to his shooting lodge near Inverness in August 1925 for the start of the grouse season, she also went by train. So did he, and his staff—valet, three footmen, and two housemaids. Thelma had barely settled into her compartment before the valet knocked and informed her that dinner was ready. She found her host waiting in a sleeping compartment, which his staff had converted into a temporary private dining room, with white tablecloth, champagne in ice buckets, and a picnic basket packed with all kinds of delicacies. "What, no plover eggs?" she asked, at which he took her in his arms and told her he loved her—a carefully planned stratagem, with a predictable outcome.

Lady Marjorie Sterling never forgot the social anxiety of arrival at a strange house. "I always found it very alarming, driving up a long drive, not knowing what to expect," she said. "The door would be opened by the butler and you were ushered into a room full of people, nearly always strangers. It made me feel quite sick."[16]

It was usual to arrive around teatime, or soon afterward. When Wallis and Ernest Simpson drove down to Fort Belvedere to spend their first weekend with the Prince of Wales, they timed their journey to arrive at six on Saturday, bringing Wallis's maid Mary with them in the car. (Sometimes guests arrived with their own personal servants, sometimes they came alone, in which case a resident footman or maid would be deputed to look after them.) The Simpsons were greeted at the door by the prince himself. He took them into the octagonal drawing room and introduced their fellow guests: Thelma Converse, whose seduction on the night train from Euston had ended in her becoming Viscountess Furness and who had been the prince's mistress for several years; Thelma's sister and brother-in-law; and Gerald Trotter, the prince's groom-in-waiting. After the introductions, the prince personally showed them up to their room.

After dressing for dinner, the Simpsons were back down for cocktails, where they found the prince dressed in a kilt (with a silver cigarette case tucked away in his sporran), working away at his needlepoint and with two cairn terriers at his feet, one of which promptly tried to bite Ernest Simpson's ankle. Dinner was simple: oysters, roast beef, salad, a sweet, and a savory. Afterward, guests were invited to try their hand at a jigsaw puzzle, the pieces of which were spread out on a long table in the drawing room, or to play a hand of cards. Bored, Thelma suggested dancing: the gramophone played "Tea for Two," and the prince took his mistress in his arms and whisked her away into the marble hall. After dancing briefly with Thelma's sister and

Wallis, he announced he was off to bed. "This being your first visit to the fort," he told the Simpsons, "perhaps I should tell you about the rules. There are none. Stay up as late as you want. Get up when you want. I go to bed early and get up early so that I can work in the garden."[17]

They came down to breakfast on Sunday morning and looked out of the window to see their host advancing across the lawn in a sweater and baggy plus fours, and wielding a billhook. He invited them both to join him in hacking back the laurels. "It's not exactly a command," said Gerald Trotter diplomatically, "but I've never known anybody to refuse."[18]

Wallis, whose experience of country-house parties had included several stuffy weekends at Knole with the Sackvilles, was unprepared for the relaxed atmosphere at Fort Belvedere and the relatively simple domesticity of the prince, whose reputation as a fast-living socialite was common knowledge. After a buffet lunch the prince showed the Simpsons round the Fort. "What fascinated me," wrote Wallis later, "was the architectural wizardry that had been exercised in imparting to the interior of this sprawling fort such an atmosphere of warmth and informality . . . For a bachelor's country house, the whole effect was astonishingly warm and attractive."[19]

The Prince of Wales' easygoing approach to his weekend guests was in sharp contrast to the formality of entertaining in some of the great ducal houses, where many of the prewar protocols remained firmly in place. Full evening dress had virtually gone out with the war, but dressing for dinner was still de rigueur, and black tie was the norm. Guests gathered in the drawing room at about seven thirty where a butler assisted by a footman served cocktails, "the worst form of drinking," according to Viscount Astor, because they were taken on an empty stomach and appealed to women and young girls.[20] Particularly popular in the early 1930s were the White Lady (gin, Cointreau, and fresh lemon juice) and the Paradise (gin, apricot brandy, and orange juice), both said to have been invented by Harry Craddock, the legendary barman at the American Bar of the Savoy Hotel from 1920–1938. If it was a big party and most of the guests were strangers to each

other, the hostess discreetly introduced each man to the woman he
was to escort in to dinner.

At 8:00 p.m. the butler announced that dinner was served, and
the guests went in. At some of the grander houses and on more formal
occasions, the strict order of precedence was followed, with the host
leading the way and escorting the woman of highest rank, the woman
second in rank with the man second in rank, and so on. The man of
highest rank would come last, accompanied by the hostess. "Always
consult a *Peerage* or *Baronetage* if in doubt as to the precedence due
to expected guests bearing titles," warned "a Member of the Aristocracy," the anonymous author of the 1916 edition of *Manners and Rules
of Good Society*, that bible of the socially insecure. "Wealth or social
position are not taken into account in this matter, it being strictly a
question of date."[21] With guests whose social rank was hard to deter-
mine, this raised all kinds of problems. Nearly two decades later,
Elizabeth Craig told "the modern hostess" that "there are no hard and
fast rules about placing ordinary people like you and me at a dinner
table."[22] She advised that the only rules to remember where no titles
were involved were to place the principal woman on the husband's
right, and the principal man on the hostess's right, and to separate
husbands and wives where possible.

Once everyone was seated, gloved footmen handed round the
first course. They were supervised by the butler, who usually stationed
himself close to his master's chair or by the sideboard from which he
dispensed wines—sherry after soup, hock with the fish, champagne
for the rest of the meal until dessert, and then claret, sherry, port,
and Madeira. White wine was served just chilled, champagne came
ice cold, and claret with a very slight warmth, which was achieved by
putting it on the hot plate in the server for a few moments.

The typical country-house dinner was a meal of Edwardian proportions. "For a big dinner party, a really posh dinner party," said Viscountess Hambleden, who entertained regularly with her husband
at their country house outside Henley in the 1930s, "you would have
either thick or clear soup, followed by fish, followed by the *entrée*—
chicken or quails. Then you had saddle of lamb or beef; you had

pudding; you had a savoury; and then you had fruit."[23] A Member of
the Aristocracy recommended that young women should steer clear of
the more highly seasoned dishes ("middle-aged and elderly ladies are
at liberty to do pretty much as they please"). They should also avoid
artichokes because it was impossible to eat them elegantly; and "as a
matter of course, young ladies do not eat cheese at dinner-parties."[24]

Servants left the dining room after dessert, and the women set off
for the drawing room ten minutes or so later. Coffee was sometimes
brought in a silver coffeepot, and a woman would pour her own while
the footman or maid held the salver. They were soon joined by the
men: it wasn't fashionable any more to linger over the port for more
than fifteen or twenty minutes, just long enough for the wine to go
round twice and for the men to smoke a cigarette.

After-dinner entertainments depended on the party. Bridge was
common, with several tables set up in the drawing room. "In most
country-house parties bridge forms the chief if not the only amusement," declared *Manners and Rules*, "and is played not only after dinner but in the afternoon also."[25] Dancing to gramophone records was
popular in some circles, as Wallis Simpson had found at Fort Belvedere. On her first evening at Eaton Hall, Loelia Ponsonby was treated
to "that harmless, world-wide, after-dinner amusement, card-tricks."[26]
Major Basil Kerr, the Duke of Westminster's agent for the Eaton
estate and one of his closest friends, was a genius with a pack of cards,
and he and Bendor entertained everyone with their patter and their
sleight of hand.

Musical recitals hadn't quite been superseded by the gramophone
or the wireless. "Mother and Sybil Thorndike used to play duets,"
recalled Lady Molly Trevelyan's daughter Pauline.[27] That's why there
were always two pianos in the drawing room at their house, Wallington Hall in Northumberland. John Christie, an Eton schoolmaster
who took over the running of his family's ten-thousand-acre estate in
1922, was so fond of musical entertainments that he built a brand-new
great hall at his rambling Sussex mansion to house a cathedral-sized
organ so that a friend of his, the recently retired organist at the Chapel
Royal in St. James's, would have something to play. The Organ Room

was the scene of concerts and operatic evenings for guests and local people throughout the 1920s, with Christie taking part along with professional and semiprofessional musicians. He fell in love with one of these visiting performers, a young soprano named Audrey Mildmay, and, after their marriage in 1931, conceived the idea of providing a larger space within the house as a showcase for her talents. The result was the Glyndebourne Festival, which opened its doors to the public for the first time in 1934 with a performance of *Le Nozze di Figaro*.

Sometimes more contemporary entertainments were on offer. Lloyd George was a great film fan, and he used to hold regular Saturday night screenings in the study of his Surrey country house for friends, farm workers, and other local people. His chauffeur had lessons in how to operate the projector, and Lloyd George made the brave decision not to select the films that were sent down from London every Friday, preferring to take potluck. "At a recent Saturday night entertainment," reported the *Guardian* in 1928, "the film turned out to be one of the crudest of love dramas, and at another it was a Charlie Chaplin picture."[28]

BREAKFAST WAS MUCH MORE INFORMAL than dinner. Women guests often preferred to breakfast in their room, as did some hostesses. Men began to assemble when the breakfast gong sounded at nine or nine thirty, but it wasn't usual to wait until everyone was seated, and some guests might not appear until ten or so. If she wasn't still in bed, the hostess would preside over the table, and footmen or maids were in attendance the whole time, serving eggs, sausages, bacon, and deviled kidneys from a hot plate and ham, tongue, and game pie from the sideboard.

When breakfast was over, which might not be until eleven or eleven thirty, the host and hostess would set out the options for the day. "The vital thing was to keep people amused without making them feel too organised," said the Countess of Rosse,[29] a sentiment endorsed by the author of *Manners and Rules*, who noted that the good hostess's "consideration and tact are so successfully exerted that somehow her guests always find themselves doing exactly what they like best and in company with those who are most congenial to them."[30] At Holker Hall in Cumbria, Lady Moyra Cavendish used to make a list of who wanted to go riding, who wanted to fish, and who wanted to play tennis or golf. "There were a great many activities to choose from," her daughter Diana remembered. Jigsaws were popular, left out on a side table in the library or drawing room for anyone to contribute a piece or two. Guests might be taken to see an interesting local church or a picturesque ruin, or shown round the house where they were staying.

During her visit to Westmorland, young Loelia Ponsonby found herself being conducted round Lowther Castle by the aged Earl of Lonsdale, whose anecdotes grew progressively more extravagant as he moved from room to room. Loelia was surprised when he pointed out a small chamber where Mary Queen of Scots had been imprisoned until she made a dramatic escape (Lowther was built by Sir Robert Smirke in 1806–1814, more than two hundred years after Mary's death), and she was frankly astonished when he showed her an iron sledge and told her he had traveled to the North Pole and back in it, pulled by six huskies. She later discovered there was a grain of truth in both stories: Mary Queen of Scots was held at an earlier Lowther after she crossed the border into England on her flight southward, and Lonsdale had undertaken an astonishing journey by sleigh to the Arctic circle and up into northern Alaska in 1888–1889.

Loelia was more impressed when her host, a keen racing man and a senior steward of the Jockey Club, showed her the Lowther stable yard:

> Every morning the grooms had to lay on it a sort of stencil of the Lonsdale arms with numbered partitions and into each partition they sprinkled coloured sawdust with the appropriate number. When the whole thing was complete the stencil was removed and there lay the Lonsdale arms in gorgeous Vistavision.[31]

And each morning the earl would come to inspect it, bringing with him his pack of pet dogs, who scrabbled around in the sand and ruined the grooms' work.

THE HYPERACTIVE PHILIP SASSOON. "THERE IS ALWAYS A SPIRIT OF RESTLESSNESS ABOUT PHILIP'S HOUSES." (Copyright: National Portrait Gallery, London)

At Port Lympne, the hyperactive Sir Philip Sassoon rarely allowed his houseguests to rest, careering around country lanes with them packed in the back of his Rolls, seeking out remote Queen Anne and early Georgian country houses. Philip Tilden, who used to take part in these architectural forays, described one occasion when Sassoon took it into his head that he simply had to gain entry to a lovely late seventeenth-century house near Tenterden on the edge of the Kentish Weald. He strode up to the front door and told the maid-servant who opened it that he was there to see Mrs. Mackintosh, and when she told him that no one of that name lived there, he ordered her to go and look. "Philip's smile, his introductions and his card (which, by the way, might have done the trick without all this scheming and plotting) led us to a pleasant meeting with hospitable people," recalled Tilden, and to a memorable glimpse of "faded rooms with their high, austere panelling, simple and dignified, the sweeping stairs, the old bits of furniture, the chintzes of fifty years before."[32]

Frances Stevenson, who as Lloyd George's mistress and secretary frequently accompanied him to house parties in the 1920s, was exhausted by the Sassoon circus. "There is always a spirit of restlessness about Philip's houses," she wrote in her diary after she and Lloyd George escaped from a boisterous party at Trent Park in May 1921, "always a crowd of people trying to be bright."[33] Their flight may have been influenced this particular weekend by Sassoon extending an invitation to the Dolly Sisters, identical twin dancers who were already as well known for their antics in the casinos and royal bedrooms of Europe as they were for their performances on stage and screen. In the late 1930s Stanley Baldwin told the Tory historian Arthur Bryant of how Sassoon entertained large weekend house parties from London at Trent, with guests including "ladies with painted toe nails." He wasn't present on these occasions, he added hastily.[34]

One constant in any country-house party was the way in which the day's activities were punctuated by lengthy pauses for meals. If there was shooting, the men often disappeared for the day, leaving at eleven and not returning much before seven that evening: on a big shoot, the women guests would join them in the field for lunch and stay on to watch the sport or to join in themselves. Otherwise lunch was served in the dining room, usually at one or one thirty. It was a light meal: a soufflé, perhaps, followed by an entrée, followed by cold meats, followed by a pudding, followed by cheese and dessert.

Then there was afternoon tea at four or four thirty, just a little something to tide everyone over until dinner. Elizabeth Craig suggested a suitable menu: buttered crumpets, buttered date and walnut loaf, cream cheese and pimento sandwiches, maids of honor, coffee éclairs, chocolate sponge roll, and queen cakes.

Early evening was taken up by the rituals of bathing, although the number and modernity of bathrooms varied wildly from one house to the next. The Earl of Strathmore's St. Paul's Walden Bury in Hertfordshire, where Elizabeth Bowes-Lyon accepted a prince's proposal of marriage during a house party, had two bathrooms for twenty-five bedrooms. Drumlanrig, one of the Duke of Buccleuch's Scottish houses, also had two, and that was only because they had been installed when the mansion was taken over as a military hospital in the Great War. "We wouldn't have had bathrooms otherwise," said his duchess.[35] Other owners adhered to the Victorian principle that bathrooms were an unnecessary luxury when there were housemaids to carry up brass cans of hot water.

At the other end of the spectrum there was William Randolph Hearst's St. Donat's Castle, which was fitted with thirty bathrooms, and the electric-lit marble-clad Art Deco delights of advanced houses like Eltham Palace. Hot water supplied from more efficient central tanks meant that, as Arthur Oswald wrote in 1931, "instead of a luke-warm trickle from the tap marked 'Hot,' a carefully tempered mixture of hot and cold wells up with a dance of bubbles."[36] It was still rare for guests to find bathrooms *en suite*, though: at Flete, where Lady Mildmay converted some of the old dressing rooms, there still wasn't a bathroom for every bedroom, "so you couldn't stay as long as you wanted," remembered her daughter rather wistfully.[37] At seven thirty, bathed, refreshed, and dressed, it was down to the drawing room again for cocktails and dinner and bridge.

AND SO TO BED. THE great nocturnal pastime of the country-house party was sex, or so it seemed from the "modern" plays put on in the West End and the testimony of the divorce courts. In the early hours, the bedroom corridors of England's stately homes were apparently filled with houseguests padding along in their dressing gowns, intent on committing some act of adultery or fornication or betrayal. Exaggerations, no doubt, but it is certainly true that in some circles a Saturday-to-Monday was seen as a good opportunity for infidelity. Servants bringing the early morning tea discovered sleeping lovers; husbands and wives fell out of love with each other and into bed with strangers, and it was vulgar to mind. A "don't ask, don't tell" policy ruled over all. One August night in 1933, a nursemaid at the Earl of Rosebery's Dalmeny House in Scotland bumped into a young man carrying a flashlight and creeping down one of the corridors.

Assuming he was a bedroom-hopping guest, she didn't challenge him. In fact he was a burglar, and he got away with a pearl necklace worth £4,000.

Memoirs of the period are full of advances repelled, both above and below stairs. There is a story (probably told of several debutantes) about how one evening at Lisadell in County Sligo young Constance Gore-Booth was nonplussed to discover her dinner companion's hand creeping up her thigh under the table. Lifting the offending hand high in the air, she said in a loud voice to the rest of the party, "Oh, look what I've found in my lap!"

Rosina Harrison, who was Lady Cranborne's lady's maid, described in her memoirs an incident when she was staying at the British Embassy in Rome and an Italian footman tried to get into her bedroom:

> That night I was getting ready for bed and was standing in my voile knickers and vest when I saw a hand come round the edge of the door. I didn't stop to think. I was over in a flash and pressing the door against the obtruding hand with all my strength. I watched it go red and then purple and I could hear some nasty Italian words uttered from the other side . . . They began getting louder and as I didn't want to wake the house I relaxed my pressure. The hand was quickly removed and there was a scuffling of feet down the corridor. I was taking no chances though so I dragged a heavy chest of drawers and pushed it against the door. After that I slept easy.[38]

The next morning she found the footman in the servants' hall, looking reproachful and wearing his arm in a sling.

There is a darker side to this carry-on-up-the-country-house bawdy, though. The predatory nature of some encounters leaves an uncomfortable taste. For every Constance Gore-Booth, confident enough to humiliate in public the man who was assaulting her, there were a hundred young women who weren't. For every Rose Harrison, prepared to slam a stranger's hand in the door rather than let him into her bedroom, there were a hundred scared maidservants who would rather risk their virtue than their job. And while there was a convention in some circles not to mind about a spouse's infidelities, it wasn't always possible to hide extramarital relationships. The marriage of publisher Sir Neville Pearson came to an abrupt end after a weekend at his country house in the summer of 1927. When the house party broke up, Sir Neville's wife left with one of the guests. Sir John Grey of Enville Hall in Staffordshire also saw his marriage founder after a house party at which his wife formed an attachment to a fellow guest. Whatever happened during their stay, when they got back to London, Lady Grey advised her husband "that she wanted a change in their relations,"[39] and sometime later Sir John received a letter from her announcing that she and the guest were living together in the Felix Hotel, Jermyn Street. There was no doubt whose side the press was on when the story broke: "Baronet Freed from Faithless Wife," was the headline when Grey obtained his *decree nisi*.[40]

WHEN THE HOUSE PARTY WAS over and it was time to say good-bye to one's host, when the maid had packed the bags and the car was waiting at the front door, there was one more ritual to be observed. A guest had to tip the servants.

There was the chauffeur, if he drove them to and from the station; the groom, if he looked after their hunters; and assorted footmen and maids, if they performed any kind of personal tasks during the stay. Most important of all was the butler. If he had unpacked for a guest, done any valeting, or run any errands, such as looking up train times or sending off telegrams, he could expect around ten shillings (fifty pence), even for a Saturday-to-Monday. That is somewhere between £25 and £125 in today's money, depending on how one does the calculation. If the butler hadn't done anything at all apart from his normal duties, a guest could perhaps get away with five shillings. A footman who acted as one's valet deserved another five shillings, and if another footman carried up the breakfast tray, he might expect half a crown. Maids who performed any of these services in the absence of male servants merited only half the male rate. In some circumstances, a guest might also tip the head housemaid.

Choosing the right moment for this little ceremony could be awkward. Leaving money on the dressing table might be all right after a stay in a hotel, but it was a little cold for a private house. If you were tipping a maid, you might ring the bell and ask to see her. As for the butler, Lady Troubridge advised leaving things until he "is putting the rug round you in the car. Then let the note slip from your hand into theirs, even although your friends are still waving from the front door."[41]

But there were parting gifts for guests, too. At Woburn Abbey, a footman stood by the front door with a tray laden with cigars and cigarettes from which guests were invited to help themselves, something to smoke in the car or in the train on their way home. At Holker Hall, they were presented with a charming papier-mâché attaché case filled with canapés and sweetmeats, little scones filled with Morecambe Bay shrimps, and other delicacies. Each item was individually wrapped and labeled for the homeward journey, and each attaché case contained a label and postage stamps, so that when the treats had all been eaten a guest could simply pop into the nearest post office and send it back.

2

EVERYONE SANG

※ ※

Everyone suddenly burst out singing;
And I was filled with such delight
As prisoned birds must find in freedom . . .

SIEGFRIED SASSOON, "EVERYONE SANG" (1919)

FOR MANY LANDED FAMILIES, THE elation felt at the end of the First World War was tempered by sadness and the prospect of an uncertain future. The loss of a son or a brother at the front, awful enough in itself, might mean the end of a dynasty, the breaking of a centuries-old connection with a great estate.

Just before lunch on Christmas Eve 1917, a telegram arrived at Stourhead in Wiltshire, the ancestral seat of the Hoare family. Over the previous weeks a flurry of messages had flown back and forth between Stourhead and the Middle East, ever since Sir Henry and Lady Alda Hoare received the news that their only son Harry had been shot through the lungs fighting the Turks at Mughar Ridge in Palestine. After a night lying out on the battlefield, Harry had been taken to a dressing station and then moved to the small British Army Hospital at Ras el Tin, overlooking the harbor of Alexandria. He was now on the mend, his parents had been told, and coping with his injury "with patience, cheerfulness and pluck." A few days earlier Harry's doctor had wired to say the boy's condition was improving, and a West Country neighbor who was stationed in Alexandria followed this up with another telegram: "Saw Harry yesterday—progressing satisfactorily." Alda Hoare recorded their relief in her diary: "we knelt and humbly thanked God for His unspeakable mercy."[1]

But Harry Hoare was dead. His wound had hemorrhaged and he had died. That was the news that the Christmas Eve telegram brought for his parents.

They didn't cry. Instead Alda fell on her knees and prayed "oh God, for strength to us, in our shattered lives." Then together they walked through the great old house and stood looking at the full-length portrait of Harry, painted when he was twenty-one. "Our only and the best of sons," wrote Sir Henry a little later. "He never grieved us by thought, word or deed."[2]

Harry Hoare's death was a blow from which his parents never recovered. Sir Henry's reaction was an urge to get away from the Wiltshire estate where his family had lived for nearly two hundred years. It held too many memories. His wife was determined to stay at Stourhead, and for exactly that reason. "I cannot bear to leave my son I everywhere see here," she confided to her diary.[3]

So they stayed. For another thirty years the couple managed Stourhead, living the life of country gentry. Sir Henry wrote letters to the *Times* and entered his animals in local agricultural shows; Lady Alda opened the house to the public at a shilling a time in aid of charities like the Queen's Institute of District Nursing and ran the household with three housemaids, a cook, a kitchen maid, a scullery maid, and three or four other staff.

Harry remained in Egypt, in the Hadra War Cemetery at Alexandria. Back at Stourhead, his name topped the list of ten local men commemorated in a roll of honor at the little medieval church of St. Peter, with an epigraph from Ecclesiasticus: "A good life hath but a few days: but a good name endureth for ever."

His parents' grief endured, too. It defined them, it engulfed them. And since Harry had never married, it left them uncertain for a future

SIR HENRY AND LADY ALDA HOARE AT STOURHEAD BEFORE THE
FIRST WAR WITH HARRY, "OUR ONLY AND THE BEST OF SONS."
(Copyright: National Trust)

without a direct heir. In 1925 Sir Henry went down to Bryanston in
Dorset, where the 4th Viscount Portman was selling up to pay the
estate duties resulting from the death of his predecessor. Sir Henry
was shocked to see family paintings, photographs, even the 3rd Lord
Portman's personal effects, all coming under the hammer. "It brought
home to me what may happen when we are gone," he wrote.[4] "Oh, had
he married, and given us a grandson to love," said Alda.[5]

Perhaps Siegfried Sassoon was right. Perhaps everyone sang
when the war was over. But so many of those songs were shot through
with sadness.

IF ALL THE PEERS IN Britain came together to celebrate the Armistice at the end of 1918, the resulting group portrait would fill a large

canvas. There would be 746 of them, arranged, no doubt, in order of precedence: dukes in front, then marquesses, earls, viscounts, and barons (not to mention two archbishops, thirty-nine bishops, and two dozen women, peeresses in their own right). Long-lineaged nobles like Charles Chetwynd-Talbot, 20th Earl of Shrewsbury, whose ancestor had fought with Henry V in the Hundred Years' War, would rub shoulders with nouveau riche press barons like Viscount Northcliffe and Lord Beaverbrook as they raised their glasses to victory. The 5th Baron Headley would have given the champagne a miss: he had converted to Islam in 1913 and, as Lord Headley el-Farooq, was president of the British Muslim Society and a staunch believer in the ability of Islam to arrest the decline of Western civilization and put a stop to suffragettism and short skirts. The 12th Viscount Taaffe, whose forebears had fought for James II at the Battle of the Boyne, might have found the toasts rather awkward, since he was currently a serving officer in the defeated Austrian army with a castle in Bohemia. In March 1919 he was one of four "traitor peers" to be deprived of their titles for "adhering to the King's enemies during the war"; the others were the Dukes of Cumberland, Albany, and Brunswick, three high-ranking German nobles whose British titles came to them through their descent from George III or Victoria and Albert.*

There were some who wouldn't have been at this imaginary gathering at all if it hadn't been for the war, the heirs of the dozen British peers who died on active service. Queen Victoria's youngest grandchild, twenty-three-year-old Maurice of Battenberg, was killed at Ypres at the beginning of the war while serving with the King's Royal Rifle Corps. Viscount Hawarden died in France in August 1914, three weeks after war was declared. Marquess Conyngham was killed forty-eight hours before the Armistice.

---

* Taaffe, who was also a count of the Holy Roman Empire, was doubly unfortunate: four weeks after losing his Irish titles, he learned that the newly established Austrian republic had abolished the nobility altogether and with it his remaining title. Land reform in the new Czechoslovakia then took away most of his Bohemian estates, and plain Mr. Henry Taaffe died in debt in Vienna in 1928.

But the psychology of loss went much deeper. One in ten titled families lost heirs in the war. Tommy Agar-Robartes, whose family owned Lanhydrock in Cornwall and Wimpole Hall in Cambridgeshire, died at Loos after being hit by sniper fire while he was bringing in a wounded private from no-man's-land. Nineteen-year-old Denis, the only son of Viscount Buxton and a second lieutenant in the Coldstream Guards, disappeared in Flanders in October 1917; all that remains of him is his name on a memorial to the missing on the Ypres Salient. Lord and Lady Desborough's eldest boy, Julian Grenfell, was hit in the head by a shell splinter at Ypres; the day after he died the *Times* published his poem "Into Battle," with its prophetic final stanza beginning "The thundering line of battle stands, / And in the air Death moans and sings." When she heard of his death, his ten-year-old sister Imogen wrote "I am glad that he is at peace and did his duty."[6] Two months later the next in line, Billy Grenfell, was killed leading a charge within a mile of where Julian had been hit.

And the roll of horror rolls on. At St. Michael's Mount, Lord St. Levan lost his brother and heir, drowned in the Mediterranean in 1916. The De Blaquieres of Brockworth Manor in Gloucestershire lost their elder son in France in the spring of 1915, and their younger two years later; with the death of Lord De Blaquiere in 1920, the male line ended, and the title, an Irish barony created in 1722, became extinct.

The survivors coped in different ways, selling up or soldiering on. In February 1917, Henry Cubitt's father died and he inherited the Cubitt family estates, which included Denbies in Surrey, a vast Italianate mansion designed by his grandfather, the famous London master-builder Thomas Cubitt, and Fallapit, a slightly more modest neo-Tudor country house in south Devon. He also inherited a title, becoming the 2nd Baron Ashcombe. His eldest son, Henry, a captain in the Coldstream Guards, was already dead, killed on the Somme in September 1916. His second son, Alick, died in the Battle of Cambrai in November 1917; he was buried in an unmarked grave.

Four months later, the Ashcombes lost their third son, William, a lieutenant in the Royal Dragoons who died of wounds in northern

France. All three boys were in their early twenties. The Ashcombes were well supplied with sons—they had six in all—but that can have been of little comfort to them. In November 1920 their fourth, Roland, married Sonia Keppel, whose mother had been the mistress of Edward VII and whose sister Violet was currently the lover of Vita Sackville-West.* In a reminder that death was not the only outcome for casualties of war, the *Times* pointed out that the wedding decorations were all being carried out by a nephew of the Keppels from the Scots Guards, "who lost the sight of both eyes during the war in trying to save his sergeant, and who has now a Victory florist shop in the Piccadilly-arcade."[7]

OF COURSE WE TAKE IT for granted that all the characters in that imaginary group portrait of British peers had stately homes—the quick and the dead, the brash profiteer and the bereaved earl, the survivors and the scarred. It might be a Baroque pile, like the Marlboroughs' Blenheim Palace and the Devonshires' Chatsworth, or a rambling romance like Broughton Castle, home to the Fiennes family since the 1440s. It might be a modest Georgian block or an outrageous piece of pathologically earnest Gothic Revivalism brimming over with turrets and battlements. Style wasn't the point. Taste wasn't the point. Big or small, elegant or ugly, a country house was a necessary adjunct to membership of that most elite of elites, the nobility of Britain. Wasn't it?

Up to a point. The 1919 edition of that great directory of the traditional landed classes and their pedigrees, *Debrett's Peerage, Baronetage, Knightage, and Companionage*, shows that the vast majority of aristocrats owned, leased, or otherwise lived in at least one country house. *Debrett's* is the roughest of rough indications of trends in country-house ownership after the war, and no more than that: those 746 peers of the realm were the tip of the iceberg, a fraction of what their Victorian parents used to call the Upper Ten Thousand. But the list is revealing.

A quarter of all peers boasted two stately homes, and several had a string of them. The main residence of Hugo Charteris, 11th Earl of

---

* The genealogically minded will already have noticed that Roland and Sonia were the grandparents of the present Duchess of Cornwall.

Wemyss and March, was Gosford in East Lothian, designed in the 1790s by Robert Adam and remodeled for the earl's father a century later. After he succeeded to the title in 1914, he chose to live there with his mistress, Lady Angela Forbes. His wife understandably preferred to live in their Cotswold home, the breathtaking sixteenth- and early seventeenth-century Stanway House in Gloucestershire. She supplemented her income by renting Stanway each summer to J. M. Barrie, of Peter Pan fame, for the considerable sum of two hundred guineas. "Lady Wemyss [has] a very clear understanding of the things that matter in life," wrote Lady Angela in her autobiography—an unnecessarily waspish comment, considering she was sleeping with the woman's husband.[8]

As well as Gosford and Stanway, the Wemyss family, whose ancestors claimed descent from Charlemagne the Great, owned four other country houses as well as a town house in Knightsbridge. The Earl of Wemyss was unusual in the size of his property portfolio but not unique. The Duke of Buccleuch also owned six country houses, and like Wemyss, five were in Scotland. As well as Wentworth Woodhouse near Rotherham, claimed as the largest private house in the United Kingdom by the *Guinness Book of Records*, William Charles De Meuron Wentworth-Fitzwilliam, 7th Earl Fitzwilliam, owned two estates near Doncaster, a Jacobean lodge on the outskirts of the Yorkshire town of Malton and two houses in County Wicklow, Ireland: Coolattin, built for his great-grandfather by Carr of York at the beginning of the nineteenth century, and nearby Carnew, a ruined castle, which was restored and reroofed in about 1817.

At the other end of the scale, one in nine peers had no country house at all in 1919. A few were living in very modest circumstances. The 3rd Lord Magheramorne, for example, gave his residence as 37 Knyveton Road, Bournemouth, and Lord Strathspey, 31st Chief of the Clan Grant, lived not in a palace but in Putney. But most of the eighty-eight British nobles without a place in the country at the end of the war had prestigious London homes in Mayfair or Park Lane or Regent's Park. Their decision to do without a rural residence was a matter of choice rather than straitened circumstances, a reflection

of the declining importance of the country house and perhaps of the
growing appeal of metropolitan life. By the 1920s many who *did* own
country houses, especially among the recently ennobled and those
who aspired to aristocracy, did not have the links with the land that
their predecessors in earlier centuries would have taken for granted.
For them, a country house, no matter how grand, was a weekend
retreat rather than a home.

And what about those who stood slightly below the nobility on
the social scale, the baronets, knights, and country squires? The press
barons, brewers, and bankers? The Americans?

Some of these bought and sold mansions with the same ease with
which they bought and sold companies or racehorses. For others,
though, the country house was a home and more—something woven
into the fabric of society, a symbol of continuity that held out the hope
of a return to normality after the slaughter.

This feeling was strong among those who came home from the
war confused, uncertain about the point of it all. The author John
Buchan, although he was never fit enough for active service and spent
the war as a correspondent, an intelligence officer, and, eventually, as
director of propaganda, wrote movingly of his first excursions into
the English countryside after being demobilized; of how throughout
the war he found it impossible to respond to nature without recalling
the scent of hawthorn and lilac vying with the stench of poison gas,
or the sound of birdsong signaling a lull in an artillery barrage. As
he tramped along the lanes of Warwickshire and Oxfordshire in the
cold, wet April of 1919, he recovered the past, he said, and with it some
hope for the future.

Finding in country life a delight "in the rhythm of nature, and in
small homely things after so many alien immensities,"[9] Buchan and his
wife, Susan, sold their London house and moved with their four young
children to Elsfield in Oxfordshire, where they bought an attractively
unassuming early eighteenth-century stone manor house with deli-
ciously haphazard additions. Here Buchan threw himself into the life
of "a minor country gentleman with a taste for letters," as he wrote
with rather deliberate self-deprecation.[10] The family employed a small

staff from the village, and sat in the front pew at church every Sunday.
John always read the lesson; Susan founded a branch of the Women's
Institute and dispensed tea on Sunday afternoons to visiting Oxford
undergraduates. She also presided over house parties where visitors
might include the poets John Masefield and Walter de la Mare, Robert Graves, who lived nearby, or T. E. Lawrence, who used to turn up
at Elsfield at odd times on Boanerges, his 1000cc Brough Superior,
and talked for hours about the Arabs, the war, his muddled masoch-
ism, and his powerful sense of disillusion. On weekdays Buchan com-
muted to his office in London, but from Friday evening until noon on
Monday, he was a country squire, riding out each morning, reveling
on winter evenings in the smell of wood smoke and the hooting of
owls in the spinneys and copses.

There were alternative and sometimes competing narratives to
the kind of rural idyll in which Buchan chose to lose himself. December 1920 saw the posthumous publication of *Poems by Wilfred Owen*:
Owen's portrayal of the soldier as victim, and in the words of one
reviewer, his "sternly just and justly stern judgment on the idyllisers,"
undercut the romantic notion of the country house as a symbol of
what England had been fighting for.[11] And two years later T. S. Eliot's
The Waste Land replaced old certainties with a kaleidoscope of fragmented and bewildering realities, turning gardens into graveyards and
teaching that, far from offering hope for the future, April was the cru-
elest month.

But the rural idyll, bred by the Romantics in the nineteenth century, nurtured by the Edwardians' quest for the heart of England, and
brought to full maturity by the war, is crucial to the conception of
country-house life in the 1920s and 1930s. In the mansions and manor
houses of postwar England, it was Buchan's view that triumphed, not
Owen's bitter sacrifice or Eliot's message of despair and redemption.
That isn't surprising—Buchan's was a view that placed those mansions and manor houses at the heart of the nation, gave them a leading role in the culture. *They* were the country in "King and country."
A house in the country, rambling, ancient, oozing tradition, with
an estate that was small enough not to be an encumbrance but big

enough for some riding and rough shooting, was the beau ideal. Those who already possessed such a thing buckled down and buried their sons, or at least memorialized them in a new stained-glass window for the local church, where St. Georges slew dragons and knights in gleaming armor gazed proudly and poignantly out at congregations whose losses might be just as great but who lacked the resources and the social status to commemorate those losses quite so graphically. Those who had no country house to connect them to the land fit for heroes could always follow John Buchan's example and buy themselves a piece of the past.

3

IT IS OURS

T he transfer of country houses from one owner to another was one of the most significant features of the property market between the wars. On March 4, 1930, the diplomat and journalist Harold Nicolson and his aristocratic wife, the author Vita Sackville-West, heard that they were to have new neighbors. The couple had lived happily at Long Barn in the Kent village of Sevenoaks Weald, "our own nestling home amid the meadows," for the past fifteen years, and neither could imagine leaving what Harold called "our little mud pie, which we both love so childishly and which for both of us is the place where we have been so happy."[1]

Now that was all changed. They discovered that Westwood, the farm next door, was being sold to "poultry people." The idea of a chicken farm on their doorstep appalled them, but neither wanted to leave Long Barn, and they immediately contacted the vendor and asked if they could buy Westwood instead. But at £16,000, her asking price was too high for them; Vita suggested offering £13,000, but Harold didn't think it was worth it, and by the end of March, Vita was reconciled to the fact that they would have to move.

On the evening of April 4, Harold, who was on the staff of the *Evening Standard* and stayed up in London during the week, had a phone call from his wife. A local real-estate agent had told her about

Sissinghurst, a sixteenth-century castle outside the little town of Cranbrook, twenty miles southeast of Long Barn, which had been on the market for two years. She had gone down to see it that afternoon and fallen in love with it.

Harold took the train down the next day, a Saturday. Vita met him at the station, and with their two teenage boys, they motored over to Cranbrook, where Harold had his first sight of Sissinghurst—or rather, of the fragments that remained. The once-great courtyard house, which had entertained Elizabeth I, had all but disappeared during three centuries of neglect: in 1752 Horace Walpole had described seeing "a park in ruins, and a house in ten times greater ruins," and it had gone downhill from there, serving as a prisoner-of-war camp during the Seven Years' War, a workhouse, and, finally, a sort of adjunct to the neighboring farm, housing farm laborers, horses, and bits of agricultural machinery.[2] Virtually all that survived intact was a low range of buildings and, beyond it, a strikingly beautiful tower, four stories high and built entirely of soft red brick.

Harold was noncommittal, but the next day he and Vita went back for another look and half-decided to offer £12,000 for the castle, its grounds, and the adjoining four hundred acres. Still they dithered. Harold reckoned they would need to spend at least another £15,000 to put it in order. By the time they had finished, they wouldn't have much change out of £30,000—a large sum, more than £4 million in today's money. For the same amount, he told his wife, they could have "a beautiful place replete with park, garage, h[ot] and c[old], central heating, historical associations, and two lodges."[3] On the other hand, Sissinghurst was in a part of Kent that they both liked. It had links, albeit tenuous ones, to Vita's family: Cecily Baker, whose father owned the place in Henry VIII's time, had married her ancestor, Sir Thomas Sackville, 1st Earl of Dorset. And, most decisively, "we like it."[4]

All through the middle of April, they hemmed and hawed. Harold's elderly mother advised them against it, saying it would cost too much to keep up. When they walked over it once more in icy winds and rain, it looked so big and dilapidated that Harold almost lost his nerve. "I am terrified of socialist legislation, of not being able to let the fields, of finding that the place is a huge hole into which we pour money, of finding that the whole thing is far more bother than it is worth," he confided to his diary, admitting that he and Vita were both depressed and worried about making the wrong decision.[5]

Finally, they made an offer and sat back to wait for an answer. After dinner one night at the beginning of May, the telephone rang, and Vita took the call. It was from the real-estate agent who was handling the sale. Harold described what happened next. "'Quite' . . . 'Yes, of course' . . . 'Oh naturally!' She puts down the receiver and says, 'It is ours.' We embrace warmly. I then go and get the plans and fiddle."[6]

It would be another five months before the couple could even camp out at Sissinghurst. They moved in permanently in 1932, letting Long Barn to the producer Sidney Bernstein and then, in 1936, to Charles Lindbergh and his wife, Anne, who had left America in search of some privacy after the media frenzy that followed the kidnap and murder of their baby son. ("No, sir, we shall not stare at the poor people," the village postmistress promised Harold when he told her the identities of Long Barn's new tenants.[7]) Sissinghurst's famous gardens were more or less complete by 1937. Even then, Harold was still looking to a future when the place would be finished. "I really believe," he told Vita, "that you will be able to make of that ramshackle farm-tumble something as personal and lovely as anything in England."[8] As of course she did.

As BUYERS IN 1930, HAROLD and Vita benefited from the fact that supply was outstripping demand as historic country houses poured onto the market in the wake of the Wall Street crash of the previous October. That summer the Marquess of Lothian let Blickling Hall, the finest Jacobean survival in Norfolk, fully furnished to Major Gilbert Russell, a great-grandson of the 6th Duke of Bedford. One of the great mid-Georgian houses, Claremont in Surrey, built for Clive of India by the impressive triumvirate of Capability Brown, Henry Holland, and Sir John Soane, came up for sale a few weeks later, as a business opportunity rather than a home: the agents said that the 210-acre estate, whose pleasure grounds included work by Brown, Vanbrugh,

SISSINGHURST: "AS PERSONAL AND LOVELY AS ANYTHING IN ENGLAND." (Copyright: Country Life)

and William Kent, was "ripe for immediate development for building purposes."[9] Broome Park in Kent, an extravaganza of cut and molded red brick dating from the 1630s, which had once been the home of Lord Kitchener of Khartoum, also came back on the market, having been sold only four months before. Claremont became a girls' school, Broome a hotel.

In the week that the sales of Claremont and Broome were announced, stories began to circulate that the Great Chamber of Gilling Castle in Yorkshire was to be dismantled and shipped off to America for a five-figure sum. The castle (actually a rather lovely house, parts of which dated back to the Middle Ages) had been bought the previous year and was being turned into a prep school. The Great Chamber, one of the finest Elizabethan interiors in the country and a riot of strapwork and inlaid flowers with an heraldic frieze

THE GREAT CHAMBER AT GILLING CASTLE IN YORKSHIRE. (Copyright: Country Life)

containing no fewer than 443 coats of arms, had been bought by "a wealthy American"—William Randolph Hearst—who also obtained paneling from Gilling's Georgian long gallery.[10]

That summer the president of the Auctioneers and Estate Agents' Institute lamented that "the large family residences, especially of the older type, are practically unsaleable." Some few country houses were being turned into schools, institutions, and local authority offices, he acknowledged, "but the demand for such purposes is very limited, and it is now found that even the moderately large house . . . is extremely difficult to dispose of."[11] At the same time concern was voiced that there was a crisis coming in the countryside. Landowners, said the Duke of Montrose, were impoverished, "mostly living on capital which, sooner or later, must become exhausted."[12] The time was coming, he argued, when the state should accept land in lieu of death duties, which since the "tax on death" had been introduced back in 1894 had risen until now it stood at 34 percent for estates valued between £500,000 and £600,000, rising to a whopping 50 percent on estates over £2 million. "The continuance of the current burdensome conditions of private ownership," said Montrose, "is quite impossible."[13]

Not everyone agreed. *Country Life*, founded in 1897 as a weekly magazine devoted to the pleasures of rural living and fast becoming essential reading for anyone who aspired to those pleasures, applauded the fact that in the past decade big houses like Stowe in Buckinghamshire and Westonbirt in Gloucestershire had found new uses as schools. Seeing their sale as evidence of an adaptable market and noting that the vast majority of sales were still to private individuals, the magazine maintained that scores of country estates, some quite large, had found buyers over the past year. By the end of the year, though, even *Country Life*'s relentlessly optimistic estate market correspondent, "Arbiter," was forced to admit that with property transactions £8 million or £9 million down on the previous year, 1930 was probably the worst since the great agricultural depressions of the 1870s.

How had it come to this? In 1918 the future looked bright for the country house and its estate. The volume of sales and prices had improved steadily right through the war, after a predictable and dramatic slump in the autumn of 1914. Farms were in particular demand: the shortage of labor as agricultural workers left for military service was more than offset by the absence of foreign competition and the fact that there was an assured market at fixed prices for every ounce of food that could be produced. True, there was a trend, first noticed before the war, for syndicates or individuals to buy up large estates and then break them up for resale, a practice that disadvantaged the tenant-farmer, who, if he or she wanted to own his or her farm, had to pay the speculators' profit on top of the market value or face the prospect of seeing it sold out from under them. The elderly Marquess of Aberdeen came in for some mildly reproving comments in 1919 when he announced to his tenants that he had sold thirty-seven thousand acres of his fifty-thousand-acre estates in Aberdeenshire to a shipbroker, Herbert Boret, who was busy buying up land in England

as well as Scotland. The marquess, who kept his ancestral home of
Haddo House (and who also owned a ranch in British Columbia),
maintained that he was merely moving with the times, which were
clearly in favor of substituting ownership for tenancy. The press reckoned he was escaping from his responsibilities as a landowner, and
when he claimed that Boret intended to give tenants the opportunity
to own their holdings, critics made pointed comments about the profit
he would expect as middleman.

Although the specter of the speculator remained throughout the
1920s, he proved less of a problem than commentators predicted. This
was partly because landowners realized that they would get more for
their estates by breaking them up themselves and selling them off in
separate lots, offering farms to their tenants privately before going to
auction; and partly because many believed quite sincerely that they
owed a duty of care to their tenants and were prepared to put their
money where their mouths were. The politician Walter Long, for
example, sacrificed a cool £20,000 by refusing an offer from a syndicate for his fifteen-thousand-acre Wiltshire estates and offering them
instead to his tenants.

In 1918 the property market saw sales of £11.38 million, an increase of
more than 25 percent on the previous year. There was a strong demand
for country houses, especially those that came without large estates.
"Today there are on the books of the leading agents scores of applicants
for properties, who cannot get what they want at the moment," wrote
Country Life's Arbiter in his end-of-year roundup of sales. "They are in
themselves a guarantee of the coming year's auctions."[14]

He was right. The most remarkable year since estate records
began was 1919, with more country houses bought and sold than ever
before and prices continuing to rise. Smaller country houses continued to be in demand, especially those within an hour's drive of London. The firm of Hampton & Sons, one of England's leading estate
agents, reported that furnished country houses were being let for the
summer at higher rents than recently and that "for country houses
with several hundred acres prices have been distinctly on the upgrade,
while for the house of medium size, with a home farm from 100 to 200

acres, the demand has been phenomenal."[15] Another prominent firm of estate agents, Knight, Frank & Rutley, recorded sales of more than three-quarters of a million acres, and total combined sales for the year reached more than £30 million. Mansions and their estates played a huge part in this boom, particularly those with historical associations. "It is striking," said the *Times*, "how many places sold this year were visited by Queen Elizabeth"; and equally striking that not a few claimed "a more or less authentic record running back to before the Norman Conquest."[16]

But there were early signs of a coming storm, as big landowners moved to capitalize on the rising market and liquidate their assets. In the final weeks of 1918, land on the edges of half a dozen estates was sold off, including a thousand acres of the Holme Hall estate near York, which realized £29,000; nine or ten of the best farms on Lord Pembroke's Wilton estate; and eight thousand acres on Earl Beauchamp's Madresfield Court estate. In fact the sale of "outlying portions"—a phrase that referred to land on the margins of an estate or perhaps separated from it—crops up again and again in the property pages, suggesting rationalization or consolidation but not financial need. Arbiter was at pains to point out that Lord Beauchamp's sale had nothing to do with Madresfield Court itself. "The sale of 8,000 acres on an extensive estate like Lord Beauchamp's has, necessarily, no more connection with the mansion and its surroundings than it has with a town house." What Arbiter couldn't know or refused to admit was that the sale of "outlying portions" would become a frequent precursor to the sale of a mansion and the departure of a family who, whether or not they had been living there since the Norman conquest, could no longer make ends meet.

Several big Scottish sporting estates came on the market in late 1918 and early 1919. The 11,600-acre Castle Menzies estate in Perthshire was offered at a reduced price of £60,000 in a sale that included five miles of salmon and trout fishing and grouse moors yielding an average of 1,200 brace of birds each year; and nearly 92,000 acres of the Duke of Sutherland's Highland property, "including Dornoch Castle," said the sale particulars, referring to a reputedly haunted sixteenth-century hunting lodge, "but not the town of Dornoch."[17] This was in addition to 237,000 acres that the Duke of Sutherland had sold earlier in the year.

A further sign that all might not be well in the country-house market was voiced in January 1919 by a spokesman for Hampton & Sons, who remarked on "the number of properties which have been disposed of together with the interior furnishings, a transaction which was comparatively rare in pre-war days."[18]

In March 1919, the Times ran a story under the headline "Ancestral Seats as Garden Cities." The report centered on Lord Middleton's announcement that he intended to sell Wollaton Hall, perched in a remarkable hilltop setting on the outskirts of Nottingham, and that he had given first refusal to the city council. Wollaton was, and indeed still is, one of the most flamboyant Elizabethan country houses. A glittering palace of turrets and towers and mannerist decoration, it was built in the 1580s for Middleton's ancestor, Sir Francis Willoughby, and designed by the greatest of all Elizabethan architects, Robert Smythson, who was buried in the local church. Its future, declared Country Life, "must be a matter of concern for all who have any admiration of the beautiful and any respect for the past."[19]

Middleton was in his seventies and without children. The council was interested in his proposal—very interested indeed. But nothing came of the plan before Lord Middleton's death in 1922, when his estates and title went to his seventy-five-year-old brother. The 10th Lord Middleton, a former major in the Indian army, announced his intention to retreat to another family seat, Birdsall House in Yorkshire, remodeled in the 1870s, and to sell off his Nottinghamshire estates, including Wollaton. But he died in 1924, and his son and heir was faced with a second set of death duties in the space of only two years. The 11th Lord Middleton sold land, some family pictures, and a library from Wollaton, which included important medieval manuscripts, hundreds of rare sixteenth- and seventeenth-century pamphlets and a First Folio Shakespeare. The four-day sale at Christies of "one of the few remaining of the old and well-matured libraries, buried in a great country house and practically unknown to bibliographers,"[20] raised over £8,300. But it wasn't enough, and he repeated the offer to give Nottingham first refusal on the Wollaton estate. The council unanimously agreed to buy the hall and eight hundred acres of parkland for £200,000.

And now it emerged that the council didn't want the mansion at all, no matter that it was one of the finest country houses in England. It wanted the park for development, and plans were swiftly unveiled to sell off the land that fronted the main Nottingham-Derby road "as sites for houses of a good class." This would enable the authorities to recoup most of the purchase price. Some land was set aside for municipal housing, for playing fields, and for an eighteen-hole golf course, which was expected "to improve the value of the adjoining building land by 2s. a yard."[21] As for Wollaton Hall itself, the council didn't quite know what to do with it. The favored option was to house the city's natural history collection there, and this was what eventually happened. "The conversion of a park so charming as this into a mass of houses has its painful side," commented the *Times*, "but the process is inevitable, and if it is carried out with taste and skill the regret is reduced to very small proportions."[22]

This tale of an unwanted masterpiece illustrates two sides to the country house in the 1920s. First, there was the obvious story of retrenchment and decline, as an established landed family was forced by death and taxes to break centuries-old links with its ancestral seat. This was sad, but hardly new: country-house-owning families had been selling up, going broke, and dying out for centuries. More novel was the notion that it was really quite difficult to find a use for a historic mansion in postwar Britain; that while its grounds were worth something as a setting for suburbia, the mansion itself was no longer any use as a home. It was as dead as the stuffed birds and animals that stared out unseeing on Wollaton's halls and galleries, as much a thing of the past as the fossils in their glass cases.

AT LEAST WOLLATON SURVIVED. TWENTY miles north of Nottingham's new natural history museum and golf course, and just across the

THE ENTRANCE HALL AT SUTTON SCARSDALE IN 1919, SHORTLY
BEFORE THE HOUSE WAS GUTTED. (Copyright: Country Life)

border in Derbyshire, lay Sutton Scarsdale, the grandest early Georgian house in the county. An enormous balustraded and rusticated
mansion facing east—always a brave choice in the wind-whipped hills
of Derbyshire—Sutton Scarsdale was the work of Francis Smith of
Warwick, who remodeled it magnificently in the 1720s. It was bought
in 1824 by Richard Arkwright, son of the inventor of the spinning
jenny and one of the richest commoners in England, and for nearly
a century the Arkwrights lived at Sutton Scarsdale without making
any major alterations to the house. Then in 1918 William Arkwright,
whose interests lay more with the breeding of pointers than architecture and elegant living, tried to let the house, having first astutely
allowed the historian Margaret Jourdain to describe its beauties to
possible buyers in a feature for *Country Life*. There were no takers. In
June 1919 a notice appeared in the press announcing the auction of the
entire Sutton Scarsdale estate, including the mansion, the local pub,

thirty farms, and seventy houses, cottages, and shops. The sale, which took place on November 6, made more than £100,000, but the mansion failed to sell and was withdrawn at £12,600. That figure, commented the *Times*, "will have to be considerably improved upon before it reaches a reasonable estimate for so stately and historic a house."[23]

But no one wanted Sutton Scarsdale—not as a country house, anyway. It was bought after the auction by a syndicate of local businessmen who gutted the place, stripped the lead from its roof, and sold off its fittings to a London antiques dealer, Charles Lockhart Roberson, whose prospectus offered paneled rooms and old chimneypieces and declared that "in these days when so many of the estates and country seats of the nobility are changing hands," his Knightsbridge gallery offered "an ideal medium through which they may be brought to the notice of possible buyers."[24] Roberson sold a stunning carved chimneypiece from Sutton Scarsdale to William Randolph Hearst, and in 1928 the new Philadelphia Art Gallery announced that three rooms acquired from Roberson from the Arkwrights' mansion, two paneled in deal and one in oak, were to form the setting for paintings by Gainsborough, Romney, and Reynolds. Sutton Scarsdale itself was left to fall into decay, a sad roofless ruin.

An even more ignominious fate befell Nuthall Temple, which stood a few miles north of Nottingham, between Wollaton and Sutton Scarsdale. Nuthall was the last of a handful of eighteenth-century English country houses inspired by the Villa Rotunda, the domed place of entertainment on a hill outside Vicenza created by Andrea Palladio in 1566–1571.* It was designed by Thomas Wright and built 1754–1757 for Sir Charles Sedley, a local member of Parliament and the grandson of the notorious Restoration rake of the same name.

By the 1920s, Nuthall belonged to the Holden family. In November 1927, Robert Millington Holden, faced with falling rents and a bill for death duties, put the temple up for auction. Advertising it as a "wonderful Palladian mansion containing [the] finest specimens of

---

* Others included Chiswick House in Middlesex (3rd Earl of Burlington for himself, 1725–1729) and Mereworth Castle, Kent (Colen Campbell for John Fane, later 7th Earl of Westmorland, 1722–1724).

Rococo decoration in the kingdom," the agents for the sale suggested first that it was "eminently adapted for club house or residential hotel," and then that its 650 acres offered "a splendid opportunity for creating a garden city."[25]

It failed to sell. The contents, including some fine Georgian furniture, a Second Folio Shakespeare, and a Zoffany of Charles James Fox, were auctioned off the following March, and in May 1929 the fixtures and fittings were sold as well—twenty-four carved marble and wood mantelpieces, 130 doors, the fittings of an Adam drawing room, and all of that Rococo work. The denuded carcass went to a local demolition contractor for £800, and at the end of July, in the presence of the local press and a crowd of onlookers, he set fire to it. "A wonderful sight," reported the *Nottingham Evening News* the next day. "What took only a few minutes to demolish by fire might have taken by the pick and shovel method a month or two."[26]

The architectural salvage trade was booming, as the breakup of estates was followed by the breakup of the mansions that had been at their heart. Some of the casualties were surprisingly modern: Wood Norton near Evesham in Worcestershire, a big Victorian house that, until 1900, had been the home of Prince Philippe, Duke of Orléans and pretender to the French throne, was offered for sale in the early 1920s. In spite of having been extensively remodeled by the duke in the 1890s, it failed to find a buyer, and in the summer of 1924, it was on the market again. Only this time it was offered for sale prior to demolition, and the auctioneers catalogued the house as so many thousand feet of oak paneling, so many oak doors, thirty-six oak mantelpieces and overmantels, and so on.

Wood Norton was saved from demolition at the last minute (it is now a hotel), but other houses weren't so lucky. Over the border in Wales, the Earl of Powis offered Lymore Hall near Montgomery, a timber-framed mansion dating from 1675, at a nominal rent of £1 a year to anyone who would repair and preserve it. It was in a poor state, and whoever leased it would have to spend around £20,000 on repairs. In 1921 there had been an unfortunate incident during a church fête at the house when the earl and twenty people fell through the floor of the Great Hall into the cellar. "Without any audible premonitory symptoms, a knot of guests were observed to disappear outright," reported the local paper.[27]

No one took the lease. So the earl offered Lymore as a gift to the town of Montgomery. The town didn't want it. Nor did the Office of Works. Nor the National Trust. Not even when an anonymous donor came forward and offered £10,000 toward saving it.

With all other avenues exhausted, the earl sold Lymore at auction in October 1929. Bidders came to the sale from all over Britain; an unnamed American museum made a big private offer for a magnificent carved Elizabethan staircase. But eventually Lymore went as a single lot to a local antique dealer, Frederick Anderson, who paid £3,500 and announced that the staircase, the oak paneling, and most of the other features were likely to go to America. (In the end the staircase only got as far as Yorkshire, where it was installed in another country house, Aldborough Hall.) The earl was too upset to attend the sale. Those who did were warned to be careful about putting too much weight on the floors.

More than 180 country houses were destroyed between the end of the war and that day in the spring of 1930 when Vita Sackville-West fell in love with Sissinghurst, and hundreds more in Scotland, Wales, and especially Ireland, where the houses of the Anglo-Irish were frequent targets for Republican gangs during the War of Independence and the civil war that followed. Casualties included Summerhill, the vast and magnificent Palladian mansion in County Meath, where the restless Empress Elisabeth of Austria had found some peace in the 1870s, which was burned by the Irish Republican Army in 1921; and the bizarre Gothic Revival chateau that was Roxborough Castle in County Tyrone, home of the earls of Charlemont and also burned down by republican soldiers. "Furniture vans engaged for nine months ahead are taking goods from the country to England," wrote Lady Gregory in 1922, when the civil war was at its height.[28]

Even in the comparatively peaceful rural landscapes of postwar England, fire was an ever-present danger. On Bonfire Night 1926, Little Bromley Hall in Essex was burned down, along with all the furniture and silver, because a window was left open in the drawing room. The cause wasn't a stray rocket or a misfiring Roman candle but a breeze that blew the curtains over an oil lamp. The same night Copythorne House, "an old New Forest mansion," was badly damaged when a can of paraffin was knocked over and caught fire. Three months earlier £25,000 of damage was caused by a fire at Caversham Park near Reading, the second at the property in less than two years. In fact around thirty country houses were either badly damaged or completely destroyed in fires in 1926 alone, with causes ranging from burglars and a painter's blowlamp to smoldering oak lintels and "an electric iron which evidently had not been disconnected the previous evening."[29] There were human casualties, too. A cook died when Crowe Hall, the residence of the Mayoress of Bath, went up in flames. (The mayoress's chain of office was saved "at great personal risk" by a local constable, who found a ladder and climbed through a window to rescue it.[30]) Four people were killed when the ceiling of the saloon at Oulton Park in Cheshire fell in on them as they were working to save furniture and paintings from the flames. A fireman was badly burned at the same time; he died later in the hospital. When Reigate Priory, the Surrey home of First Sea Lord Earl Beatty, caught fire at the end of the year, a man sitting on a branch of a tree watching the firefighters broke his leg when the branch snapped.

And 1926 wasn't even a particularly bad year. In 1929, two days after a string of country-house fires culminated in a disaster that turned the interior of seventeenth-century Lulworth Castle in Dorset into "a furnace,"[31] there were press calls for insurance companies to step in and advise owners on sensible precautions, chief of which was a proper water supply. "The water supply available at many of the most valuable and historic mansions ...," declared one expert, "is scandalously inadequate, when one considers the interests and the treasures at stake."[32]

GLANCING THROUGH THE NEWSPAPER HEADLINES of the 1920s—"Fire at Peer's Country Mansion," "Mansion Sold Piecemeal," "Wall Falls During Mansion Demolition"[33]—it seems as though big houses were being burned, dismantled, and demolished all over the country. But while the loss of some, like Nuthall, was a national disaster; others were not much missed. Few would weep over the disappearance of plodding yellow-brick Victorian piles and plain Georgian blocks, which possessed little more in the way of character and artistry than the Stockbroker Tudor suburban villas that replaced them.

Moreover, these lost country houses were only a fraction of the total. A dozen demolitions in Leicestershire ranged from the imposing neo-Classical Lindley Hall on the border with Warwickshire to the vast Victorian pile that was Bradgate House, where Edward, Prince of Wales, was entertained in the 1880s. But if we include everything from small manors to massive stately homes, ninety-five country houses survive in Leicestershire in the twenty-first century. Lancashire also lost at least a dozen mansions in the 1920s, ten more in the 1930s. But at a rough count, nearly two hundred still survive today.

The big agricultural estates whose rents had once provided the lifeblood for many of these houses were less fortunate. So although the Duke of Rutland's Belvoir Castle was one of Leicestershire's survivors, 13,300 acres of the Belvoir estate went for auction in March 1920, including seven entire villages. The duke raised nearly half a million pounds on the sale, together with another £350,000 on 14,500 acres of his Derbyshire estates, which were sold two weeks later. But most country houses survived. And if England was changing hands, as the papers frequently declared, it was not necessarily a change for the worse.

4

THE KING'S HOUSES

A t noon on a summer's day in 1927 a convoy of Rolls Royces slid out of Windsor Castle. Crowds cheered. Policemen saluted. Men removed their hats in gestures of respect as the cavalcade passed or hoisted their children high to give them a better view. Women waved handkerchiefs. From one of the leading cars a stout, gray-bearded man in a black morning coat and a silk top hat waved back. He wore a white carnation in his buttonhole.

His Majesty George V, by the Grace of God, of Great Britain, Ireland, and the British Dominions beyond the Seas, King, Defender of the Faith, Emperor of India, was going to the races.

Even kings entertained at home. Every June George V and Queen Mary moved to Windsor Castle, the sprawling labyrinth of lodgings and halls to the west of London, which had been a royal residence since the Norman conquest. They were there to host a house party for Royal Ascot Week (which actually only ran for four days, from Tuesday to Friday), the race meeting that was one of the centerpieces of the social season, and they were usually joined by some of their five surviving children: David, Albert, Mary, Henry, and George.*

---

* King George and Queen Mary's youngest child, Prince John, died after suffering a seizure in 1919, when he was thirteen years old.

Not all of the family turned up at Windsor every year. In 1922, for example, the Prince of Wales was away on a tour of the Far East, and the King and Queen and their guests settled down in the paneled Waterloo Chamber after a day at the races to watch a new film, *With the Prince of Wales Through India and Burma*. In 1923 Bertie was absent because his new bride, Lady Elizabeth Bowes-Lyon, had whooping cough. After 1930, when the Prince of Wales set up his own household at Fort Belvedere in Windsor Great Park, he entertained his own group of friends there during Ascot Week, although he still came to the Ascot opening day. And in 1929 and again in 1935, George V was himself too ill to attend.

Cousins and other relations were often invited. Princess May Cambridge, niece to Queen Mary and great-granddaughter of Queen Victoria, was at Windsor for the 1927 party. So was her mother, Prince Alice, Countess of Athlone. But the house party wasn't just for family. This particular year King George and Queen Mary entertained three ducal couples, Beaufort, Roxburghe, and Portland, and a clutch of other lesser nobles—twenty-four guests in all.

The fleet of motorcars set off for Ascot in the sunshine, which vanished by the time they reached their first stopping point, Duke's Drive in Windsor Great Park, where everyone disembarked and climbed into seven open carriages. Members of the public gathered to watch the switch, but admission to the spectacle was strictly controlled and by ticket only. The first carriage, containing the king and queen, the Prince of Wales, and Prince Henry, was preceded by scarlet-coated outriders and drawn by four grays controlled by postillions dressed in their Ascot livery of white leather breeches, dark blue waistcoats and rows of gilt buttons, a gold-laced black silk hat, and a single spur. The other carriages were each drawn by six bays, again with postillions in livery.

When everyone was comfortable, the convoy set off again through Windsor Park in the gray light until it reached the eastern end of the Ascot course. As soon as the procession came in sight, the crowds started cheering. Hats and handkerchiefs were waved from the stands, and a roar came up from the open stretches of heath. The

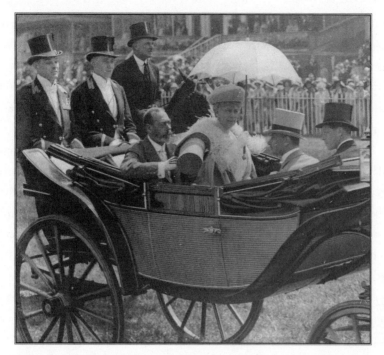

KING GEORGE V AND QUEEN MARY AT ASCOT IN 1927, ACCOMPA-NIED BY PRINCE HENRY AND THE PRINCE OF WALES. (Copyright: Associated Newspapers/REX Shutterstock)

Times noted ruefully and without explanation that this year "the cheering in the Grand Stand and the enclosures seemed a little more subdued, but if the acclamation was decorous it was cordial."[1]

The royal party usually left for Windsor Castle before the last race. They came back for the Gold Cup, which was run on the Thursday, and most years they put in an appearance on the Wednesday and Friday as well. If it rained, they dispensed with the landaus and arrived in closed cars. And each evening they entertained. Shortly before eight thirty, the king and queen and any other members of the family who were dining at the castle would set off toward the Green Drawing Room, part of a suite of reception rooms created for George IV as part of Sir Jeffry Wyatville's remodeling of the castle in 1823–1840. At the door they were met by the master of the household, who bowed and backed into the room, heralding their arrival to the other guests who were arranged in two quarter circles, men on one side and women on the other. The king, his sons, and members of the royal household wore the Windsor uniform, a tailcoat of dark blue with scarlet collar and cuffs, worn over a single-breasted white waistcoat and plain black trousers. The other men in the party wore black tailcoats and knee breeches. Women were more conventionally dressed in evening gowns and jewels.

Queen Mary moved along one line, shaking hands with the men, while George V did the same with the women. Then whoever had been commanded to escort the queen offered her his arm and led her to the table, where a Guards string band concealed behind a grille in the dining room played "God Save the King." The band continued to play throughout the meal, out of sight in a small chamber, wearing their tightly buttoned tunics and, on a warm June evening, drenched in sweat.

Each course was served by liveried footmen in scarlet and pages in blue. The meal lasted no more than an hour, and when it was over the queen would take the women back to the Green Drawing Room, each one curtseying to the king as she left the royal presence. George V would spend twenty minutes with the men over coffee, port, and liqueurs and then abruptly stand and lead them out to join the ladies. Punctually at eleven o'clock, the company reassembled in its two quadrants, men on one side and women on the other; George and Mary wished them all good night, and the royal family left the room. The evening was over.

"Nothing was lacking but gaiety," recalled the Prince of Wales, who found the abrupt and early ending to these entertainments particularly trying.[2] One night he and his brothers, determined "to enliven the atmosphere for the younger members of the party," arranged for the Guards band to stay behind in the Green Drawing Room, and after their parents had gone to bed, they returned, rolled back the carpets, and held an impromptu dance. It was a failure: the musicians could only manage some outdated foxtrots. "The ancient walls seemed to exude disapproval," the prince remembered. "We never tried it again."[3]

The episode, emblematic of a familiar gulf between generations, says something more about the world—or rather worlds—in which king, queen, and princes moved: the one immensely formal, controlled, ritualized; the other struggling halfheartedly to break free.

GEORGE V HAD A CLUTCH of castles and country houses at his disposal, ranging from Windsor, heavy with history and the accumulated remodelings of nearly nine centuries, to Sandringham, barely four decades old when the king came to the throne in 1910. The main royal residence was of course Buckingham Palace, a place with a troubled architectural history. It had undergone three major transformations since the day in 1762 when Buckingham House, as it then was, was bought by George III as a dower house for Queen Charlotte. The first, and most dramatic, stemmed from a time in 1818 when the Prince Regent, unhappy at the way his existing home of Carlton House stood exposed to public gaze on Pall Mall, decided to remodel Buckingham House. "I must have a *pied á terre*," he announced, although his notions of what constituted a *pied-á-terre* were ambitious. "The whole expense may probably be kept within £400,000, but it will be safer to reckon upon £450,000."[4]

Nothing much happened for a while because George IV, as he became in 1820, focused his passion for architecture in other directions. Another of his *pieds-á-terre*, John Nash's Brighton Pavilion, was completed in 1821; and Sir Jeffry Wyatville's remodeling of Windsor Castle as a country seat began in 1823. Then in 1825 contracts were finally signed for a massive reworking of Buckingham House, with Nash as architect.

George IV was delighted with his new home. Nash provided private and state apartments with a domed bow room at the center and, as a grand entrance, a marble arch—*the* Marble Arch—decorated with friezes celebrating British military and naval victories and crowned with Chantrey's statue of the king. He was so delighted, in fact, that halfway through the work he decided that the entire court would move to Buckingham House. Nash pointed out that his scheme had been conceived as a private residence for the king: there was no provision for the various departments of the royal household, the thousand or so members of staff. George IV simply told him "You know nothing about the matter. It will make an excellent palace."[5]

The excellent palace was still unfinished at his death in 1830, and Nash was dismissed when a select committee discovered he had exceeded the original budget of £252,690, which had been approved by the government, by £360,000. George IV's brother, who succeeded to the throne as William IV, commissioned the plodding architect Edward Blore to finish Buckingham Palace in 1831, after trying unsuccessfully to persuade his ministers that it should become a barracks for the Foot Guards. Then he offered it as a replacement when the Houses of Parliament burned down in 1834. He hated the place, which epitomized all the extravagance that he deplored in his brother, and he never lived there. In the second major remodeling, Blore was called back by Queen Victoria in 1847 to create private accommodation for the royal family in a new east front, which closed off Nash's imposing forecourt and was dismissed by the architectural press as "little more than an ordinary piece of street architecture."[6] The Marble Arch was carted off to Cumberland Gate.

Toward the end of her reign, Victoria tended to live at Windsor, and Buckingham Palace was rarely used. On her death in 1901, there were suggestions that it should be turned into a museum and picture gallery, with Edward VII and Queen Alexandra moving to Kensington Palace. That plan came to nothing, but Edward VII insisted that before he moved in the building must be redecorated, which it was, with state rooms, vestibules, and galleries all painted white with heavy gilding.

In 1911, the year after George V's accession to the throne, the unveiling of the marble and gilt colossus that is Thomas Brock's Victoria Memorial focused attention on the inadequacies of Blore's ordinary piece of street architecture, now acting as a backdrop to the 2,300-ton memorial; and over a three-month period in the summer of 1913 the entrance front was entirely refaced, without even disturbing the glass in the windows, to designs by the stolid but uninspired architect Sir Aston Webb.*

---

* The contractors, Leslie & Co., worked round the clock, employing 300 men during the day and 150 at night.

George V took a keen interest in this third remodeling. The king was personally responsible for the central balcony, which has become the most famous stage on which the kings and queens of Great Britain have showed themselves to the world. He insisted to Webb that space was needed "from time to time on occasions when the King and other members of the Royal Family wish to show themselves to the people."[7] When the news of the Armistice began to spread on the morning of November 11, 1918, five thousand people gathered in front of Buckingham Palace, "the central point of the British Empire."[8] It was on that balcony that the king appeared to them shortly after eleven o'clock, wearing the uniform of an admiral of the fleet, with Queen Mary beside him, bareheaded and wearing a fur coat. The band in the courtyard played "God Save the King" and "Rule Britannia," and everybody sang.

As the Prince and Princess of Wales, George V and Queen Mary had lived round the corner at Sir Christopher Wren's Marlborough House during Edward VII's reign. When they moved into Buckingham Palace in 1910, Queen Mary immediately began to retrieve the Regency character of the interiors. Victorian furniture was discarded, and throughout her husband's twenty-five-year reign, she had period upholstery and wall coverings made and bought good examples of Regency furniture and works of art. In the Green Drawing Room next door to the Throne Room, for example, she found a surviving fragment of green damask dating from 1832 and had fabric of the same pattern woven for new curtains. In 1928 she replaced the threadbare coverings of two sets of gilt chairs made for George IV with silk of the same date as the chairs, which had been found rolled up in a palace storeroom. She designed the canopy á la polonaise over the throne dais in the ballroom and supervised the redecoration of the Balcony Room with *chinoiserie*.

The royal household operated on a vast, feudal scale, wherever the king happened to be. When he was in residence at Windsor, hordes of servants were kept busy. Sir John Fortescue, who retired as librarian and archivist at Windsor in 1926, lovingly detailed their eating arrangements:

The royal kitchen kept sixty souls busily employed. In the stewards' room—a room contemporaneous with the cloisters of Westminster Abbey and roofed with the like vaulting—there were two dinners of one hundred each for the upper servants. In the servants' hall—a fourteenth-century building with columns and vaulting of that period—there were two dinners of two hundred each for the lower servants.[9]

Some members of the domestic staff stayed put at a particular royal residence. Others, particularly the king and queen's personal attendants, traveled with them. When Queen Mary paid a visit to the Cavendishes at Holker Hall in Lancashire, she brought with her two dressers, one footman, one page, two chauffeurs, one lady-in-waiting, a maid for the lady-in-waiting, and a detective. Before her arrival, Holker received a list of her requirements, which ranged from having a chair placed outside her bedroom at night for her page to sit on, to having fresh barley water placed in her bedroom at two-hourly intervals during the day and six clean towels to be supplied every day. She brought her own sheets and pillowcases.[10]

Even excluding the hundreds of valets and maids and footmen and cooks and cleaners, there were 205 members of George V's household, and another 22 in Queen Mary's. Some had roles that weren't exactly onerous. As poet laureate, Robert Bridges was technically a member of the royal household but was rarely required to perform at court, or even to appear there. Nor was John B. Storey M.B. often called from his bed to attend the king, even though as Honorary Surgeon-Oculist in Ireland he, too, was officially a member of the royal household. But grooms-in-waiting were regularly needed. The posts of accountant and storekeeper weren't honorary. Nor was that of postmaster at Buckingham Palace, or head of household police.

The inner workings of the royal household were arcane indeed. The operational head, the man in charge of the legions of domestic staff, was the master of the household, Sir Derek Keppel. Keppel, who was the second son of the 7th Earl of Albemarle, served the king for most of both their lives. He was appointed equerry or personal attendant to George on the latter's marriage in 1893, and deputy master of the household when his master acceded to the throne in 1910. Two years later he became master of the household, and he retained that post until the abdication of George V's son in 1936. It was Keppel who stood beside Edward VIII as his father's coffin was lowered into the vault in St. George's Chapel Windsor; Keppel who, as Archbishop Lang intoned "earth to earth, ashes to ashes," handed the new king a silver bowl containing the symbolic earth for Edward to scatter over it.

In his black frock coat, high collar, and waxed white moustaches, Keppel was in effect the general manager of a large hotel, with a staff of around 120 minor officials, clerks, secretaries, and menservants and another eighty female cleaners and maids. This hotel had to feed not only the royal family but also the hundreds of men and women who ate there every day.

The royal chef, who for most of George V's reign was the Frenchman Henri Cedard, sat down in his office after lunch every day to compose the next day's menus, writing them out in a menu book, which was sent up for royal approval. Orders for everyday foodstuffs went from the chef's office to the department of the comptroller of supply, and the comptroller's staff telephoned out for them. Deliveries were made to the Trade Door in Buckingham Palace Road and taken straight to the kitchens, where a store man noted each item in a ledger that was checked by the deputy comptroller every month. (The comptrollership was a purely political office; the work of the department was carried out by the deputy.) A massive cold storage held chicken, beef, lamb, grouse, pheasant, and partridge in season. Fruits, vegetables, and meats were regularly sent in from the royal gardens and farms at Sandringham, Balmoral, and Windsor. Whatever the chef required for the day, he had to record on a form, which the storekeeper later gave to the deputy comptroller's office for entering in a ledger, so that in theory every single item of food coming into the palace and being consumed was accounted for. Likewise, wines and champagne brought up from the royal cellars were checked in and out; although it was considered one of the perks of working in the palace that servants could help themselves to an occasional glass.

George V and his queen were careful to maintain a remoteness from the public, from their staff, even from their children. Both believed that the monarchy required it. (Their son George VI, on the other hand, was much more affable and approachable. At the private dances he gave once a fortnight at Buckingham Palace during the Second World War, he could be seen leading a conga line, followed by Queen Elizabeth, the Princesses Elizabeth and Margaret, and their guests, out of the Bow Room on the ground floor of the palace and through the maze of corridors, while the dance band played to an empty room until eventually their sovereign reappeared, slightly out of breath.) But that remoteness was, paradoxically, combined with continual exposure. A glance at the court circulars for a single week in May 1927 gives some indication of George V's engagements.

On Monday, May 2, 1927, the king and queen were driven from Windsor up to Buckingham Palace, arriving in time for lunch. The next morning the king received the prime minister, the new governor of the Falkland Islands, and an official in the Chinese service. Later that day, he and Queen Mary, together with their daughter and the ladies and gentlemen of the household in waiting, attended a charity screening of a new British war film, *The Flag Lieutenant*, at the Marble Arch Pavilion. On Wednesday, they gave lunch to King Manuel and Queen Augusta Victoria of Portugal; on Thursday, to Alexander and Lady Patricia Ramsay, the Duke of Connaught's son-in-law and daughter, before dining at the Marquess of Salisbury's town house in Arlington Street.

On Friday, the king gave an audience to the new ambassadors of Italy and Panama and his own foreign secretary, Austen Chamberlain. The queen went round to Marlborough House to inspect alterations being made there to prepare it as a residence for the Prince of Wales. On Saturday, the king was visited by the Duke of Connaught and received senior officers from the army and navy as well as the Earl of Lytton, who was giving up his post as governor of Bengal. (Queen Mary went to the pictures again, this time to a charity matinee of an American melodrama called *The Self Starter*.) When George V and Mary went to church in the private chapel at Buckingham Palace on

Sunday morning, the fact was published in the newspapers. When they toured the Royal Academy exhibition that afternoon, it was news.

Three weeks later, at the end of May 1927, enormous crowds gathered in the Mall, far more than the usual handfuls of onlookers and tourists who habitually hung around the Victoria Memorial. They were there to catch a glimpse of a living legend. George V was presenting Charles Lindbergh with the Air Force Cross, "in recognition of the valuable and distinguished service rendered to aviation by his recent flight from New York to Paris."[11] So great was Lindbergh's fame—the *Spirit of St. Louis* had been surrounded on the runway by thousands of cheering people when he landed at Croydon the previous day—that after his twenty minutes with the king and queen he disappeared into an equerry's room to sign autographs. The Duke and Duchess of York's thirteen-month-old daughter, Princess Elizabeth (later to be Queen Elizabeth II), was brought down by her nurse to see him; he patted her on the cheek.

THERE WAS A PATTERN TO the king's annual progress. Windsor for Ascot Week; the Isle of Wight for Cowes Week, where he lived aboard the royal yacht, the *Victoria and Albert*, and went racing in the *Britannia*; Norfolk or the north of England for the Glorious Twelfth of August. Then it was up to Scotland.

Balmoral in Aberdeenshire had been in the royal family since 1852, when Prince Albert bought the estate and commissioned William Smith of Aberdeen to build a rather solid Scots Baronial mansion. (An ability to choose architects with flair was never one of the British royal family's talents.) The king and queen usually spent September there for the annual Gathering of the Braemar Royal Highland Society, a celebration of Scottish traditional culture and sports, which is still going strong today.

In 1927, George V went to Balmoral from the Earl of Sefton's Abbeystead estate in Lancashire, where he had been shooting; he was joined later by Queen Mary and the Duke and Duchess of York, with little Princess Elizabeth. Every step of the king's journey was attended by ceremony. At Aberdeen Station, he was greeted by the lord provost of the city, the chief constable, and local magistrates; at Ballater, at the end of the line from Aberdeen and the nearest station to Balmoral, he was met by a guard of honor from the King's Guard of the 1st Battalion the Royal Scots and the lord lieutenant of Aberdeenshire.

Queen Mary's journey was no different. She set off from London by train the same day to visit her daughter at Goldsborough Hall in Yorkshire. A special saloon was attached to the Harrogate train, members of the public lined the barriers on either side as the train pulled out of King's Cross, and at Harrogate Station there were crowds waiting to cheer as she left by car for Goldsborough. When she arrived at Balmoral five days later, the King's Guard of the 1st Battalion the Royal Scots was there to meet her. So was the lord lieutenant of Aberdeenshire.

As at Windsor during Ascot week, George V hosted a house party and held dinners at Balmoral each night. Twenty thousand people came to the Braemar Gathering itself. George V and Queen Mary arrived in an open carriage with outriders at three o'clock for a march-past by the three clans concerned, the Balmoral Highlanders, the Duff Highlanders, and the Invercauld Highlanders. The king and queen missed the first part of the program, perhaps because it began with a ninety-minute bagpipe competition.

In the midst of so much ritual, there occurred an event insignificant in itself but all the more startling in its banality, its descent from majesty. The Saturday after the Braemar Gathering there was a charity fête in the grounds of Balmoral in aid of the parish hall in the local village of Crathie. For three hours, George V stood in the flower tent and acted as auctioneer; hundreds of people filed past to pay him for flowers grown at Balmoral or sent up from Sandringham and Windsor. Sir Derek Keppel acted as cashier. So many people wanted to buy from their king (nearly five thousand tickets to the fête had been sold at five shillings a head) that when supplies of flowers and Scottish heather began to run low, George asked his attendants to cut down the heather used to decorate the front of his stall so that he could sell that. Then he began selling off the vases and bowls that had held the flowers. Sir Frederick Ponsonby, keeper of the privy purse, auctioned off a painting of St. Paul's churchyard by Winston Churchill; it made 115 guineas after Sir Frederick pointed out that it was unique, the only picture done by a chancellor of the exchequer at the request of a sovereign. The queen and the Duke and Duchess of York sold off a collection of goods donated by various members of the royal family. And behind their stall Princess Elizabeth sat in her pram, playing with a dancing doll.

These descents from Olympus were rare. George V was not a people's king, although, by and large, the people adored him. Almost every step he took was public property: when, a few days after the charity fête, he watched a documentary about the First World War naval battles of Coronel and the Falkland Islands, the screening made the national papers. So did his conversation afterward with the film's director, his surprise that many of the incidents depicted in the film had been shot in the studio, and even the fact that he wore "conventional evening dress of the Highlander, with kilt and sporran."[12]

THE ONE PLACE WHERE THE king could find a refuge from formality and the cares of state was "dear old Sandringham, the place I love better than anywhere else in the world."[13] To George V's children, five of whom were born there, it was simply "the Big House." Edward VIII remembered that "to us 'home' always meant Sandringham."[14] George VI wrote, "I love the place."[15]

Sandringham was Edward VII's creation. When he came of age in 1862, his mother and father decided he needed a country home of his own. Lord Palmerston proposed an eight-thousand-acre shooting estate in Norfolk belonging to his stepson. Prince Albert approved; and although he died before negotiations had begun, Queen Victoria was keen to see her husband's wishes carried out. The country roundabout was plain and the eighteenth-century stuccoed house at its center was ugly, but everything was in good order; and the fact that Prince Albert had approved of the scheme was enough to convince his widow that the rather high asking price, £220,000, was worth it. The following year, Edward married Princess Alexandra of Denmark, and the couple moved in.

For a time they tinkered with the old house's inadequate accommodations. Two smaller houses were built in the grounds to take the overflow of guests, Park House and Bachelor's Cottage, and a new servants' wing was added to the main building. But it wouldn't do. By 1868 they had four children (with two more to come in the next three years), and they decided to replace the mansion at Sandringham with something fit for purpose.

With that knack that the Victorian royal family had for choosing second-rate architects, Edward went to Albert Jenkins Humbert, who had worked for Prince Albert and who was currently building the Prince Consort's mausoleum at Frogmore. Humbert came up with a design in what Pevsner calls "a frenetic Jacobean."[16] That freneticism was compounded by piecemeal additions made by the Norfolk architect Robert Edis—"a popularizer rather than an innovator," said his kindly biographer—who built on a ballroom in 1883 and a new suite of bedrooms in the early 1890s, in that florid mix of Elizabethan and Jacobean styles that has come to be known, and not always affectionately, as Jacobethan.[17] The end result was a jumble of turrets and gables and pediments and chimneystacks and a set of interiors that combined James I, Charles II, and Queen Anne in an entirely Victorian way.

But to George V, it was home. At least, the Sandringham Estate was—but that's not quite the same thing. After Edward VII died in 1910, his widow Queen Alexandra was reluctant to accept that she no longer had the status of a reigning queen. She was perhaps encouraged in this by her unmarried daughter, Princess Victoria, who lived with her and who didn't like her sister-in-law Queen Mary, describing her as "deadly dull."[18] It was seven months before Alexandra moved out of Buckingham Palace to make way for the new king and queen, and she didn't move out of Sandringham House at all.

George V couldn't bring himself to ask his mother to leave. So she shut up her husband's bedroom, keeping everything in it as it had been while he was alive, and stayed put. The king, the queen, their six children, a tutor, a governess, an equerry, a lady-in-waiting, and a private secretary all had to cram into the Bachelor's Cottage, renamed York Cottage after Edward VII gave it to George (then Duke of York) on his marriage in 1893. And there they stayed whenever they came to Sandringham, while the Queen Mother and Princess Victoria had the Big House. "It is my mother's home. My father built it for her," the king would say, whenever his exasperated wife complained.[19]

York Cottage wasn't as small as all that; it had been extended twice since 1893. But it was pokey: a Cambridge vicar who came to preach in 1924 was surprised to see that the drawing room was smaller than his own, while a future Archbishop of Canterbury, Cosmo Lang, was reminded of a visit to a curate and his wife in their own home.*

Nor was York Cottage an English Petit Trianon, an exquisite architectural display case filled with elegant baubles. In fact it was downright ugly. Harold Nicolson gave a devastating account of it in his official biography of George V, published in 1952:

> A glum little villa, encompassed by thickets of laurel and rhodo-
> dendron, shadowed by huge Wellingtonias and separated by an
> abrupt rim of lawn from a pond, at the edge of which a leaden
> pelican gazes in dejection upon the water lilies and bamboos . . .
> The rooms inside, with their fumed oak surrounds, their white
> overmantels framing oval mirrors, their Doulton tiles and stained
> glass fanlights, are indistinguishable from those of any Surbiton
> or Upper Norwood home.[20]

The situation wasn't ideal. Sir Frederick Ponsonby, who acted as the king's private secretary in the early years of his reign, had to do his work in his bedroom. Most of the servants slept out in neighboring cottages because there was no room for them. Sir Charles Cust, one of George V's equerries, said in an unguarded moment that it was absurd that a large house like Sandringham should be inhabited "by an old lady and her daughter," while York Cottage had to accommo-date a married man with a family of six, "more especially when that man happened to be the King."[21] Some helpful soul reported Cust's

---

* Visiting clergy were advised to preach for precisely fourteen minutes. Any less, and they risked being accused by the king of being too lazy to prepare a sermon. Any more, and he might say they didn't know when to stop.

remarks to Princess Victoria, and she swore she would never speak to him again; the king tore him off a strip and told him that who occupied Sandringham was none of his business.

In fact George V could have leased a decent-sized Norfolk country house at any time. There were plenty available, especially after the war. The truth was, a reluctance to upset his elderly, deaf, and formidable mother wasn't the only reason he kept the faith at York Cottage. He liked the overcrowded Christmases and the chaotic weekend parties where visiting royalty was boarded out with his mother or in neighboring houses. He liked his "glum little villa."

On November 19, 1925, the eighty-year-old Queen Alexandra had a heart attack at the Big House. Her son, who was out shooting on the estate, was sent for immediately, and the royal shooting party dispersed early the next morning after taking leave of the king at York Cottage. He and his wife spent the rest of the day at Sandringham. They were at Alexandra's bedside when she died late that afternoon.

It wasn't until the following spring that the king and queen finally made the move from York Cottage to the main house, and then it was with reluctance. "Very sad that tonight is the last night we sleep in this dear little house in which we have spent 33 very happy years," George V confided to his diary at the end of March 1926, and when it came to it even Queen Mary was sorry to leave her "very cosy and comfortable home."[22]

Sandringham was neither little nor cozy. A *porte cochère*, that drive-through carriage porch so beloved by the designers of Victorian railway stations and Edwardian hotels, led into an enormous space called the saloon, but really a Jacobethan living hall complete with a minstrels' gallery. A long, long corridor ended in the ballroom, also Jacobethan and hung with dark stamped leather. The dining room was paneled and set with a series of tapestries woven from cartoons by Goya and other Spanish artists; the drawing room was all white stucco and mirrors. A full-length portrait of Queen Alexandra presided, and still presides, over the chimneypiece.

Queen Mary took to the refurbishment of Sandringham with the same enthusiasm she had shown at Buckingham Palace. The stamped leather wall hangings came down to be replaced by wallpaper; glass chandeliers went up, and Georgian furniture moved in, while Alexandra's bric-à-brac and stuffed fauna moved out along with Princess Victoria, who went off to live in Buckinghamshire.

The king and queen spent every Christmas and New Year at Sandringham with their children, their children's spouses, their grandchildren, and a select assortment of courtiers. Nora Wigram, who came for eleven days at Christmas 1926 with her husband, Clive, a royal equerry, found the experience both charming and daunting. Daunting, because she brought with her the three Wigram children, aged thirteen, eleven, and six, and she spent most of the stay expecting them to disgrace themselves and her in front of the king. (They didn't.) Charming, because George V and Queen Mary were easy and generous hosts, constantly inquiring after the children's comfort and going out of their way to make the Wigrams feel at home. On their arrival, the guests were shown to their rooms by the king and queen, and after they had settled in, George V insisted on the children being brought down to meet him and have some tea.

Christmas Eve afternoon was taken up with the distribution of beef to all the workers on the estate in the coach house, with the entire house party in attendance. Six-year-old Francis Wigram sat on his mother's lap for an hour while men in blue butcher coats handed out the meat. "His comments had to be restrained at times," wrote Nora Wigram in her journal of the visit.[23] Christmas morning meant church and, after tea, a gathering in the Ball Room for presents. "I was overcome by the generosity of the King & Queen & these were the things I got," wrote Nora. "A Kashmir shawl, a rose bowl, antique tea-caddy of tortoiseshell & ivory, grey leather bag, an evening bag of gold tissue, 2 little enamel boxes and an ashtray."[24] Bizarrely, six-year-old Francis got a pipe, a tobacco pouch, and two ashtrays.

The big celebratory dinner was held on Boxing Day, when there were crackers and paper hats. The queen wore a pope's mitre, the Prince of Wales a penguin's head. Only the king was spared. Afterward, everyone decamped to the Ball Room again, where the Duchess of York and the four princes congregated at one end and sang rude music hall songs (in a low voice, so the king couldn't hear), while the others sat around smoking and chatting. The king turned on a gramophone and played *La Traviata*, "The Song of the Volga Boatmen," and then, just to make sure his guests were paying attention, the national anthem. Everyone leapt to their feet, while he roared with laughter.

It was from Sandringham that George V broadcast his first Christmas message to the Empire six years later. Just after 3:00 p.m. on Christmas Day 1932, he addressed a quarter of the world's population (the ones with access to wireless sets, anyway) from a tiny room under the stairs, empty except for a table and chair and two microphones in cases of Australian walnut. The three-minute speech, which had been written for the occasion by Rudyard Kipling, praised the wireless, "one of the marvels of modern science," for its ability to bring nations together, before ending with a blessing. "I speak now from my home and from my heart . . . To all—to each—I wish a happy Christmas. God bless you!"[25]

The rest of the house party—which included the Prince of Wales, the Duke of York with his Duchess, the young Princesses Elizabeth and Margaret Rose, and the Duke of Gloucester—listened in on a wireless set in another room. When it was done, everyone gathered in the ballroom for the king and queen to hand out gifts from beneath the Christmas tree.

In another sign that Sandringham was embracing modernity, this year the lights on the tree were electric.

5

REINSTATEMENT

❧❦

For the thirty-one-year-old architect Philip Tilden, the end of the
First World War offered a fresh start in a career that had all but
ended before it began. In 1914 he had been well on his way to establishing a reputation as a designer in the Arts and Crafts tradition,
with a string of small commissions and one big one—the rebuilding
of Porth-en-Alls, a romantic vernacular revival house tucked into
the cliff at Prussia Cove in Cornwall, which blended modern ferro-
concrete construction with traditional granite and oak.

Then came the war, and with it a bout of ill health, which kept
Tilden out of the army. Work on Porth-en-Alls ground to a halt,
never to be restarted. Tilden's practice faded, and he took up farming
in Devon. He didn't turn his back completely on architecture, however: a 1916 meeting at the Ritz with Gordon Selfridge led to a commission to design a 450-foot tower for the top of the latter's Oxford
Street department store. But that project also came to nothing.

Years later, Tilden recalled how he and his wife heard the church
bell ringing out across the Devon moors to announce the Armistice and
how, as they walked their land, they resolved to turn their back on "an
interlude of chaotic and incoherent years of agony" and focus instead on
the future.[1] "In the great theatre of the world the lights had vanished,
the footlights were on, the curtain lifted, and the play began."[2]

PHILIP TILDEN. "IN THE GREAT THEATRE OF THE WORLD THE LIGHTS HAD VANISHED, THE FOOTLIGHTS WERE ON, THE CURTAIN LIFTED, AND THE PLAY BEGAN." (Copyright: RIBA Collections)

Tilden was to become one of the most prolific country-house architects of the interwar period and a leading player in what he called "a veritable infection of reinstatement," the restoration and reinvention of ancient mansions. The first act in this new phase of his hitherto undistinguished architectural career was directed by Sir Martin Conway—art historian, mountaineer, prolific author, politician, and first director-general of the Imperial War Museum, who, as the war ended, was in the middle of restoring Allington Castle, a medieval ruin near Maidstone in Kent.

"More ruined castles," wrote Christopher Hussey in 1942, "have been restored and domesticated in the last thirty years than probably at any other epoch."[3] Conway and his wife, Katrina, were in the vanguard of this rage to domesticate the past. They bought Allington in 1905 after placing an advertisement in the *Times* asking for information on old houses that might be for sale—purely, Conway claimed later, so that it would give them something to do when they were out for a weekend drive in their new Panhard. They motored down to Maidstone one June morning to see the place, and as they approached, both were convinced they had wasted their time. "The surroundings were abominable," wrote Conway in 1918. There were neglected farm buildings, a tar-paving factory "with all its hideous accessories," fields of nettles, and ugly new oast houses or kilns for drying hops. "But suddenly on turning a corner the thing itself emerged before us—a dream of beauty."[4]

This dream of beauty was the crumbling, ivy-covered remains of a moated castle put up in the thirteenth century and altered by the Wyatt family in the sixteenth. The floors were propped up with scaffolding poles; the roofs were barely watertight. "Nothing was ever more picturesque," said Conway, "or less fitted for comfortable human habitation."[5] By 1914, with the help of the architect W. D. Caroë, Conway had cleared away the ivy, the farm buildings, and the factory and had diverted a public path that ran by the castle and excavated the partly filled-in moat. The Tudor long gallery was reconstructed, and after several rooms had been repaired and made habitable, the Conways moved in and sold the lease of their London house to the US president-to-be, Herbert Hoover.

Then came the war and a falling-out with Caroë, whom Conway described as having "a pugnacious disposition."[6] A month or two before the Armistice, Philip Tilden, who knew Conway's daughter Agnes, was invited down to see if he and Allington suited each other. Days later he moved to Kent on a retainer of two pounds a week, lodging first in a neighboring village and eventually in the castle itself. His job was to survey the castle, to continue the long, slow process of restoration, and to help Katrina Conway in turning a meadow that sloped down to the moat into an attractive formal garden, with a long walk, a round lily pool, and low lavender hedges of silver gray.

Tilden frequently found himself at odds with Martin Conway, who couldn't see the point in his wife's garden making (until it was finished, when he claimed the idea for his own) and whose approach to the reclaiming of Allington was too pragmatic for his architect:

> We set at naught the theories of the so-called antiscrape school [said Conway]. According to them we ought never to have replaced old work by new of the same design. Our renovations and repairs ought to have been obviously modern and of to-day. My principle was that I must retain every existing old feature, but that I was then free to do what I liked, with a view not to an attempted re-creation of what had disappeared, but to the one controlling purpose of making a beautiful thing of the whole.[7]

Tilden could complain about the way that reinforced concrete ceilings and floors, which Conway insisted on introducing as a fire prevention measure, made the bedrooms into chilly, echoing boxes. He could wince at the steel girders that replaced beams and at how windows had been cut through exterior walls: Conway's response was that "several generations had made holes in the walls wherever they needed them, and we could do the like."[8] He could disapprove of Caroë's solution to the problem of damp in the ground-floor rooms, which was to cover a bed of concrete with asphalt and carry it up the walls for a few feet. It made no difference to his client, who wanted warmth, light, and comfort. In the meantime, the Conways' daughter Agnes toiled away in the British Museum and the Public Record Office to unravel Allington's pedigree, which stretched back to the Norman conquest. The restoration took more than a quarter of a century to complete; Tilden was still working on it until shortly before Katrina Conway's death in 1933.

"During those first few years after the armistice," Tilden later remembered, "I found that my work lay mostly in the way of mending up things that had become shabby."[9] He wasn't alone. In southeast England, the great example was Hever Castle, a fortified and double-moated manor house thirty miles south of London. Hever possessed most of the prerequisites for a successful castle restoration. For one thing, it had the architectural pedigree. Parts dated back to 1270, while others were from the late fifteenth and early sixteenth centuries, when it belonged to the Boleyn family. Hever was still, as a late-Victorian guidebook put it, "an excellent specimen of the later castellated mansion."[10]

For another, it had romantic associations. Anne Boleyn spent her childhood there, and Henry VIII visited her at Hever during their courtship. (Her ghost was said to appear on Christmas Eve and drift mournfully around the grounds.) After Anne's father's death in 1539, the castle came into the possession of the king, who gave it to Anne of Cleves as part of her divorce settlement.

And it had the potential to be a comfortable country home. The Tudor mansion of the Boleyns was still habitable and partly furnished, even though, as an article of 1907 put it, it was being used by "humble farmers whose ducks and geese swam in the old moat, whose kitchens were the once proud Hall . . . whose corn and potatoes lay stacked in the chambers that were haunted by so many memories."[11*]

In 1903, two years before the Conways discovered Allington, Hever acquired the final prerequisite, a rich owner. In fact, William Waldorf Astor was more than just rich. Born in New York, in 1848, he inherited in 1890 a fortune estimated at $100 million, making him one of the wealthiest men in America. But he didn't warm to the land of his birth; that same year he decamped with his family to England, declaring that "America is not a fit place for a gentleman to live."[12] He bought Cliveden in Buckinghamshire in 1893, and ten years later, having become a naturalized British citizen, he acquired Hever.

Astor and his architect, Frank Pearson, retained the Boleyns' manor house on its original footprint and left the exterior more or less untouched. The interiors, however, were transformed. Everywhere there was paneling in Italian walnut or English oak, brand-new carved work in the style of Grinling Gibbons, and chimneypieces of Verona marble. Tapestries and Tudor portraits, bought by Astor to

---

* These "humble farmers" were showing Hever to the public in the 1890s, along with what that late-Victorian guidebook described as "some questionable Tudor relics." Visitors were allowed to view Anne Boleyn's apartments, which had the date 1584 on the outside (she was executed in 1533); and the room in which Anne of Cleves died in 1557 (she actually died in Chelsea).

evoke Hever's famous past, hung on the walls; suits of armor guarded the entrance. An entire mock-Tudor village of domestic offices and guest rooms, all designed by Pearson and built by a 750-strong army of workmen, sprang up beyond the moat, an ingenious solution to the problem of providing extra accommodation for visitors and a large staff. "I could not believe that they had been built a few short months ago," wrote Astor in 1907, "they seemed so old and crooked, and possessed such individuality as thought they had grown up one by one in various ages, as those old villages did which we sometimes see on our travels, sheltering themselves under the walls of the overlord."[13]

The picturesque charm of the arrangement is obvious (as are the feudal undertones), although Pearson maintained that the real reason for the village beyond the moat was that Astor—who went in fear of plots against his life, installed a forbidding set of electrically operated gates and kept a posse of policemen on the grounds to guard against intruders—liked to show his guests off the premises at night and raise the drawbridge behind them.

Casual sightseers were no longer allowed, causing a lot of local resentment, and his obsession with security earned Hever's owner the nickname of William "Walled-off" Astor. Philip Tilden, looking back after the Second World War, lamented the passing of tumbledown old Hever "as I first saw it in the nineties, with its grey skirts sweeping the waters of the moat, set around with the blue swords of the wild flag . . . it has now become a miniature Metropolitan Museum of New York."[14] The castle was somehow un-English, as though Astor had tried just a little too hard, creating a Gilded Age mansion in the heart of the Kent countryside without exhibiting that noblesse oblige that would have made the gilt more palatable.

"Walled-off" Astor died in 1919. In the sixteen years between his purchase of Hever and his death, that "veritable infection of reinstatement" had begun to sweep through Kent and Sussex. Tilden himself was working on Allington for the Conways. Down on the Kent coast, Henry Beecham bought the medieval Lympne Castle, perched on a spectacular site high above Romney Marsh in Kent, with views across the English Channel to France, from Frank Tennant, who had rescued the castle and commissioned a gentle and sensitive Arts and Crafts restoration from Sir Robert Lorimer, "the Scottish Lutyens."*

A few miles to the west, Bodiam Castle was being rescued by George Nathaniel Curzon, 1st Earl Curzon, 5th Baron Scarsdale, 9th Baronet, and, from 1921, Marquess Curzon of Kedleston, with a pedigree stretching back to the conquest, and a seat, Kedleston Hall in Derbyshire, that the family had occupied in its various forms for almost as long.† Curzon had already bought one castle: in 1911, when it was rumored that the fifteenth-century Tattershall in Lincolnshire was to be sold to an American syndicate that planned to tear it down and ship it across the Atlantic, he stepped in to save it for the nation: such buildings, he said, "speak to us of the valour and strength of our ancestors."[15] Four chimneypieces were discovered in packing cases at Tilbury Docks and returned by Curzon to Tattershall in a triumphal procession of wagons decorated with the Union Jack.

Curzon first saw Bodiam, a romantic fourteenth-century ruin on the border between Kent and Sussex, in about 1905. Enchanted with a building that, he said, "transports us at a bound to the days when the third Edward was fighting his foreign wars or the hunchback Richard was casting his nefarious die for the throne," he tried to buy it, but the owner, the 1st Lord Ashcombe, refused to sell.[16] He didn't give up, and in 1917 Ashcombe's son agreed to the sale. Two years later William Weir, an architect who had made his reputation as a restorer of historic buildings and who had worked for Curzon on the repair of Tattershall, began a careful program of restoration. The moat and basement area were excavated, trees and ivy were cleared away, and the stonework was repaired.

---

* Lindisfarne and Lympne both changed hands as a result of the war. Hudson, who had no children of his own, intended to leave Lindisfarne to Billy Congreve, the young son of his friend General Sir Walter Congreve; but Billy was killed in France in 1916, and Hudson sold the place five years later. The Tennants' son Mark was also killed in 1916; they put Lympne on the market the following year.

† Famously aloof, the lines of doggerel written against Curzon when he was a student at Balliol followed him for the rest of his life:

My name is George Nathaniel Curzon, / I am a most superior person. /
My cheek is pink, my hair is sleek, / I dine at Blenheim once a week.

At this point Curzon parted company from his neighboring castle owners. He briefly entertained the notion of moving into Bodiam but rejected the idea, perhaps because with his father's death in 1916, Kedleston Hall, "the glory of Derbyshire," was now his, along with its stunning Adam furnishings. He was also renting the late-Elizabethan Montacute House in Somerset. He didn't need a castle to live in. So, in a barbed response to his neighbors' veritable infection of reinstatement, he refrained, he said, "from what might have easily degenerated into an archaeological crime" and left Bodiam roofless and ruinous.[17] Philip Tilden was in complete agreement, praising the fact that no attempt had been made to reconstruct the interior of the castle. "It still remains now a permanent and austerely satisfying ruin," he wrote. "There is nothing to criticise."[18]

By now the castle habit was sweeping through southeast England. In 1911, the Unionist MP Claude Lowther came to lunch at Allington. "We discussed restoration all afternoon," Conway noted in his diary.[19] Lowther had just bought Herstmonceux Castle in Sussex, a magnificent redbrick mansion of the fifteenth century, thirty miles to the south of Allington. It had lain in ruins since 1777, when its then owner decided it was too costly to repair and pulled down a large part of it, leaving only the shell of its walls and towers.

Lowther was an eccentric character—he greeted weekend guests wearing a formal courtier's uniform of black knee breeches, black silk stockings, and buckled shoes and kept a pet ram, who was allowed to roam round the house at will among the tapestries and antique furniture he had bought for Herstmonceux. "He cared nothing about archaeology or historical correctness," commented Conway without a hint of criticism; and as they worked away throughout the 1910s and 1920s Lowther and his architect Cecil Perkins paid scant attention to the past, sweeping away courtyards, widening the moat and lowering its banks to improve the view, building a new great hall on a completely different site from the old, and introducing features that ranged from an old wall reputed to have once formed part of Hastings Castle to a great staircase that came from Theobalds, the great house

**Flamboyance at Claude Lowther's Herstmonceux Castle:
The ante-room to the drawing room in the 1930s.** (Copyright:
Country Life)

built by Lord Burghley in the sixteenth century. The result, to quote
Conway again, "is one of the most beautiful sights in England."[20]

Down on the Kent coast, thirty miles southeast of Allington, yet
another castle was being rehabilitated. On Wednesday afternoons
tourists could climb to the ramparts of Saltwood Castle to enjoy the
striking views across the Channel to France, while guides regaled
them with stories of how at dawn on December 29, 1170, four of Henry
II's knights left Saltwood for Canterbury Cathedral, where they mur-
dered Archbishop Thomas Becket. Fragments of that twelfth-century
castle survived, along with a later castellated gatehouse, although in
1580 the castle was badly damaged in an earthquake, which considerably diminished its attraction as a residence. It remained a romantic
ruin until the 1880s, when the Deedes family converted the gatehouse
into a home and moved in.

The expense of maintaining Saltwood and the discomfort of living in it eventually proved too much for them. "Water ran down the walls, there was no electricity or gas, and fires had to be lit in every room just to keep the damp at bay," wrote the journalist William Deedes, who spent part of his childhood there.[21] In 1926 Saltwood was sold to Reginald Lawson, whose family owned the *Daily Telegraph* and whose Texan wife, Iva, had a passion for castles.

One castle wasn't enough for Iva. When Claude Lowther died in 1929, Herstmonceux was put on the market, and she persuaded her husband to buy it. The couple's plans came to a sudden end one afternoon in December 1930, when Reginald failed to return to Saltwood in time for tea and a search revealed his body lying in nearby woods with a gunshot wound to the head and a discharged shotgun lying beside him. Iva put Herstmonceux on the market again, and it was bought by a one-legged baronet, Sir Paul Latham, MP, who, with his antiquarian-minded architect Walter Godfrey, finally completed the restoration begun by Lowther in 1911.

The Kent reinstaters formed an elite community, and their paths crossed frequently, sometimes in unexpected ways. In her widowhood, Iva Lawson devoted herself to restoring Saltwood, a task that in 1934 took her up to Allington Castle for advice and inspiration. Sir Martin Conway was now Lord Conway, having been raised to the peerage as Baron Conway of Allington. The last years of his marriage to Katrina had been complicated by his long-running affair with a divorcee forty-four years younger than him. Since a lot of the Conways' money had come from Katrina's stepfather, a wealthy New York newspaper owner, when Katrina died in November 1933, she pointedly left her estate, including the castle, to their only daughter, Agnes.

Conway continued to live at Allington (without his mistress, who married someone else), but the lure of Mrs. Lawson—and a fresh castle—proved impossible to resist. "Don't faint," he warned his sister a few months after Katrina's death, "I am going to marry Iva Lawson."[22] So he did, in a quiet ceremony at Caxton Hall Westminster on November 17, 1934. Afterward, Iva slipped out by a back entrance while Conway left by the front door, accompanied by one of the female guests. When he was asked if a photograph might be taken, he said, "Yes, but this is not the bride." He was seventy-eight; Iva was thirty-two.

Conway immediately brought in Philip Tilden to complete Salt-wood's restoration, and the bridge and groom had a happy two and a half years together, watching Tilden rebuild the immense Archbish-op's Audience Hall, "one of the finest great halls in England," accord-ing to Conway.[23] It was almost finished by the time of Conway's own death in 1937, and Iva filled it with tapestries and old church furnish-ings as a monument to her husband and his antiquarian taste. "Relics of the pageantry of five centuries and a dozen nationalities breathe their aroma of romance through the once bare and ruined apart-ments," enthused *Country Life*.[24]

ONE MORE CASTLE PROJECT FROM these years deserves a mention. More than a mention, in fact. When the essayist E. V. Lucas looked down from an airplane window on his native Kent during a flight from Paris to London in 1931 and saw a vast castle rising out of a lake, he was bowled over. "I had heard of such wonders, but only in the realms of grand opera and fantasy," he said. "It is incredible, unearthly. You rub your eyes."[25]

The unearthly stronghold was Leeds Castle near Maidstone, a romantic fortress built on a series of small islands in a lake formed from the River Len. Leeds had been a royal residence for much of the Middle Ages. It once belonged to Eleanor of Castile: her widowed husband, Edward I, honeymooned here in 1299 with his second wife, Margaret of France, and it became a tradition for English kings to grant the castle to their queens as part of their dower. Major building work was carried out in the early sixteenth century for Henry VIII and Catherine of Aragon and again in the 1630s, although by then it had passed into private hands.

In 1822 parts of the castle were in a ruinous condition, and the owner, Fiennes Wykeham-Martin, spent a fortune replacing them with a battlemented and turreted piece of Georgian medievalism, which nearly ruined him. His son's judicious marriage helped to restore the family fortunes, but by the 1920s, the Wykeham-Martins were losing the battle to maintain Leeds. In 1921 Charles Wykeham-Martin tried without success to let the furnished "beautiful and historic castle," on either a long or a short lease.[26] He tried again in 1923, when he let it be known that if no private tenant could be found he would be prepared to accept offers from a school or other institution. But again there were no takers.

Two years later he tried for a third time. The agents, Knight, Frank & Rutley, did their best. Leeds was "a Plantagenet and Tudor Royal Residence . . . one of the most beautiful inhabited castles in the country." (The Wykeham-Martins hadn't actually inhabited it for years.) Set in "an undulating and timber park," it boasted "imposing Halls, a fine suite of six Entertaining rooms, Chapel, twenty Principal and Secondary Bedrooms."

Still, there were no takers, and it seemed that the castle was doomed to continue its spiral of decline. But suddenly, in February 1927, an announcement appeared in the national press that Leeds had been sold privately to a Mr. and Mrs. Wilson Filmer for £200,000. The new owners planned to turn it into a comfortable modern residence.

Olive Wilson Filmer, who was to make Leeds Castle her home for the next half a century, was well connected. Born in America in 1899, she could trace her ancestry to Henry Paget, the 1st Marquess of Anglesey, who commanded the cavalry at Waterloo and lost a leg in the process. Olive's first husband and the father of her two young daughters was the Hon. Charles Winn, second son of Lord St. Oswald of Nostell Priory. If her second husband, Arthur Wilson Filmer, had a less aristocratic pedigree, he was still perfectly eligible, a big game hunter with a town house in Mayfair and a rambling Tudor country house, East Sutton Place in Kent. Not as eligible as Olive, though: her American mother Pauline was a Whitney heiress, and when she died in 1916, she left Olive a fortune in the region of $2 million.

Olive divorced Charles Winn in 1925 and married Arthur Wilson Filmer the same year. They began their life together by renting Bawdsey Manor, an extravagantly turreted example of Victorian Tudor Revival in Suffolk. Olive's pet monkey caused £2,000 worth of damage to the furnishings and landed the newlyweds in court as a result, so they had to move. Arthur knew Leeds, and with the prospect before them of so many other Kent castles being reclaimed and restored and remodeled, they began negotiations to buy it in 1926. Their decision may have been prompted not only by the example of neighbors like the Conways at Allington but also by an unpleasant incident that took place that year, when a disgruntled former servant threatened Arthur's father with a revolver and then swore he was going to burn his house to the ground. Under the circumstances, a fortified mansion surrounded by a lake had its advantages.

Leeds was in a poor state, and the Wilson Filmers laid out hefty sums—around £100,000, according to one account—on its modernization. Their architect, Owen Cary Little, was an unexceptional man in his sixties. Much more distinguished was the architect-designer that the Wilson Filmers brought in to collaborate with him— Armand Albert Rateau, whose Pavillon de l'Élegance, designed in partnership with a longtime client, the couturier Jeanne Lanvin, had caused a stir at the 1925 Exposition Internationale des Arts Décoratifs et Industriels Modernes in Paris. The Frenchman hadn't worked in England before (Leeds Castle would be his only commission in this country), but he was well known in Paris, where his Levallois workshops employed two hundred metalworkers, cabinetmakers, sculptors, and weavers, and also in New York, where his work was featured in 1925–1926 at the Metropolitan Museum. He worked in expensive materials—ivory and silk, giltwood and bronze—and in a kind of stripped-down neoclassical style, which benefited every now and then from dashes of hard, high Art Deco and a sinuous Art Nouveau.

Rateau's distinctive brand of urban sophistication wasn't particularly appropriate for an old castle in the middle of Kent. Nor was he an obvious choice for Arthur Wilson Filmer, whose own tastes tended toward the antique. We don't know who brought them together, although Cole Porter was a mutual acquaintance. However, aided by Owen Little and guided by his clients, Rateau managed to introduce into the reinvented Leeds Castle an oddly satisfying blend of Arts and Crafts medievalism, French Gothic, and Hollywood theatricality.

His main task was the transformation of the Gloriette, a D-shaped building on an island of its own and linked to the rest of the castle by its own two-storied stone bridge. The Gloriette had a complicated past. Built in the late thirteenth century on the site of a Norman keep, it was remodeled by Henry VIII in the 1520s, burned by Dutch prisoners of war in 1665, and converted into domestic offices by the Wykeham-Martins, when they built the new castle in 1822. Rateau gutted it and created an entirely new bedroom suite, a set of guest bedrooms and a set of reception rooms. The chapel was converted into a paneled writing room, with a radiogram that piped music around the castle. The great chamber built by Edward I and used by Henry VIII was converted into an evening saloon, although the way Rateau treated it—introducing carved oak beams and a massive sixteenth-century stone chimneypiece—suggested a Tudor great hall. By way of contrast, Olive's dressing room was elegantly neo-Georgian, while her onyx-lined bathroom was pure Art Deco.

Most of the ironmongery, the linen-fold paneling, and the oak beams were brand new, straight from Rateau's workshop. And they were good. A few years after it was installed, a timber-framed stair tower was mistaken by *Country Life*'s Christopher Hussey, who certainly knew his stuff, for a Regency copy of an original feature; and the staircase itself was presided over by a battered crusader, sword and shield in hand, who perches on the newel post with a lion at his feet and pretends to be the real thing. But in a manner entirely typical of the period, Rateau and his clients combined the new work with genuinely old pieces. Some chimneypieces came from different parts of the castle; others were imported from France, imparting a faint air of Fontainebleau. Antique furniture was also brought in: seventeenth- and eighteenth-century tables, beds, and cabinets from France, Spain, and England and nineteenth-century candelabra. The most impressive introduction was that of the paneled parlor from Thorpe Hall in Cambridgeshire, which was built in 1653–1656 for Cromwell's lord chief justice, Oliver St. John; it was bought in 1928 from the firm of White Allom and installed in the castle's main drawing room.

Leeds Castle was a hive of activity in the late 1920s, with local laborers mixing with contractors from London and Bath and specialist craftsmen from France and Italy. Mains for electricity and water were brought in. A new bridge was built across the lake to take a light railway, which moved materials to the site and took away the unwanted rubble. The works office was on floating pontoons. The main contractor was the London firm of Keeble & Sons, whose men lodged in the neighborhood during the week, traveling down to Maidstone by train on a Southern Railways coach marked "Leeds Castle only." The Wilson Filmers spent the week in London, coming down on weekends to inspect the work, sometimes with Olive's two young daughters from her first marriage.

Work went quickly, so that by 1928, only a year after the sale of Leeds Castle went through, the Gloriette was sufficiently finished for Arthur and Olive to entertain there; Rateau was one of their first guests. Zebras and llamas were introduced into the park, along with twenty-four flamingos, who spent a few months enjoying the lake before flying away.

Architect Owen Little died in 1931. So did the Wilson Filmers' marriage. They divorced; Arthur moved to Yorkshire, and Olive, the Lady of the Lake, kept her fairy stronghold in Kent. Her third husband, whom she married the same year, was a Scottish baronet, Sir Adrian Baillie. They had a son, whom they christened Gawaine—an appropriate name for the heir to a fantasy castle.

AT THE OTHER END OF the scale from a vast moated castle like Leeds was the manor house, late medieval perhaps, or Elizabethan or Jacobean. Most likely all three, with some Georgian paneling thrown in for good measure and a Victorian addition it would have been better off without. These smaller country houses were more numerous than their bigger brethren and more affordable. They attracted a different class of savior.

The Rev. Frederic Meyrick-Jones is a perfect example. Cultured, sporting, with antiquarian tastes and a strong social conscience,

Meyrick-Jones exemplified muscular Christianity in the early twentieth century. After Marlborough, where he didn't distinguish himself
academically, he went up to Cambridge, where he got his cricket blue
in 1888. He went on to play first-class cricket for Kent and Hampshire. He became a legendary squash amateur and an ordained priest
in the Church of England. For eight years from 1899, he ran a mission
in west London, where he gained a distinguished reputation as a billiards player, and that "by the exacting standards of a working men's
club," according to the *Times*.[27]

In 1908 Meyrick-Jones, now married with children, leased Home
Place in Norfolk, a masterpiece of the Arts and Crafts movement
designed by Edward Schultz Prior. He filled it with antiques and ran
it as an establishment for "difficult" boys.* "Although he never again
resumed a cure of souls ecclesiastically," recalled a friend, "he never
ceased to inculcate, more by example than precept, a real standard of
Christian life on all who enjoyed his friendship."[28]

Soon after the end of the First World War, Meyrick-Jones and his
wife moved to the West Country and decided to restore Woodlands
Manor, a medieval manor house at Mere in Wiltshire. Woodlands had
been in the Meyrick family since the late eighteenth century. It was
reckoned to be "one of the quaintest old world dwellings in Wiltshire."[29]
However, it was let to a local farmer and in a poor state: floors were rot-
ten, walls were bulging, and some elaborate geometrical plasterwork,
which had been introduced in Elizabethan times, was disintegrating.
The tenant used the fourteenth-century chapel as a cheese store.

In 1920 Meyrick-Jones and his wife began what he called "the restoration of this small, very old home by two amateurs."[30] The chapel
was no longer needed for a cheese store—cheese production on local
farms had petered out during the war—so the farmer, whose lease
would in any case be up in April 1921, allowed the couple to tear out the
shelves that lined the room and remove a modern stove, which filled an

---

* Home Place, also known as Voewood and Kelling Place, was built for another clergyman, Rev. Percy Lloyd. Shortly after it was finished, a sanatorium opened next
  door, and Mrs. Lloyd, concerned about contracting tuberculosis from her neighbors,
  insisted that her husband let the house.

Elizabethan fireplace. They replaced an iron tie-rod, which was preventing the walls from bulging outward, with a carved sixteenth-century beam. They repaired the ceiling and replastered the walls, and they introduced small panes of seventeenth-century glass into the windows.

A blocked doorway, which had originally given out onto an external stair, was reopened, fitted with an old studded door, and turned into a little balcony, with an Elizabethan balustrade they had acquired years before in Worcester and some medieval tiles with the arms of Richard, Duke of Cornwall, that came from a priory in neighboring Somerset. Over the chimneypiece they fixed a large carved angel bought in Cambridge. "If we happened to have among our gatherings some fine carved bit of grey oak," wrote Meyrick-Jones in his 1924 account of the restoration, "it was not always easy to refrain from inserting it somewhere!"[31]

And Meyrick-Jones did have quite a collection of "gatherings." There were tapestries, pewter and ironwork, Caroline tables and early Georgian walnut chairs, oak bedsteads, and fragments of medieval painted rood screens. He also acquired architectural fragments and salvage, mainly in the West Country. "Whenever possible, old doors—especially studded ones—were collected from any possible source," he wrote. "Also windows, hinges, latches of the 16th and 17th centuries, 'durns' or door-frames, 'Crown' glass and anything else 'early,' domestic and likely to be of use—the older the better."[32]

The patient tenant-farmer, a Mr. Day, allowed Meyrick-Jones's builder to get to work on the chamber below the cheese store chapel, which was currently fitted out as a kitchen. The range was ripped out, a cupboard with doors of linen-fold paneling was removed to reveal another blocked doorway, and Meyrick-Jones installed a Henry VIII oak frame and an early studded door—more of his gatherings.

In April 1921, having lost his cheese store and his kitchen, Mr. Day finally vacated the premises. That same evening, Meyrick-Jones personally took a sledgehammer to the walls, and over the summer, his small army of laborers and masons worked to remove the later introductions, which had turned Woodlands' two-story-high great hall into an assemblage of bedrooms and reception rooms:

The glory of housebreaking, of letting in more light, started. Partitions were ruthlessly knocked to pieces—good firewood! The floorboards of the bedrooms above were torn up. This floor sliced the height of the hall in two. The ceiling of these bedrooms which hid the roof was torn down. The nineteenth century staircase . . . which jutted out into the hall was taken down—to be used again elsewhere.[33]

With advice from the ubiquitous Philip Tilden, the clergyman reinstated the minstrel gallery overlooking the hall, making use of three bedroom doors, which turned out to be the original linen-fold panels of the gallery screen.

By 1924 the Meyrick-Joneses had moved into Woodlands, filling it with their eclectic collection of English furniture and recycled historic fittings. There were some casualties among the manor house's own fittings: in 1929, for instance, one of its best Elizabethan chimneypieces found its way to the Wilson Filmers' Leeds Castle, reputedly sold to fund the continuing restoration of the house.

By the end of the Second World War, the couple, now quite elderly, moved to another historic house, this time at Shaftesbury in Dorset, and because they had no room, or because they had no money, Frederic sold off some of their gatherings, including five seventeenth- and eighteenth-century oak bedsteads, one of which was a four-poster with a tester or canopy dating from the 1630s. He offered the lot for £185.

IT WASN'T ONLY MUSCULAR CLERGYMEN like Frederic Meyrick-Jones who rescued smaller country houses and turned them into shrines at which to worship the cult of the antique. Within a twenty-mile radius of Woodlands, Meyrick-Jones had two excellent examples to inspire him. One was Lytes Cary in Somerset, the remains of a medieval manor house that had been lovingly restored from 1907 onward by Sir Walter Jenner, son of the famous Victorian physician. The other was the exquisite Westwood Manor near Bradford-on-Avon in Wiltshire, a lovely mixture of late medieval and Jacobean, which, after spending much of the nineteenth century as a farmhouse and apple store, was bought in 1911 by the diplomat Edgar Lister, who, according to James Lees-Milne, a frequent visitor to Westood, "cordially disliked and despised" the present and "positively immersed himself quite contentedly in the past."[34]

Like the Meyrick-Jones' at Woodlands Manor, both Jenner and Lister made free use of fittings and furnishings from different periods to create an ambience, a romantic evocation of the past, with no attempt at authenticity or at establishing a period. That isn't a criticism: they weren't making museums.

But the obsession with the past could be carried to extraordinary lengths. All over England, old stone tiles were removed from ancient barns and cottages and recycled, along with the moss that covered them and provided a patina of authenticity to the roofs they covered—roofs that were carefully repaired so that they sagged in the right places. Chipped and broken bricks were no longer discarded: instead, they were put to one side until some eager antiquarian came along to turn them into new walls, laying them crookedly, of course, and making sure there was no uniformity of color. Warped and weatherworn old timbers were placed in prominent positions; clean, smooth-cut wood was only used where it couldn't be seen. Every detail of these "restorations," inside and out, had to be old. More important, it had to *look* old.

Country Life, in an article of 1924 describing Basil Ionides's restoration for himself of Howbridge Hall, a small Elizabethan country house at Witham in Essex, noted with admiration that nothing new had been used, right down to the door handles and hinges, the finger plates, and the tiles in the grates. Ionides, later to dispense with the antique dramatically in his Art Deco work at Claridges and the silver and gold interior of the Savoy Theatre, wouldn't have an electric or pneumatic bell system to summon the servants, only bell pulls in all the rooms—"they tell who is pulling and in what temper they pull."[35] Every pull was of old needlework, Queen Anne petit point in the dining room and Victorian cross-stitch everywhere else. The architect Sir Albert Richardson refused to have electricity or any modern conveniences at Avenue House, the Georgian house at Ampthill in Bedfordshire that he bought in 1919 and made his home for the next forty-five years, preferring candles and lamps and immersing himself in the past, like Lister. He was also fond of dressing up in Georgian costume around the house.

Why did they do it? Why did politicians and heiresses and clergymen sink their fortunes and their futures into refurbishing ruins? "We have had to stint and screw from year to year," wrote Conway in 1932. "I ask myself on looking back whether it was worth while."[36]

It is tempting to put it all down to the war, to assume that the crumbling stones and silver-gray oak beams somehow epitomized England and that after 1918 they were so much more precious for having been threatened. But many of the great postwar restorations— Allington and Herstmonceux, Lympne, Westwood Manor—had been started before 1914. They are best seen as part of an antiurban, anti-industrial, and antimodern tradition with a pedigree reaching back to nineteenth-century Romanticism and its offspring, the Arts and Crafts movement. Yet the war certainly honed this sensibility. The sense of reconnection with something profound that John Buchan found in Elsfield was shared by others, who, having gone through the war, opted for tea in the great parlor and swans on the moat instead of a hedonistic Jazz Age binge. Some chose both.

There was also a heightened awareness of what was being lost and of what was and was not being done to save it. In 1912 a spate of architectural scandals, including the removal of Tattershall Castle's fireplaces, led to calls for central government to be given powers to purchase threatened historic monuments, and this passed into law the following year as the Ancient Monuments Act, which also included plans for the compilation of a list or schedule of monuments reckoned to be of national importance. Once a building was on the schedule and the owner had been informed, it would be a crime to damage it. But houses were exempt from the provisions of the act; their inclusion would have been regarded as "domestic interference of the kind which is intolerable to the Englishman."[37]

As the schedules of ancient monuments began to appear after the war, there were calls for state intervention to rescue historic mansions. In 1920 an Ancient Monuments Advisory Committee was set up, and the following year it recommended that the powers of the 1913 Act should be widened to include residential buildings, with owners being compensated:

> Old country houses and manor houses are undoubtedly of first-rate importance, and should be included in any scheme of protection. The upkeep of a large country house is likely to be an ever-growing burden. The State should be prepared to recognize the services of an owner who maintains on account of its historic and artistic value a structure which is ill-suited for modern requirements.[38]

In 1923 Viscount Lascelles, later the 6th Earl of Harewood, argued that either an organization like the National Trust should try and find the money for the upkeep of unwanted historic houses, or the State, "recognising the social and artistic value of noble architecture, should afford relief to owners who allow the public to visit their heritage."[39]

All of these strategies would be adopted, but not in the near future. In the meantime, public discussions raised the profile of the historic house, while a property market in which supply continued to exceed demand meant that for those with antiquarian tastes and deep pockets there were bargains to be had.

A common thread is that so many who came to the rescue of castles and manor houses were new to country-house life. Frederic Meyrick-Jones was a clergyman; Martin Conway was a clergyman's son, only able to buy Allington Castle through the generosity of his wealthy American father-in-law. Frank Tennant's money came from chemical manufacturing, that of his successor at Lympne Castle, Henry Beecham, from patent medicines. Claude Lowther was the son of a naval officer—although admittedly he was the grandson of a peer, since his father was the illegitimate son of the 2nd Earl of Lonsdale and an opera singer. Olive Wilson Filmer was half American, Iva Lawson wholly so.

The old order was doomed, complained the Duke of Marlborough in 1919, in a reference to Tennyson's "The old order changeth, yielding place to new." Death duties were killing it. What new order would replace it? he asked. "Are these historic houses, the abiding memorials of events which live in the hearts of Englishmen, to be converted into museums, bare relics of a dead past?"[40]

Martin Conway had the answer. "If the old order changes," he wrote, "it is not to give permanent place to barbarism and civil night, but to some other equally great manifestation of that divine power which . . . always pours forth something new."[41]

6

A NEW CULTURE

N ot surprisingly, it wasn't everyone who yearned to live in a
draughty old castle or a half-derelict manor house. A country
house didn't have to boast an ancient pedigree or towers or a moat: it
could be brand new and still be attractive.

Sir Philip Sassoon, who was one of the greatest connoisseurs of the
twentieth century, built himself one new country house and remodeled
another so dramatically that he may as well have built it from scratch.
For projects like that he needed to be rich, and he was. His family
had been bankers to the caliphs of Baghdad for a thousand years. His
great-grandfather moved from Persia to Bombay in the nineteenth
century, establishing a trading empire so powerful that it was said
"silver and gold, silks, gums and spices, opium and cotton, wool and
wheat—whatever moves over sea or land feels the hand or bears the
mark of Sassoon & Co."[1] His grandfather's philanthropy earned him a
baronetcy, and his father Sir Edward married a Rothschild, Aline. The
Prince of Wales, later Edward VII, named his yacht after her.

Sir Edward Sassoon died in 1912, three years after his wife. He
left behind an eighteen-year-old daughter, Sibyl, and Philip, who was
twenty-three. He also left his enormous Park Lane mansion, built in
the 1890s for the Randlord Barney Barnato, and an even more enormous fortune. Sir Edward's estate was valued at over £750,000.

Within a year of her father's death, Sibyl married George Cholmondeley, Lord Rocksavage, who was heir to the marquessate, of Cholmondeley and vast estates in Norfolk and Cheshire, including the Palladian masterpiece Houghton Hall. She received a quarter of the Sassoon fortune; the rest went to Philip, now Sir Philip Sassoon, Bt., to be held in trust until his thirtieth birthday. In the meantime, he had to make do with an annual allowance of £12,000, well over a million pounds in today's money. When the Rocksavages set off to India on their six-month honeymoon in November 1913, Sir Philip sent them a white Rolls Royce as a wedding present to get around in while they were there.

In 1912 Sir Philip stood for parliament as MP for Hythe in Kent, succeeding his father. He was to be Hythe's Conservative MP for the rest of his life, successfully fighting seven general elections. And rather than choosing to occupy Shorncliffe Lodge, the Regency-Gothick villa in Sandgate that his father had used as a base in the constituency, Sir Philip bought a 270-acre site overlooking Romney Marsh, with a view across to the Channel and the lights of France. He commissioned Herbert Baker to build him a weekend retreat, to be called Belcaire. It was "on the lip of the world," he used to say, and so peaceful that "one can hear the dogs bark in Beauvais."[2]

Belcaire was a pleasant enough house of red brick, with the kind of Dutch gables that recalled Baker's twenty years as an architect in South Africa. It was barely finished in 1914 when Sassoon went out to France, spending most of the war as private secretary to Douglas Haig, commander-in-chief of the British armies. Even in a foreign country and in the middle of a world war, the young man (he was twenty-five when war broke out) continued to direct work on the gardens at Belcaire and managed to commission a striking series of allegorical murals for his new drawing room from a Catalan artist, José Maria Sert. In gold and sepia and black, they depicted France being harried by German eagles while her allies, in the form of naked children, came to her aid with cannon spouting flames and a pair of huge elephants reared up unaccountably to perch on the mantelpiece.

"Elephants in different attitudes": José Maria Sert's curious allegorical mural at Port Lympne. (Copyright: Country Life)

The prime minister, Herbert Asquith, who dropped in to see Belcaire in 1915 while its owner was away, was appalled at walls "of highly burnished mustard-gold, on which are frescoes of a darker shade, representing elephants in different attitudes"; his fellow tourists, Lady Desborough and Sir John Simon, the attorney general, couldn't find words to describe "their horror and disgust."[3] Sassoon, when he came home on leave, was more measured, but even he couldn't disguise his shock at what Sert had done. He was only half joking when he called the murals "monstrous" and told his friend Sir Louis Mallet they had made the drawing room so dark "that you have to whip out a pocket torch at midday or you're as good as lost."[4] Disappointed or not, after the war he still commissioned Sert to decorate the enormous ballroom at his Park Lane mansion with an even more fantastic concoction, this time in blue and silver, showing camels and more elephants making their way past temples and across desert wastes.

Sassoon held on to his Hythe seat in the general election of December 1918 with a majority of 5,382 over the Labour candidate. (Rumors that his cousin Siegfried might stand against him proved unfounded.) Having come into his inheritance that same month, he decided to extend and remodel Belcaire and to rename it Port Lympne, a reference to the ancient Roman Portus Lemanis, which stood close by before Romney Marsh was drained. Herbert Baker was busy working with Lutyens on the government complex at New Delhi, and Sir Philip brought in Philip Tilden to replace him.

One suspects that artistic direction remained with the client. Certainly Tilden never had created, and never would create again, anything as satisfyingly theatrical as the country house that took shape over the next couple of years. Tilden believed Port Lympne was Sassoon's response to the war, a challenge, a declaration that "a new culture had risen up from the sick-bed of the old, with new aspirations . . . [a] mind tuned to a new burst of imagination."[5] Other reactions ranged from astonishment to sneers. The unnamed *Country Life* correspondent who reviewed the house in 1923 was ecstatic: "An example of the artistic power and ability of its own generation . . . The splendid success of Sir Philip's bold experiment should be a great encouragement to all who have faith in the future of British art and architecture . . . The rooms at Port Lympne are a compact fairy palace in which one walks, wide-eyed, as though on air."[6] The house enchanted him. Honor Channon, on the other hand, said it reminded her of a Spanish brothel.[7] Her husband, Chips, the American-born British politician, was mesmerized by its oddness, describing it as "a triumph of beautiful bad taste and Babylonian luxury, with terrace and flowery gardens, and jade green pools and swimming baths and rooms done up in silver and blue and orange."[8] Max Beerbohm called it an "extraordinary elaboration of Persian fantasy, controlled by Etonian good taste."[9]

Glyn Philpot decorated the dining room with a frieze of white bullocks and naked black Egyptians against a chocolate-brown ground; the walls were paneled with lapis lazuli, "a living wall of moving colour" beneath a ceiling of opalescent pink. The dining chairs and table were gilded. (Legend has it that Philip called Philpot back in 1936 at short notice to add loincloths and skirts to the naked Egyptians in preparation for a visit by Queen Mary.) Paintings by Sargent, Nicholson, and Steer hung on the walls.

The Wrenaissance woodwork in Philip's small library was silver tinged with gilt; in the drawing room, reached through sliding bronze doors, Tilden set off the elephantine Sert murals by covering the walls in a dramatic black and gold faux marble, created for the purpose in a workshop at the back of Marylebone station. He also hit on the clever idea of lightening the darkness by matching the real windows with trompe l'oeil versions of black-and-oyster-colored mirror-glass in gilded lead cames. Halfway up the main staircase there was a large plate-glass window that, at the press of a switch, slid soundlessly up into the wall to give access to an enclosed Alhambra-like patio built over the domestic offices, where seven fountains played around a central well-head. "At night," said *Country Life*, "the stars are always visible from this enchanted garden and golden lights flood the arcades with mysterious radiance."[10]

Unable to bear the Sert elephants, even with the marble composition and the mirrors, Sir Philip eventually had them painted over in a range of creams, brilliant whites, and off-whites, but he compensated for their absence in grand style, commissioning the young Rex Whistler to decorate his billiard room in 1931. Sassoon was a trustee of the Tate Gallery, where Whistler had come to prominence in 1927 with his mural of *The Expedition in Pursuit of Rare Meats* for the restaurant there. Whistler transformed the Port Lympne billiard room into a Tent Room, its ceiling a huge painted trompe l'oeil canvas awning, perhaps in reference to the house's main function as a summer home for Sassoon. Around the walls the young artist created a strange riverside landscape, populated with real and imaginary figures: their mutual friend Gerald Berners, as a small boy; the proprietor of Whistler's favorite Soho restaurant, Le Tour Eiffel; and a mysterious woman in mourning leaning against an urn marked "In Memoriam."

James Gibbs's St. Martin-in-the-Fields is prominent in this urban riverscape, towering behind the Palladian Bridge from Wilton. Berners's own country house, Faringdon, can be seen in the distance, so can a group of black-robed priests and a well-dressed woman in an eighteenth-century carriage. As so often with Whistler's murals, one has the impression that somewhere, just out of reach, a story lurks, a linking narrative that would make everything clear, if only we could find it.

The sense of theater that pervades the interiors spilled out into the fifteen acres of gardens. Sassoon masterminded the planting, with advice from the garden designer Norah Lindsay. Behind the house, Tilden cut a steep stone stairway into the cliff, with classical pavilions and fountains. On the terrace below, where Baker had marked out a site for a swimming pool before the war, he created one of the most dramatic bathing pools in England, flanked by raised quadrant pools and balustraded steps and fountains, the whole seeming to float above the marsh, with spectacular views to the Channel and the thin line of the Pas de Calais coast on the horizon.*

Port Lympne was the antithesis of both the carefully constructed historicism of Allington Castle and the romantic myth of rural England that men like Buchan reached out to grasp after the war. It was the archetype of the outsider's country house, a stage on which its owner could act out the role of English baronet and, more important, could direct the characters who flocked to take advantage of his lavish hospitality at Port Lympne, from Winston Churchill and Lloyd George to Lawrence of Arabia and Charlie Chaplin, all willing players in his extraordinary fantasy.

Sassoon shimmered through almost every memoir of the period. He never married—indeed, had no obvious sexual inclination in any direction, in spite of persistent rumors that he was homosexual. His was the kind of life that attracted legends: in 1930s Folkestone, for instance, it was whispered that he was attended by black eunuchs and that he bought his shirts at Marks & Spencer. The one story was

---

* The bathing pool didn't float quite well enough: when Tilden filled it with water, it showed signs of sliding down the hill and had to be reduced in size.

about as likely as the other. His Jewishness and his Indian blood were constantly referred to by those who knew him, not often in the ugly way Virginia Woolf had with words (she called him "an under-bred Whitechapel Jew") but in the coded, casual racism of the day.[11] He was "exotic," "oriental." "A strange, lonely, un-English little figure," wrote Harold Nicolson.[12] Robert Boothby, who knew him as well as any man, said that he was "not part of England, and whatever gods he worshipped were not our gods."[13] Interestingly, Sibyl Sassoon's marriage into the ranks of the English nobility meant that none of this sense of otherness clung to her at all.

Chips Channon, a fellow outsider, albeit one who tried a great deal harder to belong, was intrigued, unsure, admiring of Port Lympne's owner, calling him at various times "this strangest of sinister men" and "one of the most exciting, tantalizing personalities of the age."[14] When Sassoon died at the age of only fifty in June 1939, from complications following a bout of influenza, Channon wrote a measured obituary in his diary, praising his wit and his amiability, noting his hunger to be in the society of the great—"royalties haunted his house always, and he was loyal to them as he was to no-one else"—and judging, rightly, that while Sassoon's political career was less than glittering, his taste and his passion for the arts were his great achievements. "What he really loved were jewelled elephants and contrasting colours—the bizarre and the beautiful."[15]

Sassoon was also capable of restraint at times, especially when, alongside the jeweled elephants and contrasting colors, he sought to add to his collection that most ephemeral of art objects, Englishness. Port Lympne wasn't his only country house: on the death of his father in 1912, he had inherited the leasehold of Trent Park in Hertfordshire, an enormous Victorian house built of mauve bricks that stood in five hundred acres on the southern edge of Enfield Chase. Modernized in the 1890s, Trent Park boasted thirty bedrooms, a large lake, Japanese water gardens and tennis courts, and a tower "of peculiarly hideous appearance."[16] It was only forty-five minutes from London by car ("thirteen miles from the Bank of England"), and every conceivable modern comfort was installed: electric light, elevator, telephones, and central heating. There were also "ten furnished rooms for visiting chauffeurs."[17]

Having made a half-hearted attempt to soften the worst Victorian excesses of Trent, in 1925 Sassoon gave up and embarked on a wholesale remodeling. The result, as Christopher Hussey reported in 1931, was "a great country house in the pure English tradition," with none of the Palladian tricks or self-conscious period features that marked out so many other examples of the period. Everyone has assumed that Philip Tilden acted as Sassoon's architect at Trent Park, although Tilden—not normally slow to take credit—failed to mention the fact (or even the house) in his memoirs, and Hussey spoke as if Sassoon himself were responsible. There is another name in the frame, Lieutenant-Colonel Reginald Cooper, a shadowy figure who designed the orangery in 1923 and who restored a number of small country houses for his own use in the 1920s and 1930s. But whoever was responsible for the new Trent Park, they did a beautiful job of reinventing it. The peculiarly hideous tower came down; rose-red bricks from the demolished Devonshire House were used to reface the exterior, punctuated with stone window surrounds, stringcourses, and cornice from the same source. Inside the house, Sassoon installed an oak staircase with spiral balusters from Devonshire House and paneled the main reception rooms and painted them soft blues, grays, or yellows. There were no elephants, no Moorish patios. Rex Whistler was brought in again, but this time his work was confined to overmantel panels with classical trophies (and a lovely painting of the house with Sassoon and his cousin Hannah Gubbay, who often acted as his hostess, made while the artist was staying at Trent in May 1934). The furniture was good quality, but the kind of quality that might have been accumulated over the years by a family who had lived at Trent since the early eighteenth century.

If Trent were another stage, the subject of the play was English landed life, with Sassoon in the leading role. "Sir Philip has produced a building at once dignified and unpretentious, practical yet civilized," wrote Hussey. It "can be regarded as an ideal example of English domestic architecture unalloyed by fashion or fantasy."[18]

Trent Park: The drawing room in 1931. (Copyright: Country Life)

But the fantasy kept on breaking through, even at Trent. Sassoon was powered by a desire not to impress, exactly, but to please; and that, coupled with his immense wealth and an impetuous nature, had startling consequences. Rex Whistler suggested one day in 1933 that some of the statuary in the gardens might look well with gilded highlights: the next time he visited, an enormous lead gladiator had a gleaming golden sword and a shield that looked like a gold dish cover. "I must say he has gone further with the idea than I should have dared!" Whistler wrote to a friend.[19]

The gilded statues gave rise to all sorts of stories about Trent. The drainpipes were golden; the antlers of the stags in the park were golden because their owner liked the way they glittered in the sunshine. On one occasion Sassoon was supposed to have had the Union Jack lowered from its flagpole on the roof because he felt its colors clashed with the sunset.

These stories may have been true: one never knows with Sir Philip Sassoon. It *was* true, for instance, that he kept scarlet ibis and pink flamingos on the lake at Trent and that he made a point of personally feeding his small flock of king, rock-hopper, and black-footed penguins whenever he was there. It *was* true that when the Duke and Duchess of Kent honeymooned at Trent Park in 1934, Sassoon bought three monuments to eighteenth-century dukes of Kent at the Wrest Park sale and had them set up to make the newlyweds feel at home, and that he had his flowerbeds planted overnight. Robert Boothby spoke of an occasion when he arrived at Trent late one night, ahead of the rest of the house party. Early the next morning he was woken by the sound of cart wheels on the drive. "I got up and went out in my dressing gown to find six horse-drawn carts coming up the avenue, laden with flowers from Covent Garden in full bloom. An army of gardeners [there were eighteen] was waiting to plant them out in borders which had been carefully prepared. By the time the [other] guests began to arrive for lunch, they were all in."[20]

SCORES OF NEW COUNTRY HOUSES were built between the wars as architects and clients groped toward a new definition of the country house, one which took account of changing requirements, changing social structures, and a world in which the past was no longer the only style manual.

Yet the uncertainty which characterized postwar architecture in Britain meant that no one style dominated the field in new country-house building. Old stagers who had carved out careers for themselves as builders of Wrenaissance mansions before the war continued to design in much the same vein after it, although inevitably, that side of their practices tended to decline as more and more country houses came onto the market. And the Arts and Crafts movement continued to appeal to those who liked to bury themselves in rural romance.

The greatest Arts and Crafts country house of the 1920s, Rodmarton Manor in Gloucestershire, was designed and started before the war but not completed until 1929. Claud Biddulph had been given the 550-acre Rodmarton estate by his father in 1894, when he was eighteen. There was no mansion to go with it, but Claud preferred a career in the city to life as a country squire until 1906, when he and his new wife, Margaret, decided to make a home for themselves in Gloucestershire. They commissioned Ernest Barnsley to come up with designs for what Claud called their "cottage in the country"— half-jokingly, because for all its quiet charm and its studied references to the farms and manor houses of the Cotswolds, Rodmarton is a substantial country house.

Barnsley, who had moved to the Cotswolds from London with his brother Sidney and Ernest Gimson in the 1890s to rediscover and reinvigorate traditional crafts, produced his first designs for Rodmarton in 1909, and shortly afterward work began on the kitchen court and domestic offices in the east wing and progressed slowly westward. Although the shell was roofed by about 1912 and the Biddulphs were able to move in in 1915, the house wasn't finished until 1929, three years after Barnsley's death, when his son-in-law Norman Jewson completed the chapel in the west wing. The long gestation period was due entirely to Barnsley's insistence on traditional working practices. No contractor was employed, something that by the early twentieth century was most unusual for such a large project. All the stone and slate was quarried nearby and brought to the site by wagon, to be worked by local masons. Timber for beams and rafters was cut and seasoned on the estate; Barnsley wouldn't allow planks to be shaped with a circular saw—that smacked of an industrial process and came between the workman and his materials. So a sawpit was constructed onsite, and two men slaved away sawing every single plank with a two-handed saw. Metalwork was made by the local blacksmith; the Rodmarton foreman acted as clerk of works.

The emphasis on local involvement continued inside the house, with furniture made by estate joiners and designed by Ernest Barnsley, his brother Sidney, and the cabinetmaker Peter Waals. The workmen also produced oak paneling from drawings by the designer Alfred Powell, whose wife, Louise, contributed pottery and the decoration of a piano designed by Waals. Both the Powells were regular visitors to the house, as was the Labour politician Ramsay MacDonald. The main hall was often given over to craft classes in cane work, needlework, and woodwork for the villagers, presided over by Margaret Biddulph.

CRAFT CLASSES IN CANE WORK AT RODMARTON MANOR. (Copyright: Country Life)

There was a serious point to all this. Rodmarton was an educational enterprise, a quiet attempt to change the world. If traditional crafts were dying out they must be revived, and their revival depended not on city-bred reformers like Barnsley and the Biddulphs but on people like the Biddulphs' estate workers and on the women who lived in the surrounding villages. Give them the skills and the confidence to make beautiful things, and they would pass their knowledge on to others.

This was the sort of radical social adventure that the Arts and Crafts movement had always dreamed about. It was rare to see it made real, but other architects, motivated less by a desire to change the world than by the picturesque possibilities of the vernacular, continued to work in the same tradition well after the war. Oswald Milne, who was articled to Sir Arthur Blomfield at the end of the 1890s and worked for a couple of years in Lutyens's office, was one such, continuing after the Armistice the vaguely Arts and Crafts country-house practice he had established in 1904, when he first set up on his own. In 1919 he went into partnership with Paul Phipps, whom he knew from Lutyens's office, and produced a series of pleasant but hardly inspiring country houses, of which the most interesting—as much because of the site and the clients than Milne's treatment of the project—was Coleton Fishacre on the south Devon coast.

The site of Coleton Fishacre is dramatic, a narrow valley descends to a little cove. It is best appreciated from the sea, which is how Milne's clients, Rupert and Lady Dorothy D'Oyly Carte, first came upon it, while they were yachting between Brixham and Dartmouth in 1923. D'Oyly Carte's father was the impresario Richard D'Oyly Carte, whose exclusive business arrangement with Gilbert and Sullivan had led to the formation of the famous opera company and the building of both the Savoy Theatre and the Savoy Hotel, all of which Rupert now managed.

Coleton Fishacre was a weekend retreat for husband and wife and their two teenage children. It is old-fashioned for the 1920s, unadventurous: Milne took rather too much to heart Philip Webb's dictum that "I never begin to be satisfied until my work looks commonplace." Nevertheless, the walls of shale stone (quarried on the estate in best Arts and Crafts fashion), the unpainted oak window frames, and the steep roofs of Delabole stone slates do give a sense of tranquility, of a house that is not too quaint and not too modern.

And the weekend retreat became a residence, a country house rather than a seaside holiday home. It was big enough to accommodate an indoor staff of four—butler, housekeeper, housemaid, and cook—as well as a chauffeur and six gardeners. Soon after the house was finished, Lady Dorothy came to live there permanently, while her husband lived in London and motored down on Friday evenings. They spent their time yachting—Rupert had a cutter named *Content*—and gardening. By the 1930s the gardens at Coleton were well enough established to be opened to the public in aid of the Queen's Institute of District Nursing. The family swam in the sea or in a concrete tidal pool they had built down in the cove and entertained friends from the world of the arts. There were bridge parties and concerts, everything, as it turned out, except happiness. The D'Oyly Cartes's son, Michael, was killed in a motoring accident in 1932, and their marriage didn't long survive his death: they separated in 1936, and Rupert divorced Lady Dorothy on the grounds of her adultery five years later.

In their different ways, Rodmarton and Coleton Fishacre suggest that the postwar country-house tradition was backward looking, locked into a quiet and self-effacing love affair with the past. And in the hands of some architects, it was. There were too many thatched mansions, the twentieth-century equivalent of the Regency *cottage ornée*, with catslide roofs and leaded lattice windows, turning their back on the brave new world of the future, while their owners listened to the latest news of financial disaster on the markets and the march of terror across Europe on wirelesses that were disguised in distressed oak "antique" cabinets and powered by generators hidden away in half-timbered Stockbroker Tudor garages.

But there were also the modernists. A scattering of Modern Movement country houses sprang up between the wars, their gleaming white walls, flat roofs, and horizontal bands of glass meeting with a public response that was always amazed, often downright hostile. Local councils were reluctant to grant planning permission for these experiments, while the older generation of architects condemned the style as inappropriate, foreign, out of step with tradition. In 1934 Sir Reginald Blomfield, whose prewar practice had turned out numbers of conservative Wrenaissance mansions, launched a savage attack on what he called "Modernismus," condemning houses that looked like oblong boxes on posts, covered in birthday cake icing, their interiors "like the operating-rooms of a hospital." "What is the particular advantage of a flat roof?" asked *Country Life* in 1930, immediately providing the answer to its own question. "There isn't any."[21] A couple of years later it announced that "houses of this type . . . can never fit into the English landscape in the same way as buildings constructed of local materials and in traditional styles."[22] Ironically, this was exactly the kind of criticism that two centuries earlier had been leveled at Palladianism, now the most revered of country-house styles.

There was something dangerously un-English about both Modernism and its supporters. Many of the leading Modernist architects working in England were, or at least *sounded*, suspiciously foreign—Eric Mendelssohn, Walter Gropius, Ernö Goldfinger, Serge Chermayeff, Berthold Lubetkin. Many were Jewish; most were left wing and pro-Soviet.

And there was no doubting the fact that Modernist buildings looked unusual, especially when they reared up out of the rural landscape. One of the first big Modernist houses to appear in Britain was Crowsteps, near Newbury in Berkshire, designed by Thomas S. Tait of the Scottish firm of Sir John Burnet and Partners. In 1927 Tait had begun work on Silver End, a Modernist settlement for workers at the factory of Francis Crittall, whose firm manufactured the metal window frames that seemed to grace every modern building of the period. The housing—flat-roofed with triangular oriel windows and rendered walls—included terraces of three-bedroom "cottages," each with sitting room, living room, and scullery; four-bedroom detached houses, presumably intended for senior members of the Critall staff; and the grandest house in the village, Le Château, sleek and elegant, the horizontal lines of its roofs and balconies emphasized by steel casement windows (by Crittall, of course) without vertical glazing bars.

Tait's client at Crowsteps, Dr. Alan Simmons, had been inspired by Silver End. The white ziggurat that Tait gave him, more a villa in its own grounds than a country house (it stands in glorious isolation in early photographs, but it actually formed part of a leafy new suburb on the edge of town), was equally uncompromising. "This house not only invites criticism," wrote the architectural writer Randall Phillips, "it challenges it."[23] A stepped series of boxes with sundecks and balconies looked out onto a long concrete-lined pool. The cement render that encased the entire house was mixed with a little ochre to give a cream finish. The doors were single panels, the dining table, specially designed for the house, was coated in black cellulose paint, "proof against marking by hot plates and dishes," and the staircase had solid walls in place of balusters, with a vermilion handrail. The maids, whose bedrooms were at the top of the house, had a sitting room of

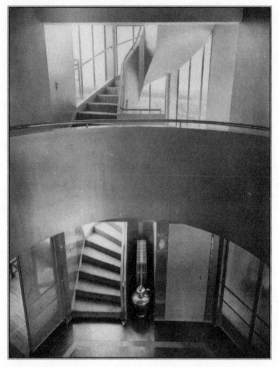

THE STAIRCASE AT HIGH AND OVER IN 1931: NOT WHAT AN ENGLISH
COUNTRY HOUSE IS SUPPOSED TO LOOK LIKE? (Copyright: Country Life)

their own next to the kitchen, which in turn was next door to the dining room, a piece of practical planning that by the 1920s was becoming
common in new houses, even the biggest and grandest.

It is hard today to recapture some of the astonishment that
greeted a house like Crowsteps. There was more. If anyone wants an
illustration of just how thoroughly un-English the new architecture
could be in the interwar years, High and Over is it. Even today, more
than eighty years after it was finished, its hard white angles and blind,
staring windows startle the eye. This is exciting, we think; it is architecture at its most provocative. But it is not what a country house is
supposed to look like. Not an *English* country house, at any rate.

The client for whom High and Over was designed was as English
as they come, and a man, moreover, who cared more than most about
historical precedent. Essex-born Bernard Ashmole (1894–1988) was
thirty-five years old when he decided to build himself a new house at

Amersham, deep in the heart of commuter-belt Buckinghamshire. He was married with a young family and had just been appointed professor of classical archaeology at University College London.

Ashmole, who had established a reputation as an expert on numismatics and classical sculpture, took up the chair at University College London (UCL) in 1929, shortly after returning from a three-year stint as director of the British School in Rome. It was while he was there that he first met his architect, the brilliant young New Zealander Amyas Connell. Connell had trained in an architect's office in Wellington before working his passage to England as a stoker on the SS *Karamarin* in 1923, in company with his friend and fellow student, Basil Ward. Further studies at UCL led to his winning the Rome Scholarship in architecture in 1926, which is how he came to meet Bernard Ashmole.

Ashmole's decision to choose Connell as the architect for his new house was quite courageous. The younger man had built nothing of any substance, his views were extremely progressive, and the designs he *had* produced were heavily influenced by Le Corbusier, whose work provoked reactions ranging from rage and horror to blank incomprehension among the British architectural establishment.

One of the most intriguing things about High and Over is its plan. As its name implies, the house stands high on a hill overlooking the Misbourne valley. It is built in the shape of a Y, with three more or less equal arms radiating out at 120-degree angles from a hexagonal hall. Stark, flat-roofed, and clad in cement-rendered brick over a frame of reinforced concrete, it is carefully asymmetrical, in spite of its broadly symmetrical plan. The fenestration varies from one wing to another; an angular oriel window projects out over Ashmole's library in the south wing, and a low single-story extension containing domestic offices unbalances the northeast wing, which houses the dining room and kitchen. Most striking of all is the pair of flat concrete hoods or canopies supported on columns that hover above the south and northwest blocks like giant airplane wings: in spite of the obvious associations with the machine age, they were intended primarily to provide shade and support for the Ashmole children's hammocks. The rest of the roof was taken up with an airy (and suitably remote) hexagonal day nursery, a night nursery, and nurse's bedroom. A dumb-waiter brought meals up from the kitchen on the ground floor.

The three faces of the hexagon that don't connect to the living room, dining room, and library were still made to do some work. One took the chrome-plated steel front door; the second opened onto a terrace that led to the gardens; and the third was filled with a polygonal glass staircase, which on the rare occasions when the sun shone in Amersham, would let sunlight flood into the hall and the landing above. Four main bedrooms led off this landing: the master bedroom and dressing room were in the south wing, over the library, and included a built-in shower—quite a novelty in 1931.

The hall itself formed the most elegant interior in the whole house. In the center of a black marble floor inlaid with pieces of glass, Connell sunk a glass basin with a fountain that could shoot a stream of water as high as the first-floor gallery. This lit up at night. The sets of doors to the dining room, library, and living room—all capable of being folded back to create a single large space for entertaining—were made of steel and glass, with the inside surfaces of the glass sprayed with translucent patterns of cellulose. The main rooms had lighting concealed behind glass panels set into the ceilings, and decoration varied from plain orange walls in the dining room to chrome and jade green cellulose in the living room, which also had a built-in wireless. Blomfield asked very publicly what on earth was the point of the Rome Scholarship if Connell ended up by "flouting the face of authority" in such a way.[24]

MODERNIST COUNTRY HOUSES WERE SOMETHING of an anomaly. Their owners had to grapple with the fact that not only did their new rural retreats flout the face of architectural authority but they also ran counter to the English country house's most powerful attraction, its ability to evoke stability, continuity, sanctuary, a still point at the center of a maelstrom of cultural and social change.

Sometimes those owners couldn't reconcile the tension between the shock of the new and the pull of the past. That, ultimately, was what happened at Joldwynds in Surrey, arguably the greatest Modernist country house of them all. Joldwynds came with all the trimmings: twelve bedrooms, six baths, five living rooms, domestic offices, garage and stables with three flats, a swimming pool, a hard tennis court, and twenty acres of woodland to explore in the unlikely event that the fifteen acres of beautiful gardens lost their charm. The polished white mansion was "the striking country house of the future," to borrow a phrase from the agent's particulars.[25]

Its architect, one of the most intriguing country-house architects of the period, was Oliver Hill, whose work immediately after the war tended to be either romantically thatched and picturesque or formal and neo-Georgian in the mold of Richard Norman Shaw, Reginald Blomfield, and Sir Edwin Lutyens. (Lutyens was actually a friend and neighbor of his parents). After a visit in 1925 to the Paris Exposition Internationale des Arts Décoratifs et Industriels Modernes, Hill's work began to show affinities with Modernism, although never to the exclusion of traditional styles. It seemed as if he were eager to experiment but lacked the opportunity and the necessary supportive client.

He found him in 1930, when a prosperous barrister, Wilfred Greene, and his wife, Nancy, commissioned a weekend retreat at Holmbury St. Mary, about ten miles southeast of Guildford in Surrey. There was already a Victorian mansion on the site, a rather splendid thing surrounded by parkland, with gables and outrageously tall chimneystacks. It had been built by Philip Webb in 1873. But it was too big, too impractical, and too old-fashioned for the Greenes, and they decided that it had to go. In the machine age, people like the Greenes demanded more from their houses than picturesque skylines. Mere charm of appearance had no place in their brave new world.

The Joldwynds that replaced Webb's house was a gleaming monument, one of the best Modernist houses in Britain. Hill used brick, rendered with cement and carborundum, and then polished until the walls shone like white marble. On the entrance façade, which faced north, the effect was set off to perfection by a green copper door flanked by gazelles and, as the notional pivot around which the dynamics of the building revolved, a two-storied semicircular staircase tower of glass. The whole entrance front is effectively a single sweeping curve, and the theme was taken up by the staircase, by the circular drum on the roof (which held a water tank), and by gently concave parapets.

Hill had a penchant for rich and exotic materials, something that caused his more ideologically correct contemporaries to view his work with suspicion. At Joldwynds he indulged himself to the full. The floor of the ivory-colored entrance hall was inlaid with coral and jade. This led into the sitting room, which was floored with Australian walnut and filled with furniture designed by Hill and made of white birch, eucalyptus, and Burmese padouk. The dining-room furniture was upholstered in white calf and veneered with ivory-colored shagreen.

Unfortunately, the Greenes didn't like it. Wilfred was cross about the cost of all those exotic woods and the poor quality of the building work. He complained that a piece of tar had fallen through a skylight and landed on his lavatory seat, "where it still remains"—until Hill came in person to remove it, presumably. He also criticized the oil central heating, which was spewing out fumes and smuts in equal measure. Nancy Greene confined her comments to the interiors, sending Hill a devastatingly detailed account of the "merits and demerits of the furniture which you designed for us." There were no merits: everything was too high, too hard, and too heavy. The end result was undeniably photogenic, she said, but "unfortunately Joldwynds was meant for a house to live in, not a lovely film set."[26] In 1937, after only four years of living in this loveliest of lovely film sets, the Greenes sold up and left.

7

LUTYENS

❦

T he name most frequently associated with country-house architecture in the twentieth century is that of Sir Edwin Lutyens.
Although he was born back in 1869, Lutyens was an Edwardian,
with an Edwardian love of opulence, an Edwardian romanticism, an
Edwardian sense of England's past. With a few exceptions, his greatest houses were designed before 1914. The Lutyens archetypes had
all been invented and perfected by then: the severe neo-Georgian of
Nashdom in Buckinghamshire (1905–1908), a whitewashed hotel of
a house built for the Princess Alexis Dolgorouki, whose exotic name
belied her origins as a Lancashire heiress called Fanny Wilson; the
free Tudor and tall, twisting chimneys of Marsh Court in Hampshire
(1901); and the elegant, excellent William and Mary and "dear little
Queen Anne" of houses like Great Maytham in Kent (1907–1909) and
Ednaston Manor, Derbyshire (1912–1914).

Above all, he had refined the oak-beamed lyrical romance of Old
England, which would remain such a potent cultural force throughout the 1920s and 1930s—a romance that had its roots in the anti-
industrialism and antiurbanism of William Morris and the early Arts
and Crafts movement but that was taken to new heights in houses
like Munstead Wood (1896, for his longtime collaborator Gertrude
Jekyll) and Great Dixter (1910), a house of the fifteenth century, which

EDWIN LUTYENS. (Copyright: Punch Limited)

Lutyens extended by adding a timber-framed yeoman's hall-house from neighboring Kent.

Lutyens's great contribution to post-Armistice England came in other forms. His most acclaimed domestic building of the postwar period boasted a marble staircase and a suite of state apartments, hot and cold running water, a garden by Gertrude Jekyll, and portraits by leading artists of the day, including Sir John Lavery and Glyn Philpot, Alfred Munnings and William Nicholson, but no one ever mounted that staircase or strolled through the state rooms. Queen Mary's Dolls' House, a one-twelfth-scale piece of Wrenaissance designed by Lutyens in 1921–1924, was praised to the skies when it went on show at the British Empire Exhibition at Wembley in 1924. More than 1.6 million visitors viewed the "miracle in miniature," as the *Times* called it; "a model for the ages of the best the twentieth century can do in domestic architecture, decoration and furnishing."[1]

Other postwar Lutyens works were iconic in the true sense of the word: the Cenotaph, Britain's official national war memorial; the Great War Stone, which was placed in all the larger military cemeteries in France; India Gate, the seventy-five-foot-high All India War Memorial Arch, which stands, as big as the Arc de Triomphe, at the heart of New Delhi; and the moving and magnificent Thiepval Memorial to the Missing of the Somme, unveiled in 1932 and the largest British war memorial in the world, inscribed with 72,099 names.

By the 1920s Lutyens's output of country houses was declining as corporate architecture, fame, and the struggle to complete the government complex at New Delhi occupied so much of his time. (And, of course, as the demand for new country houses fell: it was a great deal cheaper to buy an old one, and there were plenty on the market.) He had reached that curious stage in an architect's career where clients were moving on and selling the houses he had built for them: Edward Hudson sold Lindisfarne Castle to the banker Oswald Falk in 1921; Goddards in Surrey, one of Lutyens's loveliest houses, came on the market three years later.

And slowly, work resumed on a prewar masterpiece. The client, Julius Drewe, was a tea importer whose successful grocery business (in 1883 he founded the Home and Colonial Stores, and by 1890 it had 107 branches around the country) enabled him to retire, first to a castellated Georgian mansion in Kent, then to a redbrick Victorian pile in Sussex, and, finally, to Devon. In his retirement, Drewe became absorbed in the task of tracing his family's ancestry. An older brother who shared his interest consulted a professional genealogist, who told the Drewes that they were descended from Drogo or Dru, a Norman baron who had come to England with William the Conqueror and whose descendant, Drogo de Teigne, had settled in, and given his name to, the parish of Drewsteignton in Devon. Julius was convinced. By 1910 he had bought lands at Drewsteignton, and in that year he made the decision to build himself a seat on a spectacular site nine hundred feet above sea level and two hundred feet above the wooded gorge below.

Lutyens started to sketch out designs for Drewe that summer. It was the architect's biggest commission to date. Drewe's budget was

£50,000 for the house and another £10,000 for the grounds—a huge sum, but then Drewe wanted a huge house. A castle, in fact, that would commemorate (and publicize) his centuries-old connections with the area. "I do wish he didn't want a castle," Lutyens wrote to his wife, "but just a delicious lovable house with plenty of good large rooms in it."[2]

In the event, only half of Lutyens's original scheme for Castle Drogo, a splayed U-plan with a central great hall, was built, and even then the budget was trebled, partly as a result of Drewe's decision that Lutyens's cavity walls should give way to more authentic solid granite.

The war brought the building work to a halt. Materials were scarce, and Drewe actively encouraged the workforce to enlist. (He refused to employ any single men at Castle Drogo, for example, maintaining that they should all be fighting.) In 1917 his eldest son Adrian was killed at Ypres; Drewe's daughter recalled that "the joy very much went out of life as far as my father and mother were concerned, and things were very much quieter."[3] But work resumed in 1919, and Castle Drogo was ready for the Drewes to move into by 1927.

And it *is* a castle, complete with battlements and towers, a heraldic Drewe lion above the front door and a 644-pound working portcullis behind it. But Drogo is more than a toy fort built on the shifting sands of an outmoded historicism. Whatever Lutyens's private desires for the maintenance of a social and architectural status quo, which was already beginning to fragment around him, he achieved a new, raw, and very modern elementalism, defining the very essence of a castle, stripping it of its externals, and then reinterpreting it to suit the needs of a landed family in the twentieth century. Drogo is a dramatic and ambiguous *tour de force*, which simultaneously conjures up and repudiates the past. Its composition and materials establish links with the medieval, while at the same time rejecting the hazy, idealized romanticism of the late nineteenth century in favor of a wholly contemporary conception, which is every bit as cold and hard-edged as the granite blocks from which it is built.

Inside, there are surprises everywhere. Wide passages punctuated by shallow saucer domes disappear round unexpected corners or fade

CASTLE DROGO: A REAL CASTLE, AND YET A WHOLLY TWENTIETH-CENTURY CONCEPTION. (Copyright: Country Life)

into the distance—and quite a distance it can be, since the kitchens are some fifty yards away from the dining room. Walls rear up like cliffs as the floor suddenly falls away in long flights of steps. Vaults and arches intersect like medieval undercrofts, while above the main staircase, which revolves around an apparently solid core but in fact conceals a complete servants' stair within it, the ceiling alters at each turn, changing from coffered vault to dome to arches to oak beams but remains at its original height, so that by the time one reaches the bottom, the distance from floor to ceiling is a towering twenty-seven feet.

The more you get to know Drogo, the more you come to realize the extent of Lutyens's achievement. The almost unnatural precision of the masonry, the perfect regularity of the vaults and arches and domes, the great windows breaking through the walls and flooding the rooms inside with light, all remind us that it is a wholly twentieth-century conception. At the same time, the restrained treatment, the absence of ornament, the grim granite of the interiors demonstrate that this is no Scotch-baronial exercise in historicism. The house is neither a "real" castle nor a sham folly: Lutyens managed to create a building that was modern, while still conveying that sense of timeless solidity that Julius Drewe needed to validate his ancestry.

LUTYENS WAS INVOLVED IN TWO hundred projects between 1919 and his death in 1944, but only half a dozen or so were country houses. There was Drogo, conceived in Edwardian England, stripped down and simplified for a postwar world. There was a startling and austere extension that he made to Penheale Manor in Cornwall in the early 1920s—itself an indirect consequence of the war, in that the owner, Captain Norman Colville, M.C., had been gassed and bought the house after being advised by his doctors to move south from Scotland for his health. And there were several remodelings of older buildings, such as the work he carried out in 1928 at Plumpton Place in Sussex, a romantic timber-framed manor house that he repaired and enlarged for his old patron Edward Hudson, proprietor of *Country Life*.

Lutyens only built two new country houses after the war, both in collaboration with other architects and for very different clients. Yet at a time when the country house was meant to be in crisis, they were among the largest he had ever designed.

The first, Gledstone Hall, was for a cotton lord so self-made that his career borders on caricature. Amos Nelson was born into a working-class family in Lancashire in 1860. He went to work at the age of eight, and by the time he was twenty-one, he had saved enough from his meager earnings to set up in business as a small-scale cotton manufacturer in partnership with his father, a weaver. He sold that business in 1946 for £3.7 million, one of the biggest ever mill transactions.

In 1919 Nelson bought the nine-thousand-acre Gledstone Park estate in Yorkshire, which had at its core a classical country house of the 1770s, said to have been designed by Carr of York. He commissioned a local architect, Richard Jaques, to modernize the house and then, as the scale of the task grew, persuaded Jaques that it would be a good idea to enlist the help of a more experienced country-house architect. Lutyens worked up a design aboard the SS *Caledonia* in

December 1920 en route to India, after finding himself in the unenvi-
able position of having his client as a fellow passenger. "I have to work
to keep his interest to a pitch higher than the toss of waves," he wrote
to his wife. "But Lord! how I sweated in that little red hot room at the
top of the ship."[4]

He sweated in vain. Nelson decided that the cost of remodeling was going to be prohibitive. But he still wanted a country house
that would reflect both his status and his political aspirations: he was
knighted in January 1922 and stood unsuccessfully for Parliament as a
Conservative in the November election of that year. So between 1922
and 1926, the old Gledstone Park was replaced by a new house on a
new site, designed by Lutyens but with Jaques giving a helping hand.
(The old hall remained in limbo for a couple of years before being
demolished in 1928. The stable block survived and has since been
turned into a house.)

Lutyens opted to give visitors the kind of grandly eclectic introduction they might have expected from a cotton lord's unancestral
pile in the nineteenth century: a rigidly symmetrical neo-Palladian
mansion with steep, rather French roofs, flanking pavilions, and an
enormous Ionic *porte cochére*, the only portico Lutyens ever built in
England. This entrance front, half chateau, half house of parade, conceals the fact that Gledstone is smaller than it seems and, in its planning at least, more modern. There are only seven bedrooms, for one
thing. The kitchen was placed almost next door to the dining room—
no long processions of lukewarm food—and while the kitchen, servants' hall, and other domestic offices filled one wing, its companion
was false, not much more than a screen wall hiding a little courtyard
and garaging for Sir Amos's cars.

The interior was simple and only one room deep with a cross-
corridor running east to west. There was a low-ceilinged central
entrance hall, a dining room, a drawing room, and a big games room
with a billiard table, all looking out over the south-facing garden. A
morning room and library were tucked into the angles formed by the
two wings. Lutyens made a great thing of the black-and-white marble flooring. The hall had a typical Palladian checkerboard; the main

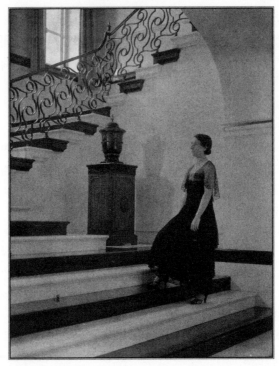

THE SECOND LADY NELSON ON THE STAIRCASE AT GLEDSTONE PARK. (Copyright: Country Life)

staircase, alternating black-and-white steps, which were, as Pevsner commented, "handsome to look at and neck-breaking to walk on."[5] In a nod to the Jazz Age, the ground-floor corridor was given a striking pattern of swirling black and white, culminating in a cluster of teardrops.

Despite touches like this, there is something a little humorless about Gledstone, which has none of the wit, none of the sense of playing with a genre that characterizes Castle Drogo. But Nelson was happy with the result. A series of photographs of the house taken for *Country Life* in 1935 show the rooms peppered with good-ish antiques and reproduction furniture, a refectory table in the entrance hall, a small mahogany dining table and a circular rug in the dining room. Several of the Georgian chimneypieces from the old house found their way into the new one. And judging by the number of times she appeared in the photoshoot, posing on the staircase, sitting on sofas, talking to the nurse who held her baby, Nelson was just as proud of his new wife. The first Lady Nelson, to whom he was married for fifty-two years, had died in 1931, and within six months he had found and married her successor, who promptly gave him his seventh child in his seventies.

Lutyens's last great country house was Middleton Park, near Bicester, for the twenty-five-year-old 9th Earl of Jersey. Completed in 1938 (and given statutory protection as a building of exceptional interest only thirteen years later, which must be some kind of record), it was another collaboration, this time with the architect's son Robert.

For a long time, the two Lutyens men had endured a difficult relationship. In 1920 the teenage Robert left Cambridge and eloped with a research chemist called Eva Lubryjinska, who was seven years his senior, painted her fingernails, and was a Polish Jew. They were married in Edinburgh, and the anti-Semitic Lutyens found it hard to forgive his son.* The fact that the marriage turned out to be unhappy didn't help their relationship: being proved wrong does little to make an erring son forgive his disapproving father. In the 1920s Robert made a living as a journalist (he was a lead writer on the *Daily Mail*) and then as an interior designer before going into architectural practice in 1933 without any formal training. He produced interiors for several members of the board of Marks & Spencer and their relatives, and as a result he was involved in the design of a string of Marks & Spencer stores in the 1930s.

Their client at Middleton Park succeeded to the Jersey earldom in 1923 when he was only thirteen years old, and he also married young. "Grandy" (the Earl of Jersey was also Viscount Grandison of Limerick in the Irish peerage) was twenty-one, and his wife, Patricia Richards, was eighteen when they married in January 1932. They had three country houses. Their main home was Middleton Park, then an impressive Georgian mansion with a domed central block and two wings linked to it by curving colonnades. There was also Osterley Park in Middlesex, an Elizabethan house remodeled by Robert Adam in the 1760s and opened to the public by the Earl in 1939. And they

---

* Eva was the niece of Chaim Weizmann, later the first president of Israel.

owned Baglan House in Glamorgan, another Georgian house where the family spent a couple of weeks each summer.

Like many others, Jersey appeared to be feeling the financial pinch in the Depression years. In 1933 the head gardener at Middleton Park was dismissed "owing to curtailment of expenses,"[6] and the following year Hampton and Sons held a nine-day sale at Middleton, attracting buyers from all over the country. Jersey sold off thousands of items: a set of twenty-four Chippendale mahogany chairs, Adam side-tables and George I giltwood torchères, a pair of Indian ivory arm chairs (which alone fetched a considerable 280 guineas), and the contents of the guest bedrooms—all forty-four of them. The family library, including rare works on costume and travel, first editions by Charles Dickens, and an eight-hundred-volume set of Parliamentary Debates, went under the hammer. So did a mixed bag of pictures and drawings. The highest price for a painting was ninety-four guineas, paid for a portrait of the fifth Earl's sister, Lady Sarah Bayly, by a nineteenth-century president of the Royal Academy, Sir Martin Shee.

Rather than heralding the breakup of the Middleton Park estate and a flight to Monte Carlo or Happy Valley, the sale helped to finance a new beginning of a different sort. In 1935 the old house was demolished and work began on a brand-new mansion. Jersey initially consulted Robert Lutyens, but Edward Hudson advised him to bring Lutyens senior in as well. The partnership cemented an uneasy rapprochement between father and son, with Robert later explaining generously that it was far from being a union of equals. Writing of himself in the third person, he acknowledged that his role was to mediate between "disparate generations" and that "his chief desire . . . was to stand sufficiently close to his father to be able to watch him actually at work. The work that mattered was all the father's."[7]

Middleton Park is big and meant for entertaining. The north-facing eleven-bay entrance façade is 120-feet long, and behind it lie rooms of a scale and number that wouldn't be out of place in a country house built a century earlier. Tall windows with shutters, and a row of flat-topped dormers in the hipped roof, contrive to give the house a faintly French air, contradicting Robert Lutyens's opinion that with Middleton Park his father achieved a "quintessential Englishness."[8]

The interiors, all arches and vaults and filled with the kind of playful, stripped-down geometries that showed that Lutyens was still at the top of his game as he approached his seventies, were carefully zoned. On the west there was a traditional male complex of interconnecting study, smoking room, and library. A huge drawing room filled the center of the south front, with a dining room finishing off the sequence of ground-floor reception rooms. Above there were eight principal bedrooms, each equipped with its own *en suite* bathroom. A substantial service wing was supplemented by four detached lodges for visiting valets, maids, and chauffeurs. In lieu of stables there was garaging for nine cars.

In January 1937, with Middleton Park still unfinished, the Earl and Countess of Jersey divorced, and six months later Grandy married an American film star.* Virginia Cherrill is best known today for two roles: one as the blind flowergirl in Charlie Chaplin's 1931 classic *City Lights* and the other as Cary Grant's first wife. She left Grant after seven months of marriage.

Edwin Lutyens didn't like her. He called her "a common little woman without brain [who had] no idea of what an Englishman's house should be."[9] Robert also found her difficult, complaining that she insisted on having a cocktail bar and other Hollywood features included at Middleton Park. However, it was probably Virginia who was responsible for one of the house's finest interiors: her bathroom, which was rightly described by *Country Life* in 1946 as "a notable instance of the between-wars cult of the tub."[10] With walls of pink onyx and white marble, taps of gilt bronze, and a shower enclosed in mirror-glass, it was a magnificent piece of English Deco. One suspects this was an instance where Robert stepped in between those disparate generations and took a hand in its design.

---

* Grandy's first countess also remarried that summer. By the end of their lives, they had amassed seven spouses between them.

The earl and his Hollywood countess weren't destined to enjoy Middleton Park. They spent only two nights there before war broke out. Then Grandy went off to join the army. Virginia went off with a Polish airman. The couple divorced in 1946, and the same year the earl sold Middleton Park to an industrialist, A. C. J. Wall.

Middleton was Lutyens's last country house. He died of lung cancer on New Year's Day 1944, eulogized as England's greatest architect since Wren, the inventor of the modern English country house, and the best-known British architect in the world. But among all the praise was the occasional acknowledgment that he had outlived his time. "He appears as the last great exponent of the architecture of an age that had passed," observed one obituarist.[11] And in truth, the grandiose classicism of Gledstone and Middleton already seemed to belong to another age when they were still brand new. Most of those who chose to build themselves a country house between the wars might like the *idea* of marbled halls and Ionic porticos: but when it came down to it, convenience and practicality meant more to them than grandeur.

8

MAKING PLANS

ne of the trickiest problems for the owner of an ancient ancestral pile was how best to use the great hall. This cavernous space
might be medieval and open to the rafters, with a screens passage at
one end and a dais at the other; it might have a grand carved staircase,
marble floors, and an Adam ceiling. But no stately home with any pre-
tension to the name was without one.

Yet what was it *for*, exactly? The medieval hall had been a place
where the lord presided over gatherings of the entire household,
seated beneath a canopy of state—an act that even the most theat-
rically inclined antiquarian would find rather hard to pull off in the
twentieth century. Over the centuries the great hall had evolved into
a quasi-public entrance space, a waiting area for servants, until the
introduction of effective bell-pull systems in the early nineteenth century consigned those waiting servants to the netherworld behind the
green baize door. Victorians who looked wistfully on a mythical mer-
rye olde England peopled by benevolent landowners and grateful tenants sought to keep something of the communal function of the great
hall, holding tenants' dinners here and summoning village children to
receive their oranges at Christmas in front of a blazing Yule log. The
old halls presented, as Pugin put it, "a standing illustration of good old
English hospitality."[1] The prolific Victorian architect George Gilbert

Scott agreed. "The residence of a great landed proprietor should never be without [one]," he declared in 1857. "Its disuse was accompanied by the decay of that ancient hospitality which is impossible without it."[2]

By and large, the twentieth century was of the same mind as Pugin and Scott. Some few country-house owners partitioned their great halls, perhaps horizontally to create an extra bedroom or—less commonly—vertically to create reception rooms of manageable proportions. But in the 1930s it was still common to see old armor, antlers, and ancient weapons decorating the walls of a baronial great hall, interspersed in that more well-traveled age with the occasional head of an ibis or a rhinoceros, with a tiger-skin rug spread out beside the hearth. A lick of paint might brighten things up: the Marquess of Lothian, who moved back into Blickling Hall in 1932 after years of letting his Norfolk estate, removed the stained glass from his great hall, a remarkable mixture of Jacobean and Georgian Gothick, took down most of the portraits, and painted it white. The English hall had become "the centre of great memories of a proud past," Hermann Muthesius told German readers of his *Das Englische Haus* in 1911.[3]

The twentieth century also understood that there was an easy answer to the question of what to do with the great hall—live in it.

It was their parents and grandparents who made the discovery. The gender-based zoning of the Victorian country house—drawing room and boudoir for the women; library, smoking room, and billiards room for the men—meant that here and there families and guests began to use the hall as neutral territory. An organ or a grand piano might be installed—there was plenty of space, after all—and from here it was a short step to adding chairs and sofas where guests could listen to the music. In the 1930s Sir Charles Trevelyan often held dances, charades, and other party games in the top-lit hall at Wallington, although the acoustics were so bad that house parties usually decamped to the drawing room for recitals.

"Halls of this sort always house a grand piano for music-making and sometimes a billiard-table," Muthesius reported. "The hall tends to become the comfortable all-purpose room of the house, in which each member of the family can follow his favourite pursuit and spend his time as he likes."[4] It was precisely this flexibility, this absence of a defined function that appealed: in smaller country houses the lounge hall, as it became known in the 1920s, might even contain a dining table, returning it to its medieval roots. With high-backed sofas, writing tables, and that must-have Arts and Crafts feature, an ingle nook, the hall was another reception room, to the consternation of the architectural critic Harry Goodhard-Rendel, who complained about the curious fashion of sitting "not in one's sitting rooms but in the hall outside them . . . with a stream of housemaids issuing with slop-pails from the bedrooms after breakfast in full view."[5]

THE BALANCING ACT, WHICH SO many owners of older country houses had to perform, was to live in a congenial "muddle of museum carpets [and] ruined castles"—Harold Nicolson's description of life at Sissinghurst[6]—and yet still have modern conveniences and home comforts. The older the house, the harder that was. By the 1920s, light, sun, and air were prized in a way that medieval and Tudor forebears would have found incomprehensible. So were bathrooms.

One agent of change was the fast-moving property market. Families who had lived content for generations with all the inconveniences of inadequate or labor-intensive heating, lighting, and plumbing gave way to less tolerant new owners, "people for the most part keen and alive to the priceless heritage of architectural beauty which these houses represent, but conscious also that the defects . . . shall be remedied."[7] It is easy to imagine a Duke of Rutland or a Duke of Bedford being prepared to put up with candles and oil lamps at Belvoir or Woburn; much less easy to think of a Sir Philip Sassoon or a Lady Baillie doing so at Port Lympne or Leeds Castle. Even the dedicated restorers demanded a degree of comfort. At Allington, Sir Martin Conway was clear from the start that while he set out to preserve every old feature of the castle, he wouldn't scruple to insert new doors, windows, staircases, and the like wherever they were needed, or "to make the place into a thoroughly warm, dry, light, and comfortably fitted home."[8]

Change was in the air. By the 1920s, it seemed ridiculous to put the kitchens in a basement or even in a separate building, as the

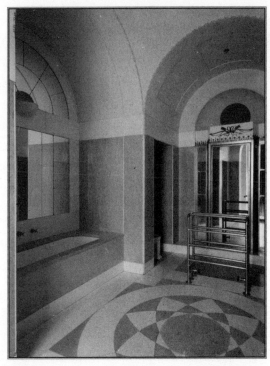

THE BATHROOM AS ART FORM: THE COUNTESS OF JERSEY'S BATH-
ROOM AT MIDDLETON PARK, PHOTOGRAPHED IN 1946. (Copyright:
Country Life)

Tudors had done, or to adopt a favorite Victorian scheme of linking
them to the dining room by a deliberately circuitous route that kept
cooking smells out of the main house. The modern country house was
planned for modern living.

But for people blessed with a sprawling old mansion that had
been built in the days when servants were cheap and convenience not
a consideration, the options were limited. An owner could demolish
his or her house and start again, as Amos Nelson did at Gledstone or
as Wilfred and Nancy Greene did with Philip Webb's Joldwynds. Or
they could remove the inconvenient bits. The paint was scarcely dry on
the High Victorian Tyntesfield, near Bristol, before the Gibbs family,
who had just built it, began to dismantle it. An immense domed conservatory that had been inspired by the Crystal Palace went in 1917,

falling prey to storm damage, wartime labor shortages, and changing horticultural fashions, and in 1935 the splendid Gothic clock tower that loomed over the entrance porch was dismantled after it was found to have dry rot, and the roofline was adjusted accordingly.

Less radical, less expensive, and therefore more popular was a tendency to tinker and make do, changing or blurring the historic function of a room. A billiard table or bookcases might be installed in a seventeenth-century long gallery or a Tudor great chamber. (Books do furnish a room.) A gallery might become a corridor; partition walls and false ceilings could make huge bedchambers more manageable and also provide opportunities for introducing a bathroom or two.

As far as other requirements for the modern country house were concerned, there was general agreement that size mattered; rather less agreement on what constituted the *right* size. In 1919 it was possible to announce that the big country house was a thing of the past and still to suggest that, for a man of moderate means, the bare minimum accommodation must consist of three or four sitting rooms and ten bedrooms, with day and night nurseries for young children and servants' quarters to match. Sixteen years later, the Conservative politician Sir Samuel Hoare sold his family seat, Sidestrand Hall in Norfolk, and twenty acres of gardens, complaining that it had all the inconveniences of a big house and "none of the spaciousness that is so essential to country life."[9] He and his wife would rather have "a Petit Trianon in the middle of my woods and far away from the roads and noises of the modern world,"[10] and in 1938 they commissioned John Seely and Paul Paget to design for them a pretty single-story villa in the remaining grounds of Sidestrand, a shooting box, which they planned to use in the summer.

The heart of Templewood, as it was called, was a central saloon about forty feet by thirty feet. "It is a single big room that is needed in a small country house, and not the network of *cabinets particuliers* that Victorian England seemed to prefer," said Hoare.[11] The saloon opened onto a south-facing covered loggia, with all the other rooms grouped around it. To the west there was a small entrance hall, cloakroom, and toilet, with maids' rooms and a guest bedroom. The east range consisted of separate bedrooms for Sir Samuel and his wife, Lady Maude, a small dining room, and in the northeast corner a kitchen, connected to the dining room by a small serving area. And the rest of the north side was filled with pantry, wine cellar, broom and linen cupboards, and a servants' hall. The house was equipped with four bathrooms, for Sir Samuel, Lady Maude, their guests, and the servants. If critics complained that Templewood was too small, said Sir Samuel, "my answer is that no house can nowadays be too small."[12] In any case, there was also a large garage block with more accommodation for staff and extra guests.

There was only one possible architectural style for this villa. During the Great War, when Sir Samuel headed a British intelligence mission in Rome, he took the opportunity to travel up to Vicenza to explore the architecture of Palladio. Ever since then he had worshipped him "as the great master of the art of country life." After Nuthall Temple, Nottinghamshire's own Villa Rotunda, was stripped and demolished in 1929, Hoare bought the portico, the ironwork for balustrading, swags, sphinxes to guard the drive, and other pieces of stonework. Herbert Baker's demolition of Sir John Soane's Bank of England in the late 1920s provided Ionic columns for the loggia and the entrance façade. Seely and Paget did the rest.

The trend in new country houses was all toward compactness and convenience. Monsters like Middleton Park were rare. So were brand-new houses that functioned as their forebears had before 1914, as the headquarters of great agricultural estates. The large-scale country house was giving way to a more manageable house in the country, still with extensive gardens, perhaps, but without the tenanted farms and cottages that had been the norm at the beginning of the century. Homes with a smaller footprint were cheaper to heat and required fewer staff (and that meant lower wage bills and lower food bills), and they were generally easier to manage. Natural light was important, even for those who objected to the optimism of a liner-style sundeck on the roof: tall windows and well-lit bedrooms and corridors were the order of the day. "Our first thoughts today," declared an anonymous *Country Life* critic in 1937, discussing what shape the contemporary country house should take, "are of the amenities and technique of living—how a house shall be planned, not only to make the most of the site, of light and air and the view, but also to be efficient and economical in running."[13]

The hall still had a part to play. It should be "not too large as to be wasteful," said another *Country Life* writer, Randall Phillips, "but yet sufficiently ample to give a generous welcome to the visitor and to serve as a household rendezvous."[14] At Ashcombe Tower on the south Devon coast, built in 1933–1936 by Brian O'Rorke for the local MP, Major Ralph Rayner, the great hall was simply renamed. O'Rorke, who is best known for his modernist designs for the liners of the Orient Steam Navigation Company, produced a house that was all Arts and Crafts on the outside and Modern Movement on the inside and tied the knot between past and present with a central great hall, forty feet by twenty-two feet and entered at one end, which he called simply "the Big Room." Concealed lighting and low sofas, rugs and curtains by Marion Dorn and an electric clock over the fireplace set the contemporary tone, but those contemporaries were quick to note the similarities between the position and function of the Big Room and its counterpart in a Tudor mansion. The introduction and reinvention of such a traditional space was, said one, "natural today when we have abandoned many of the formalities that we have inherited from the eighteenth century."[15]

Ashcombe incorporated typical 1930s flourishes: built-in bedroom furniture, flush walnut paneling, a cocktail bar tucked away beneath a half landing, a newel post capped with a chromium-plated ball finial. But it was basically an Elizabethan H-plan, adapted to twentieth-century use. A morning room and study occupied most of one upright of the H, a dining room the other, with kitchens and domestic offices leading off it, and the cross-bar was the Big Room.

Attached to the house was a purpose-built squash court with shower and changing rooms, one of half a dozen that appeared in Devon country houses in the 1920s and 1930s. (The court at Hazelwood House, Loddiswell, was made out of one-half of a disused Congregational chapel next to the entrance drive; the other half, formerly a Sunday school, was converted into a billiard room.)

The upper floor of Ashcombe Tower was filled with guest rooms; the Rayners' bedroom suite, which came with built-in wardrobes and a blue-and-pink bathroom; and, at the opposite end of the house from their bedroom, a pair of day and night nurseries for their children. There were five servants' rooms in the attics along with a playroom for the children and another bathroom. Outbuildings included a garage for four cars, complete with petrol pumps.

In one other respect Ashcombe Tower was also entirely of its day: and that was in its relationship with the outdoors. The dining room had huge double French windows that opened onto a south-facing loggia where the family could breakfast, with views out to sea, and just beside it, in the angle formed by the dining room and the service wing, O'Rorke supplied a swimming pool.

It sometimes feels as if the post-Armistice generation invented fresh air. In California, theorists like the naturopath Dr. Philip Lovell, author of *Diet for Health by Natural Methods*, advocated fruit, vegetables, and plenty of sunshine as a recipe for the good life, while Swiss clinics pioneered heliotherapy as a treatment for tuberculosis. In Germany, Hans Suren's *Der Mensch und die Sonne* went through sixty-seven editions between its publication in 1924 and its appearance in an English translation as *Man and Sunlight* three years later.[*] Suren turned sun worship into a religion, and he played the part of high priest with a messianic zeal. "Greetings to you, you who are sun lovers," he wrote in his introduction. "You bear ardent longings in your hearts! Longings after warm sunshine, blue skies, light and nature; after victorious strength, spiritual loftiness and childlike faith."[16] In England Oliver Hill, who combined interests in nudism, adolescent girls, and photography in a way that doesn't sit comfortably with twenty-first-century sensibilities, predicted that "a maximum of sunlight and such facilities for recreation and exercise, dancing, swimming, and squash, will be large factors to be provided for in the modern house."[17]

---

[*] One of the more plausible reasons for the phenomenal success of *Der Mensch und die Sonne* was the fact that it contained copious illustrations of seminaked men and women.

Sun worship had some curious impacts on the country house and its architecture. The most advanced Modernist houses came supplied with big balconies and roof-top sundecks: the airplane-wing canopies that hover over the flat roof of Amyas Connell's High and Over are one of the more extreme examples. A few houses, and not only those built by Modernists, were provided with sleeping porches, an import from the more reliable climate of California. The Biddulphs' bedroom at Rodmarton Manor, which was about as un-Modernist a country house as one could imagine, was equipped with one.

Landfall, an Oliver Hill house of 1938–1939 set among pines overlooking Poole Harbour in Dorset, is a sun worshipper's house like no other of the period. The main living areas—a big staircase hall and an even bigger living room—quite literally opened onto a south-facing terrace, in that they were equipped with plate-glass screens in cedar frames running on tracks that could be rolled back. On the floor above, the principal bedrooms, also south-facing, gave onto a continuing balcony, while above them Hill created a glazed sunroom and roof terrace. As if all these opportunities for open-air living weren't enough, an external spiral stair of concrete linked the terrace with the balcony. Landfall caught the zeitgeist in other ways: Marian Dorn rugs, fitted furniture, a cocktail cabinet-cum-radiogram, and a projector "lodged under the stairs [and] throwing through two apertures in the wall on to a screen in front of the windows."[18]

Then there were the swimming pools. They were a rare but not unknown feature of the late Victorian and Edwardian country-house landscape, when they tended to be called "bathing pools" and were tucked discreetly out of sight in a woodland or inside a temple in a park. There were always ornamental lakes, of course, but they were often visible from the house, which made them inappropriate for swimming or bathing. After the First War, purpose-built swimming pools began to appear in increasing numbers. By the 1920s, two pre-war Lutyens' houses had them: Marsh Court in Hampshire and the neo-Georgian Wittersham House in Kent, which also boasted an "outside room." At Port Lympne, Sir Philip Sassoon had that fabulous hanging pool that perched precariously over Romney Marsh.

They also made a splash in more historic mansions. The Duke of Gloucester's Barnwell and the Prince of Wales's Fort Belvedere both had pools. E. Guy Dawber added one to Wormington Grange, a big Georgian pile in Gloucestershire with nineteen bedrooms, when he was creating a loggia and formal garden there in 1921. Sixteen years later, Olive Baillie installed an open-air swimming pool at Leeds Castle with underwater lights and a wave machine, one of the first in England. And Shortgrove Hall in Essex, a Queen Anne house used by Adele, Lady Meyer, as a base for her work campaigning for women's health and better working conditions, had a pool, a hard tennis court, a croquet lawn, and a cricket ground. The Meyers obviously took their recreations seriously.

"Beautiful swimming pool 35ft by 20ft surrounded by gaily flowered gardens" was the headline of one advertisement in the *Times* for a country house near Esher. By the 1930s estate agents were touting the swimming pool, or even the potential for one, as a huge asset. An old timber-framed manor house on the Sussex downs came with an old quarry in the park, and the agents were keen to point out that this would be a perfect spot for a pool. A sixteenth-century house in twenty acres between Canterbury and Folkestone was advertised in 1938 as possessing "a warm-water swimming pool in the grounds."[19] And a five-bedroomed fifteenth-century house in two hundred acres outside Chelmsford could offer not only a swimming pool but also a Turkish bath house.

The Chelmsford house also possessed a "Vita glass sun lounge," a feature that puts one in mind of King's Thursday, the "surprising creation of ferro-concrete," which the Hungarian Otto Silenus designed for Margot Best-Chetwynde in Evelyn Waugh's 1928 novel *Decline and Fall*. There, too, "the aluminium blinds shot up, and the sun poured in through the vita-glass, filling the room with beneficent rays."[20] Vita glass was a British invention developed in the 1920s that, unlike ordinary glass, allowed the passage of ultraviolet rays, the "vital" rays that tanned the skin and produced vitamin D in the body, assisted the formation of sound bone and teeth, and, it was claimed, even increased the bactericidal power of the blood, helping it to resist infection. Vita glass lured the outdoors into the house. It was possible to absorb all those warming, health-giving, therapeutic rays without even stepping out onto the terrace—no bad thing in a miserable English summer.

ELECTRICITY, ACKNOWLEDGED TO BE THE cleanest and most efficient domestic energy supply, if ever so slightly vulgar, was usually installed in new country houses after 1918. For the progressives, it was an integral part of the brave new world of Bakelite and brightly colored cellulose that promised a domestic and aesthetic revolution, powering the indoor fountains with their changing lighting displays, the built-in wirelesses and built-in heating panels, the drawing room curtains that glided apart at the touch of a switch. For the old guard it at least meant less grime and not having to employ a lamp boy.

The first public electricity supplies, used for street lighting, had been made back in 1881, around the same time that a handful of country houses was being fitted with some form of electric lighting. One of the first of these was Cragside in Northumberland, where its owner, the inventor, industrialist, and "modern magician" William Armstrong, installed hydroelectricity and lit a number of living rooms by December 1880. (Cragside also boasted an electric dinner gong.) The Marquess of Salisbury at Hatfield House in Hertfordshire followed a year or so later, and in spite of emitting blue sparks, failing at frequent intervals, and electrocuting a gardener, the supply was stable enough to impress August Hare when he visited the house in 1890. "All the windows blazed and glittered with light through the dark walls," he recalled. "The Golden Gallery with its hundreds of electric lamps was like a Venetian illumination."[21]

Electricity usage soared in Britain between the wars. The number of users rose from three quarters of a million in 1920 to nine million in 1938, the fastest increase in the world. In 1926 the Electricity (Supply) Act created a Central Electricity Board for the UK, which began to standardize the services (and the different voltages) that were provided by six hundred or so private companies and local authorities.

But these advances benefited the town, and not the country. By definition, the location of a country house often meant that it remained resolutely off the grid, and it simply wasn't economical to connect to a mains supply that, if the nearest distribution point was any more than a quarter of a mile from the house, could increase the price per unit from a penny to six pence or nine pence. Frustrated landowners watched pylons and power lines trooping across their parks, only to be told they were too far from the mains to benefit from the march of progress.

Even when electric light *was* available, owners often mixed new and old technology. Electric light was installed at the Tudor Long Melford Hall in the 1930s, for example, but only in the Great Saloon, the drawing room, and the dining room; other state rooms were still lit by gas, and the kitchens and bedrooms by gas and candles. For a time in the early 1920s, petrol lighting enjoyed a vogue. The *Times* commented in February 1921 on its increasing popularity, citing the case of a Tudor country house in Buckinghamshire, where "beamed ceilings and walls and open fireplaces are the old, and central heating and petrol lighting some of the new, attractions."[22]

The only option for most country-house owners who were set on an electrical supply was to install a private generating plant. By 1905, at least four hundred houses had their own. In 1938, a private generating plant was installed at the 9th Duke of Manchester's ancestral home of Kimbolton Castle in Cambridgeshire. Kimbolton is a monster of a house, dramatically remodeled by Vanbrugh and Hawksmoor for the 1st Duke in 1707–1714. The fact that the new plant had to power 350 lighting points gives some indication of its scale. The system, which was fully automatic, consisted of a battery and two gleaming Lister engines, one generating 7.5 kW and the other 16 kW, which were housed in a converted stable. By itself the battery supplied the load for up to forty lamps; if more lamps were turned on, or if an electric fire was connected to one of eighteen heating points scattered about the house, or if the battery charge dropped, then the smaller plant started automatically. If the castle required more power, the larger plant kicked in and the smaller one shut down; and on those rare occasions when even that wasn't enough, both plants operated simultaneously, generating 23.5 kW.

"As is usual with a large country house," went an enthusiastic review of Kimbolton's system in 1939, "electricity takes its full share of those domestic services which it can do so well." Water was pumped round the castle's central heating system, which was presumably oil or coal fired; a small workshop was fitted with a powered lathe and a saw bench; and "in the kitchen a small electric cooker has been installed for occasional use and a large refrigerator is operated electrically."[23]

With a smaller house, and especially one that was close enough for a direct connection to the mains, it was possible to be even more ambitious. The Manor House at West Wick near Marlborough, a lovely five-bay ex-farmhouse with a Georgian façade and thirteenth-century innards, was connected to the mains and made all electric in 1938. A combination of electric fires and low-temperature convection heaters did away with the need for a central heating system that would involve cutting through the structure of the house and also got rid of "that chilly feeling which is generally present in winter in a spacious house of this type."[24] Light fittings in the reception rooms were either central electroliers or candle-type wall sconces. Concealed lighting was used in the bedrooms, and four water heaters were installed, including a one-hundred-gallon heater for the main bathrooms upstairs and a more modest thirty-gallon heater for servant bedrooms and the kitchen.

Getting an electrical supply was only one-half of the story. Not for nothing did an advertisement for a firm specializing in the installation of electrical equipment for country houses claim that its system "can be carried out without damage to the fabric of the buildings or to the decorations."[25] An owner also had to have the building wired—easy enough in the case of a new house, or a major restoration, but not a task to be undertaken lightly if it involved chasing out rococo plasterwork or cutting a channel through a baroque mural. The guides at Stanford Hall in Leicestershire used to tell the story of how in the 1920s Lord and Lady Braye were baffled by the prospect of having to run cables through their long ballroom without wrecking its delicate eighteenth-century stuccowork. Then someone had a bright idea: they prized up a floorboard at one end and dropped a dead rabbit into the

ALL LIT UP: A BY-PRODUCT OF THE GENERAL AVAILABILITY OF ELEC-
TRICITY WAS THE FLOODLIGHTING OF COUNTRY HOUSES. (Copyright:
Country Life)

void; then they prized up a floorboard at the other end and unleashed
a ferret, with a string tied to his collar. When the ferret had managed
to negotiate the joists and reach the rabbit, the string was used to pull
through a cable and, hey, presto! The problem was solved.

ONE UNUSUAL BY-PRODUCT OF THE general availability of electricity was the floodlighting of country houses. In 1931 the International
Illumination Congress was held in Britain to mark the centenary of
Michael Faraday's discovery of electromagnetic induction, the principle behind the electric generator and transformer. As part of the celebrations, the organizing committee arranged for the floodlighting
of an eclectic array of landmarks and monuments across the country, from Edinburgh Castle to the façade of the municipal baths in
Stoke Newington and the new Art Deco Carreras cigarette factory
in Camden Town, where three hundred powerful electric lamps gave
two-color effects with four color changes each minute. In all, fourteen

London boroughs and fifty-four towns and cities took part in the scheme, along with hundreds of castles, cathedrals, and churches.

In central London, hundreds of thousands of people turned out on the first night to see the capital "touched by a magic wand," as a journalist from the *Illustrated London News* put it.[26] Throughout September, army searchlights illuminated St. Paul's Cathedral and the steeples of Sir Christopher Wren's city churches. St. James's Park was transformed (by gaslight rather than electricity) into "a nocturnal fairyland."[27] The Tower of London, Tower Bridge, Big Ben, Nelson's Column, and the National Gallery were all floodlit. The Houses of Parliament, said the *Times*, was "the color of old ivory, built into the gentle darkness." Westminster Abbey "wore a more mysterious look, as though all of it had vanished except the hollow, white, enclosing walls."[28] Buckingham Palace, moon colored and lit by 250 electric floodlights, was the most beautiful sight of the evening. From the top of the 273-foot campanile of Westminster Cathedral, the public could look out on the pockets of bright light that flared across the city, an eerie dress rehearsal for the Blitz ten years later.

A few disapproving voices were raised. Complaints about the cost were silenced by an announcement that everyone—the manufacturers of the equipment, the contractors who installed them, and the electricians who serviced them—had given their services for free. The *British Journal of Ophthalmology* huffily dismissed some of the illumination as "merely a glare," before grudgingly admitting that "occasionally, it rendered visible architectural features which are not ordinarily observed."[29] The principal of the Architectural Association, Howard Robertson, announced with his tongue firmly in his cheek that if the practice became general it would be disastrous for architects because it would show up their deficiencies.

Everyone else loved the idea. Why not floodlight the portico of a country house or a fountain in the grounds? Why not wire up a temple in the park or string rows of colored lamps between the trees?

I can think of plenty of reasons why not. But in the Britain of the 1930s, emerging from years of depression to find itself lurching toward another war, a light in the darkness was as much of an escapist fantasy as a Busby Berkeley musical, especially when it was tied in to a celebration of British culture. There was a bright joy in electricity. In 1935 the round tower at Windsor Castle was illuminated as part of George V's Silver Jubilee celebrations. So was Hampton Court Palace, and St. James's Palace, and Buckingham Palace, where George V opened the Jubilee Day celebrations by pressing an electric button to light a huge beacon in Hyde Park, signaling a chain of similar beacons all over the country. "In all this finery of fire no violence is done to the veritable forms," declared a lead in the *Times*, "and the new beauty supplements, not ousts, the old. Flood-lighting will surely do great things in days to come."[30]

And so it did. Over the border in Scotland, Edinburgh Castle, Inverness Castle, and the Duke of Roxburghe's Floors Castle were all floodlit in the 1930s. Chatsworth was floodlit to celebrate the succession of the 10th Duke of Devonshire. So was Blenheim Palace, to mark a reception attended by British and German officials. "Its grand baroque beauty could be seen for miles," wrote Chips Channon.[31] When the nation was gearing up for the celebrations to accompany George VI's coronation in May 1937, writers urged the owners of country houses to join in the fun and illuminate their mansions and parks. "Bonfires, laboriously built up, exhaust their glamour in a single night; a flood-lighting installation is available for a week or a month or as long as festivities continue."[32]

CONVERSATION PIECE: REX WHISTLER'S 1938 PORTRAIT OF THE FAMILY OF THE 6TH MARQUESS OF ANGLESEY AT PLAS NEWYDD (Rex Whistler/ Plas Newydd, Anglesey, UK/The Collection of the Marquess of Anglesey/National Trust Photographic Library/John Hammond/Bridgeman Images)

THE HALL ORIEL WINDOW AT STANWAY MANOR, ONE OF SIX STATELY HOMES BELONGING TO THE 11TH EARL OF WEMYSS AND MARCH (Copyright: Country Life)

VITA SACKVILLE-WEST'S WRITING ROOM AT SISSINGHURST. "I REALLY BELIEVE THAT YOU WILL BE ABLE TO MAKE SOMETHING AS PERSONAL AND LOVELY AS ANYTHING IN ENGLAND," SAID HER HUSBAND, HAROLD NICOLSON. (Copyright: Country Life)

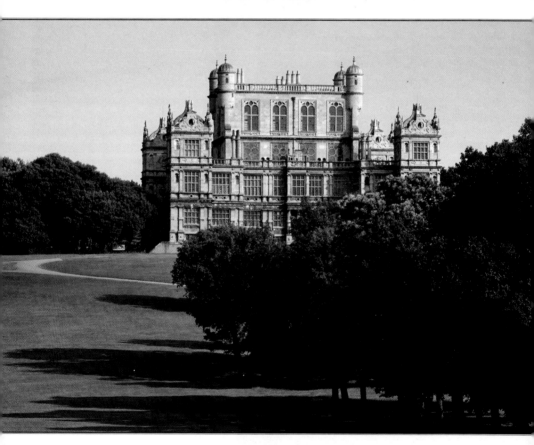

WOLLATON HALL, NOTTINGHAMSHIRE—AN UNWANTED MASTERPIECE
(Copyright: Country Life)

ALLINGTON CASTLE, KENT—A DREAM OF BEAUTY (Copyright: Country Life)

GLYN PHILPOT'S FRIEZE IN THE DINING ROOM AT PORT LYMPNE.
LEGEND HAS IT THAT SIR PHILIP SASSOON CALLED PHILPOT
BACK AT SHORT NOTICE TO ADD LOINCLOTHS AND SKIRTS TO THE
NAKED FIGURES IN PREPARATION FOR A VISIT BY QUEEN MARY.
(Copyright: Country Life)

REX WHISTLER'S TENT ROOM AT PORT LYMPNE. ONE HAS THE
IMPRESSION THAT SOMEWHERE, JUST OUT OF REACH, A STORY
LURKS. (Copyright: Country Life)

CASTLE DROGO—A DRAMATIC AND AMBIGUOUS TOUR DE FORCE, WHICH SIMULTANEOUSLY CONJURES UP AND REPUDIATES THE PAST
(Copyright: National Trust Images/Dennis Gilbert)

SIR PHILIP SASSOON AND HIS COUSIN, HANNAH GUBBAY, ON THE TERRACE AT TRENT PARK IN 1934 (Rex Whistler/Private Collection/Bridgeman Images)

Blenheim Palace, Oxfordshire (Copyright: Country Life)

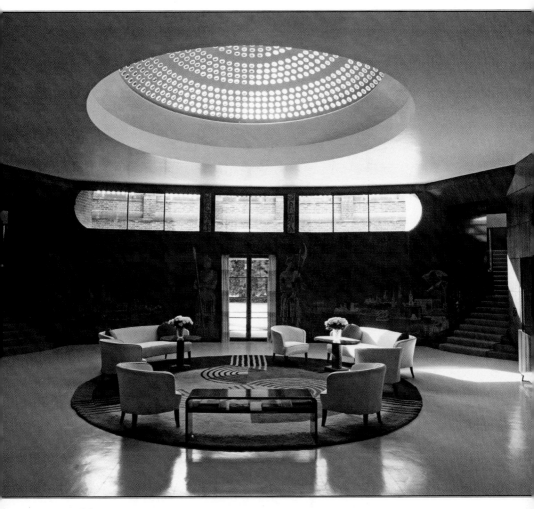

THE TRIANGULAR ENTRANCE HALL, A STARTLING INTRODUCTION
TO THE DECO DELIGHTS OF STEPHEN AND GINIE COURTAULD'S
ELTHAM PALACE (Copyright: Country Life)

LORD FAIRHAVEN: AN ENGLISH ARISTOCRAT WITH GILDED AGE TASTES (Copyright: National Trust Images/John Hammond)

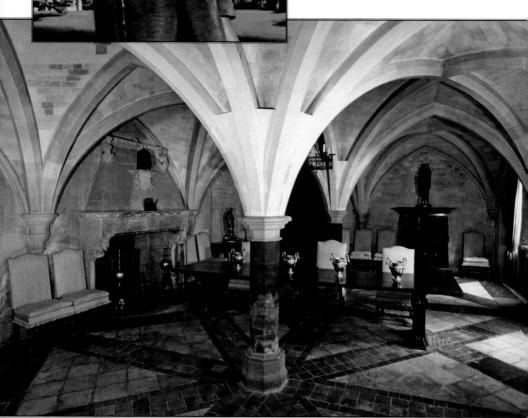

LORD FAIRHAVEN'S DINING ROOM AT ANGLESEY ABBEY, ONCE THE MONKS' PARLOUR OF THE ORIGINAL MEDIEVAL PRIORY (Copyright: Country Life)

9

HOME DECORATING

❧ ❦

I n 1913 the *Post Office London Directory* listed 4 interior decorators, none of whom traded from fashionable West End addresses. One was in Hackney, another in Brixton, the third in Putney, and the fourth in Fulham. Eight years later, that same London Directory contained no fewer than 122 interior decorators, more than half of whom had premises in Mayfair and other fashionable West End addresses.

What was the reason for this explosion in taste making? *Vogue* put it down to the rising divorce rate. "Someone once said that a woman is either happily married or an Interior Decorator. Whether the rise of the Society decorator can be attributed to the present slump in married felicity, it is as certain that it is as fashionable now to be doing up the house of one's acquaintances as it was to open a hat-shop in pre-war days."[1] More plausibly, people's uncertainty about their own taste opened the door to the professional and the confident amateur. And that in turn points to the role played by the hesitant nouveaux riches in English high society between the wars—and also to the fluid property market, with houses changing hands more frequently and each new owner keen to reinvent his or her new home.

There was already a smattering of well-established firms who didn't appear in the prewar listings, simply because although they offered an interior decoration service they regarded themselves

primarily as furnishers or upholsterers or antique dealers or architects. The doyen of country-house decorators was White, Allom &
Co., "decorative artists and contractors" of London, Montreal, and
New York. White, Allom was founded in 1893 by Charles Carrick
Allom, grandson of the artist and architect Thomas Allom. Nothing is known of White, who disappeared from the scene early on.
The firm's main premises were at 15 George Street, Hanover Square,
and here Allom, himself an architect, assembled a team of craftsmen and specialist consultants who offered "interior decoration of a
distinguished character." Their style was conservative and generally
neo-Georgian with an occasional foray into sturdy Jacobethan oak.
From early on, White, Allom had a working relationship with the legendary art dealer Joseph Duveen, who subcontracted them to provide
suitable historic interiors as settings for the works of art he sold.

White, Allom's reputation, both before and after the First War,
had a great deal to do with the firm's connections with the British
royal family. In 1904 they did some work at Marlborough House for
George, Prince of Wales, and three years later they were working for
his father Edward VII at Buckingham Palace, where they redecorated
the Ballroom, East Gallery, and Bow Drawing-Room. After Edward's
death in 1910, they were back at the palace, setting silk panels taken
from the Brighton Pavilion into *chinoiserie* panels for the Centre
Room, from which the royal family emerged onto the balcony overlooking the Mall. White, Allom held a Royal Warrant until 1960, a
fact that in itself recommended the firm to private clients.[2]

ANOTHER CATEGORY OF DECORATOR WAS essentially a furniture
dealer. So in 1912 Francis Lenygon, already well known as a cabinetmaker to the country-house-owning classes, merged with the upholsterers Morant & Co. to form Lenygon & Morant, trading out of 31
Old Burlington Street, where he built a showroom in the back garden. Lenygon & Morant provided authentic and reproduction furniture, with a strong emphasis on Baroque and Early Georgian, and
even entire salvaged interiors. In 1910 the firm's stock list offered no
fewer than seventeen rooms for sale, with, at the top of the list, a

remarkable Dutch Baroque interior taken from a house in Gronin-
gen that included painted ceiling, walls, overdoors, and chimneypiece.
Charles of London, which also sold antiques and salvaged architectural fittings, was set up in Brook Street, Mayfair, in 1903, by Charles
Joel Duveen, brother of Joseph, who was said to pay him $25,000 a
year not to trade under the Duveen name.

The postwar London Directory lists also included the big furniture stores—Maples and Waring & Gillow—and one or two firms
whose presence in the list is frankly odd, like the Mayfair Window
Cleaning Co. on Park Lane and the Nautilus Fire Co. of Oxford
Street. But the elite were now there, too: Lenygon & Morant, Charles
of London, and White, Allom had all decided that they were interior
decorators after all.

But by far the biggest group was composed, as *Vogue* suggested,
of talented amateurs (and some were not so talented) who moved from
decorating their own homes and the homes of friends and acquaintances
to opening their own premises and carving out careers, while never jet-
tisoning that sense that theirs was a relationship of social equals.

The great society decorator was Sibyl Colefax, famous all over
London as a hostess, and infamous as a collector of scalps, gathering
celebrities to her "as a parrot picks up beads," in the words of Virginia
Woolf, who was one of the beads.[3] Memoirs of the period are full of
stories told at her expense about her relentless pursuit of this name or
that, usually recounted by people who were happy enough to accept
her hospitality at the time. Margot Asquith, exasperated at her determination to know everyone, said one couldn't talk about the birth of
Christ without Sibyl saying she was there in the manger. And Gerald
Berners mocked her lion hunting by inviting her to dinner "to meet
the P. of W." When she turned up, she found herself being introduced
not to the Prince of Wales but to the Provost of Worcester.

One evening in June 1936, Lady Colefax held a dinner party. It
was by way of being a farewell to Argyll House, the Chelsea villa
designed by Giacomo Leoni in 1723, which had been her home for fifteen years. Sibyl's barrister husband had died four months previously,
and she was about to move to a much smaller house in Westminster.

Her guests of honor were the couple that the whole of smart society was eager to be seen with—Edward VIII and Wallis Simpson, no less. Several members of the king's inner circle were also there: Perry Brownlow, who six months later would take Wallis into hiding in France while the abdication crisis played itself out in Britain, and the prominent politician Lord Stanley and his wife, Portia, who had once been touted as a bride for Edward. Tom Lamont, chair of the board of J. P. Morgan, and Robert Vansittart, the foreign office official who was exasperating everyone with his dark prophecies of a coming war with Germany, were also there with their wives, as was the Polish pianist Arthur Rubinstein.

As the evening wore on, other guests arrived: Winston Churchill, Noel Coward, Gerald Berners, forgiven for his P. of W. joke, and the society beauty Lady Diana Cooper, who was just about to go cruising down the Dalmatian coast with Edward and Wallis. Rubinstein played Chopin after dinner, which bored the king so that he stood up to take his leave; then Noel Coward sang "Mad Dogs and Englishmen," which persuaded him to stay. It was a triumph, Harold Nicolson (who was there) reported to Vita (who was not). "I was glad for Sibyl's sake, since I fear it is her last party in that charming house and never has it looked so lovely."[4]

Sibyl Colefax's entertaining had a purpose. As well as being a society hostess, she was one of London's most successful decorators, a dealer in chintzes and wallpapers, in "the most charming and carefully designed modern furniture," as her business card declared, and in "antique furniture, glass, china, with a special feature of Regency pieces." Customers who visited Sibyl Colefax Ltd., her shop at 24 Bruton Street in fashionable Mayfair, were told that "Everything here is different."[5] And as Nicolson's comment revealed, the Bruton Street premises weren't her only showroom. She was adept at displaying her talents at Argyll House. "From the moment that one arrived in the small panelled hall and savoured the aroma of dried rosemary burnt on a saucer," said Cecil Beaton, "one knew one had arrived in a completely different atmosphere."[6] Argyll House was decorated with "all the restraint of an eighteenth-century intellectual," he thought,

SIBYL COLEFAX'S BRUTON STREET SHOWROOM. (Copyright: Colefax and Fowler. Photography: Millar & Harris/English Heritage Collection)

although he reckoned that Sibyl never managed to achieve the same relaxed restraint in her work for clients. And those clients were the people she mixed with, artists and actors and noblemen. They were the friends who came to dinner.

The blurring of social and commercial boundaries between decorator and client was used ruthlessly by the decorator. Soon after the dinner for Edward VIII and Mrs. Simpson, Sibyl was lobbying Wallis, who was a good friend, to use her influence with the king on her behalf. "As far as I know," Wallis wrote back, kindly but firmly, "neither Buckingham Palace nor the Fort [Fort Belvedere, the king's country house in Windsor Great Park] are having anything done in the way of 'face lifting.'"[7] In Charles Allom's case, the division between tradesman and social equal was even more blurred. Allom was knighted in 1913, had a country house of his own—Westbury Court in Gloucestershire—and sailed regularly with George V. Allom's ability to mix business with social life did a good deal to raise the status of the decorator between the wars. Of course that meant that when it came to the delicate matter of presenting his bill, there was occasionally some awkwardness. When he was working on William Randolph Hearst's St. Donat's Castle in the 1930s, he supplied hundreds of items while politely leaving the matter of payment up to his client: ten years later Hearst still owed White, Allom £222,000—the equivalent of tens of millions of pounds today—and the decorator had to sue to get his money.

The big difference between a professional architect-furnisher, like Sir Charles Allom, and society decorators, like Sibyl Colefax, was training. Most Mayfair decorators didn't have any, relying instead on their experience of remodeling their own homes and for inspiration on visiting the homes of their friends, on browsing antique shops and auctions, and on the high-quality halftone illustrations, particularly of historic interiors, which had been coming onto the market for the past decade or so. In 1909 Francis Lenygon allowed his name to appear on the title page of *The Decoration and Furniture of English Mansions during the Seventeenth and Eighteenth Centuries* and five years later on two volumes for Batsford on historic interiors, *Decoration in England from 1660 to 1770* and *Furniture in England from 1660 to 1770*, although all were in fact ghost-written by the furniture historian Margaret Jourdain. A. D. F. Hamlin, professor of architectural history at Columbia, produced a two-volume *History of Ornament* (1916, 1923) expressly commending it to "teachers and students of architecture and decorative design, and to designers generally."[8] Then there were the magazines: *Vogue* to find out what period was in fashion; *Country Life* to understand why.

It was the business of actually decorating one's own home that set so many society decorators on the path to their own little showroom off Grosvenor Square. Sibyl Colefax's interest dated back to 1912, when she and her husband took a long lease on Old Buckhurst in Sussex, the remains of a mansion built by the Sackvilles in the early sixteenth century. Little was left except a gatehouse, an oast house, and some nondescript stables; but "the place was full of magic," remembered

Sibyl, and their architect, Cecil Brewer (best known today for his designs with partner Arnold Smith for the National Museum of Wales in Cardiff), managed to maintain that magic while turning the tumbledown country house into a comfortable modern home. Sibyl bought up oak furniture "which in time and in character complete the picture," wrote an approving H. Avray Tipping when Old Buckhurst was written up in *Country Life* in 1919.[9] Two years later, their finances looking a little rocky, the Colefaxes sold the lease on Old Buckhurst, moved out of the town house they also occupied at Onslow Square in South Kensington, and consolidated their fortunes by moving to Argyll House, which was within easy reach of central London and at the same time functioned as what its architect Giacomo Leoni had called "a small country house."[10]

By 1930 Sir Arthur Colefax's practice at the bar was shrinking, a result of his increasing deafness, and Sibyl began to think of interior decoration as a way of propping up the Colefax fortunes. She first began to "help" her friends and quickly found that they liked her ideas and were prepared to pay for them. She worked for a time for another London decorator, Dolly Mann, and then took up an offer from the antique dealers Stair & Andrew to open a first-floor showroom at their Bruton Street premises, in return for sharing her contacts with them. "I do hope the shop is doing well," wrote one of her friends in September 1930. It was: on Christmas Eve 1931 she told Harold Nicolson over lunch at Boulestin's in Covent Garden that she had made £2,000 that year.

Time hasn't been kind to Sibyl's interiors. Only one is known to have survived from these years: the pink-and-white bedroom she created for the Marchioness of Anglesey at Plas Newydd in Wales. There are also photographs of work she did for Evelyn Waugh's brother Alec at Edrington, a Queen Anne rectory in Hampshire. She was recommended by Evelyn, who told his brother, "you'll be saved the kind of mistakes that are made by decorators who are not used to dealing with persons of quality, and she's very businesslike."[11] In fact she wasn't. She was always late for appointments, and the Waughs were bewildered by the way she filled their house with pieces of furniture that she wrongly thought might fit and annoyed to find that the curtains in their library looked odd. It was because they had been hung inside out.

Interior decoration was an intense and competitive business. At the height of her success in the late 1920s and early 1930s, Syrie Maugham, that other great doyenne of society decorators, who was saluted by *Vogue* "for teaching us to use white in our houses . . . and for being one of the few lady decorators who kept her head during the modernistic deluge by consistently combining old and new,"[12] spent six months of the year in England and six in America. She had warehouses and workshops in a four-story factory building in Chelsea, a stone's throw from the Embankment. Altogether Syrie Ltd. employed more than twenty people, as well as contracting out work and buying in antiques, papers, and other items. Textiles and wallpapers were imported from France. Syrie bought used furniture from a shop just off Marylebone Road and replicas of seventeenth-century pieces from a firm in High Wycombe. She used a north London firm to make her curtains and pelmets from textiles bought in France. She rarely designed items herself. Like Sibyl Colefax, her skills lay in combining things to create a look and in promoting herself. She cultivated Wallis Simpson, never quite achieving the same intimacy as Sibyl, but profiting in other ways. She sold furniture to Mrs. Simpson and decorated several rooms at the Prince of Wales's Fort Belvedere, using huge mirrors to reflect the swans that floated on the lake.

PIERO MALACRIDA DE SAINT-AUGUST WAS the epitome of the society decorator, a figure who would have been invented if he hadn't already existed. He was artistic, aristocratic, and Italian, with an equally aristocratic British wife, Louisa, who played the part of bright young thing to perfection. He was an ex-cavalry officer. She was an aviator, a race-car driver, a poet and playwright, and a theater designer. Her portrait, by Flora Lion or in miniature by Alfred Praga, hung in the Royal Academy; gossip columnists took care to mention her in their columns, where she was always "the beautiful Marchesa Malacrida," always "the loveliest figure in the room."[13]

This golden couple was seen in the right places. When the Court Circular mentioned a musical party in Portland place, they were there, chatting to the Duchess of Rutland and the Egyptian chargé d'affaires. Another night they might be at a reception at the Polish embassy, or a Belgrave Square fund-raiser for the League of Nations, or a charity garden fête in aid of a children's hospital. It seemed that whenever there was a masked ball or a society wedding or a fashionable Mayfair tea party in the late 1920s and early 1930s, the Marchese and Marchesa Malacrida were on the invitation list.

Like other semiprofessional decorators of the period, Malacrida was a master of social connection and self-publicity. In an article on "Modern Tendencies in Decoration," which he wrote for *Vogue* in 1928, he set out his stall, half smiling, tolerant, urbane. Applauding the new, more intelligent interest that people were taking in their homes after the "colouristic blunders" of their Victorian and Edwardian forebears, he nevertheless lamented that taste seemed locked in the past. All that seemed on offer were

> [t]he cottagey-inglenooky-pickled-oak school; the walnutty-Queen-Annish, real or false, but chiefly false; a few sporadic cases of Adam and Regency, decorous mahogany being tolerated if believed to be extremely good; a few endemic cases of Victorian-papier-mâché-dogs-in-the-hearth-glass-shaded-flowers for the aspidistra section of the community; and then, above all, triumphant and unchallenged, the Hollywood-Italo-Spanish.[14]

At least these looks were safe, he said, and both client and designer pretty much knew what the end result would be. Things weren't so simple for decorators like him, who cast the past aside and worked in the modern manner. Materials weren't obtainable in the right colors; furniture had to be specially made; every "dreary little detail," from the door handles to the tassels on the end of a blind cord, had to be designed from scratch. Plumbers and plasterers and carpenters and electricians informed you that "they have worked for twenty years for Sir Blankety Blank and that pipes or switches or what-nots as you want them are simply not done." And always in the background was the client, wanting to know exactly what you were going to do to their dining room or bathroom—"a very difficult and embarrassing question this, because, at that stage of things, one often has only very hazy ideas about the finished article one is going to turn out."[15]

There is something endearing about the bewildered, self-deprecating tone that Malacrida adopts here, especially his honesty in admitting, as he does, that his pleasure at completing an interior is always marred by the knowledge that in ten or twenty years' time someone is going to walk in and say, "Isn't it pathetic? The poor fellow thought he was doing something new."[16] But there is nothing self-deprecating about the photographs that accompany Malacrida's essay. They all show his recent work at 20 Portman Square for the immensely rich industrialist Samuel Courtauld, perhaps the greatest collector of French Impressionism in the country. Courtauld had taken over the lease at Portman Square the previous year and begun a careful restoration of the Adam state rooms. His wife, however, clearly wanted something modern. Malacrida provided it, in the form of a large studio-boudoir at the top of the house, with wall lights by Oliver Messel and a trompe-l'oeil blind by the painter and set designer John Armstrong, showing nude figures cavorting on tightropes and clambering up ladders into open windows. A bathroom had enormous fish-scale panels on the lower walls, beneath a ceiling in which more figures by Armstrong danced and juggled and worshipped the sun.

Malacrida's career as a designer is mysterious, the narrative fragmented. He indulged in a little property speculation on his own account, buying flats in smart London addresses, remodeling them, and selling them. But most of his work seems to have been undertaken for White, Allom & Co. Between 1926 and 1929, the Malacridas lived in and decorated an eighteenth-century house in Upper Brooke Street, Mayfair. As so often happened with the decorators of the period, none of this work has survived, but according to the *Survey of London*, the marchese created "an exotic ambience with a strong Italianate flavour," painting the ceiling of the main staircase as "the underside of an arboreal bower."[17][*] Around the same time he did some unspecified work for Nancy Cunard, who lived nearby in Grosvenor Square.

In 1929 the Malacridas moved to Grosvenor Street, just off the square, and their apartment was featured in another *Vogue* article that November. The anonymous writer was intrigued by a set of interiors that were relentlessly modern, without a hint of Sibyl Colefax's muted neo-Georgian pastels or Syrie Ltd.'s off-whites and painted Spanish wood carvings. Instead, there were steel furniture and black glass in the marchese's bedroom, built-in furniture and shelving—and a bar with washable white walls, so that the Malacridas and their friends could draw pictures on them with colored crayons and then wipe them clean and start again. "The idea is typical of the modern restlessness of spirit." said *Vogue*, "and the execution is also typical of the times, as it encourages a more or less artistic self-expression."[18]

It must have been through his links with Samuel Courtauld that the marchese obtained his only country-house commission and the work for which he is best known today. In 1933 Samuel's brother Stephen Courtauld acquired a Crown lease on Eltham Palace, six miles from Westminster on the outskirts of London. Eltham had once been the residence of kings: a vast, moated complex of lodgings and courts where Edward IV celebrated Christmas with two thousand guests and retainers, where Cardinal Wolsey took his oath as Lord Chancellor of England, and Henry VIII walked in the allées and arbors with Catherine of Aragon. But it had never recovered from being stripped by Oliver Cromwell in the 1650s. Now only the medieval Great Hall was left, and there were plans to surround it with a housing estate.

Stephen Courtauld was happy to restore the hall, but he didn't want to live in a medieval ruin. He and his wife, Ginie, decided to attach a modern house to the remains of the palace. Their architects, John Seely and Paul Paget, produced a splayed U-plan, with the hall as one arm, the new house as the other, and a triangular entrance

---

* A photograph of this staircase in 1926 survives, showing lanterns perched on tasseled posts, painted plaster figures in robes perched in alcoves, and the arboreal bower. It all looks very odd.

hall in the angle formed by the two wings. It was only partly successful: Seely & Paget opted for a slightly old-fashioned exterior based
on Wren's work at Hampton Court, all red brick with stone dress-
ings, and although the Courtaulds were pleased, critical opinion was
not favorable. "An admirably designed but unfortunately sited cigarette factory," was the verdict of historian G. M. Young.[19] Sir Herbert
Baker, Lutyens's partner at New Delhi and the first architect of Port
Lympne, spent a pleasant day picnicking with Seely and Paget in the
garden and then went away and announced that "Romance has gone
from Eltham."[20] "Very unusual" was as far as Christopher Hussey was
prepared to go in *Country Life*.[21]

The interiors were a different matter. Stephen Courtauld was
reserved and deeply introspective. His half-Hungarian, half-Italian
wife, Ginie, was not. She was a marchesa herself, on account of a
previous marriage to an Italian nobleman, and had a pet ring-tailed
lemur, which she had bought in Harrods, and a snake tattoo above
her right ankle. No doubt both the Courtaulds were responsible for
the fact that Eltham was a very modern mansion, with electric fires,
gas central heating, internal telephones, a loudspeaker system to relay
the sound of gramophone records around the house, and a centralized
vacuum cleaner system in the basement. But one suspects that the
vitality of the interiors owed most to Ginie.

The triangular entrance hall, a startling introduction to the
house, was the work of the Swedish designer Rolf Engströmer, who
also produced the black-bean and walnut furniture, which stood on a
circular rug commissioned from Marion Dorn, whose bold, geomet-
rically patterned carpets and textiles could be found in fashionable
London interiors, from the famous White Room in Syrie Maugham's
Chelsea house to the lobby of Claridges. But the two most spectacular
features of the hall are the shallow glass dome that lights it, and the
black-bean veneer that lines it, with marquetry panels by Engströmer's
fellow countryman, Jerk Werkmäster, depicting buildings in Italy and
Scandinavia. The room is guarded by two larger-than-life marquetry
figures, also by Werkmäster—a Roman soldier and a horned Viking
bearing a halberd, who flank the glazed entrance doors.

Seely & Paget decorated the guest bedrooms, fitting them out with built-in liner-style laminated furniture. But if one had to identify an *ensemblier* who defined the Eltham look, it was Malacrida. Paget resented his arrival, later claiming ill-naturedly that the commission came because of Sir Charles Allom, "who sailed a yacht in Cowes week and was very much received by royalty"; and explaining that "Mrs Courtauld . . . was of Italian-Rumanian extraction" and was thus friendly with the marchese. Whatever the reason—and the connection with Samuel Courtauld still seems the most likely—Malacrida was given the task of designing the drawing room, the dining room, the library, and Ginie's bedroom suite.

He had hardly begun to think about the commission when tragedy struck. At the end of September 1934 he and his wife went down for the weekend to a cottage they had borrowed in the Chilterns, just north of Henley-on-Thames. He went back to Grosvenor Street on Monday morning, leaving Louisa to follow on in their car later in the week.

On Wednesday morning the marchesa was driving along the Henley-London road with their pet spaniel in the passenger seat when, for no apparent reason, she swerved and braked hard. The car skidded through a hedge and rolled down a forty-foot embankment. The marchesa broke her neck. The jury returned a verdict of accidental death. Louise was thirty-eight. Stephen and Ginie Courtauld came to the funeral.

Malacrida went abroad for a month. He sold off his library and published *Finale*, a collection of his wife's letters to him. "Under their brilliant and witty surface is hidden a beautiful love-story," wrote a reviewer in the *Observer*.[22] And then he disappeared. No more mentions in *Vogue* or the Court Circular. No more appearances at receptions and charity balls. Nothing, really, to earn him more than a footnote in history.[*]

Except for Eltham Palace. The drawing room, which like Malacrida's other Eltham interiors was executed by White, Allom & Co. to his designs, was comfortable rather than exciting, with antique

---

[*] Malacrida died in 1980.

rugs, cream walls, and painted faux ceiling timbers, although it looked rather like the triumphant and unchallenged Hollywood-Italo-Spanish interiors he had dismissed in the 1920s. But it was specifically designed to show some of Stephen Courtauld's collection of Italian pictures and furniture, so perhaps he can be forgiven.

The dining room was all Malacrida—black marble and ebonized woods inlaid with bold geometrical patterns, concealed beam lighting to show off Stephen's landscapes by Turner and Crome, and, most remarkable of all, a ceiling of shining aluminium leaf. "Not really quite our taste," recalled Paget, still smarting from having the interior decoration of Eltham taken away and given to Malacrida. "It had a silver ceiling."[23]

On the first floor was Ginie's suite, "the outstanding decorative achievement," according to an admiring Christopher Hussey. The marchese lined Ginie's oval bedroom with pale pinkish maple and weathered sycamore veneer, punctuated with pilasters, like some shrine to an ancient goddess. The walls were inlaid with exquisite marquetry in patterns that led Hussey to strive so hard for definition that he invented an entirely new style—"modern Swedish rococo." Curved doorways opened onto the landing and into the goddess's inner sanctum, a bathroom lined with onyx and gold mosaic, its bath set back in a golden recess and presided over by a marble Psyche. Even in an era that excelled in the creation of beautiful bathrooms, an era in which *Vogue* declared that "bathrooms nowadays look more expensive than any rooms in the house," and academics shook their heads at the folly of their "hypertrophied magnificence," Ginie's bathroom—her entire suite, in fact—stood out as a redefinition of country-house style: modern without falling into the easy vocabulary of the Moderne or the stark white austerity of Modernism, opulent without vulgarity, making use of traditional materials but refusing to bow down to tradition. It makes one wish that more of Marchese Malacrida's interior designs had survived.

"We would have done something much better," said Paget.

10

THE NEW GEORGIANS

❦

M alacrida's taste, urban and urbane, helped to make Eltham Palace the outstanding example of High Deco country-house design. But its sleek lines were a step too far for most owners, as they were for Seely and Paget. The pull of the past was just too great to resist: not a scholarly, "authentic" reconstruction of the past but a more lyrical evocation of a world that had been lost—if indeed it had ever existed at all.

The most influential country-house decorators of the interwar years, then, were not marchesas with flair or society matrons with an eye for modernity but an unlikely young American couple with a taste for the English eighteenth century.

Ronald Tree and Nancy Field were twenty-one when they met aboard the Cunard liner *Mauretania*, bound for England on the return leg of its first transatlantic voyage since returning to private service after the war. Nancy, already a widow, was on her way to spend Christmas 1918 with her aunt and namesake, Nancy Astor, at the latter's Buckinghamshire country house, Cliveden. Her husband, Henry Field, the grandson of a Chicago department store magnate, had died the previous year after only five months of marriage. Ronnie, who was Henry's cousin, had known Nancy for some time.

Their shipboard romance outlasted the voyage. Eighteen months later they were married at Wren's St. James's Church, Piccadilly. The bride was given away by her uncle, Viscount Astor.

Fox hunting was one of Ronnie's passions, a legacy of his adolescence spent in England. The Trees lived in America but each winter they crossed the Atlantic to ride to hounds with the Quorn and the Cottesmore. In 1926 they came to live permanently in England, partly so that Ronnie could pursue a political career—he had been told that his English accent precluded anything of the sort in America—but also because he had been invited to become joint master of the prestigious Pytchley Hunt, which met in some of the finest hunting country in England, along the border between Northamptonshire and Leicestershire.

Northamptonshire is one of those not-quite-in-the-Cotswolds counties that have been overlooked by topographers and seekers after the picturesque. Dismissed by travelers in the eighteenth century as "disagreeable . . . [all] wide pastures, and hopeless views" and known mainly in the twentieth for its fox hunting and its boot and shoe factories, it has always been somewhere to pass through on the way to something more exciting, unless one was interested in boots or shoes or chasing foxes.[1]

Yet Northamptonshire's country houses rank with the best. There are rambling Elizabethan beauties like Deene Park and the ruined Kirby Hall; Baroque splendor at Boughton and Hawksmoor's Easton Neston; gentle classicism in Lamport Hall and Cottesbrooke. And for reticent, quiet beauty Kelmarsh, which the Trees leased in 1927, is hard to beat. Designed by James Gibbs and built c. 1728–1732, it is a two-storied, redbrick house of seven bays, the center, which contains the hall and saloon, breaking out very gently under a triangular pediment. When the Trees moved in on a ten-year repairing lease, the place was run down and disfigured with various Victorian accretions. Its owner, Claude Lancaster, was two years younger than them and happy enough to let his tenants tidy it up while he pursued his family interests in coal and iron in Nottinghamshire.

THE HALL AT KELMARSH IN 1933. A PORTRAIT BY ALFRED MUN-NINGS OF RONALD TREE AS MASTER OF THE PYTCHLEY HUNT HANGS OVER THE FIREPLACE. (Copyright: Country Life)

The remodeling of Kelmarsh—and it was more of a gentle facelift than a wholesale reinvention—was a collaboration between the Trees and a stable of artists and craftspeople. The architect Paul Phipps, who had worked in Lutyens's office and was married to Nancy Astor's sister Nora, was put in charge of the modernization work, and it was he who installed modern heating, plumbing, and electric light. William Adams Delano, who had remodeled Mirador in Virginia for Nancy Tree, designed the library paneling. A painter called Mr. Kick advised on color schemes, and for help with textiles, the Trees went to Elden Ltd. on Duke Street, one of Mayfair's best-known firms of interior decorators.

The proprietrix of Elden Ltd., Ethel Bethell, was a "genius in the arrangement of old damask, brocades and painted or embroidered stuffs,"[2] and she as much as the Trees and their craftsmen was responsible for the Kelmarsh look. She provided the brocade curtains in the hall and a set of more elaborate swagged silk curtains in blue gray for the saloon. She also supplied a complete dressing room—created for a decorators' exhibition at Olympia in 1927 and bought in its entirety—and decorated Nancy Tree's bedroom, which had walls hung with white silk and curtains to match and a specially made bed hung with white damask trimmed with silver lamé. Old gilt mirrors and gilt finials to the bed created an effect that Nancy called "ice with a glint of gold."[3]

Elsewhere there was Chinese hand-painted eighteenth-century wallpaper acquired from a house in Norfolk, Aubusson carpets, Chippendale dining chairs, and Italian painted furniture. The colors were generally pale, and the overall effect was comfortable without clutter, restrained, and in keeping with the spirit of the place. It spoke of a sophisticated and complex relationship with the past rather than slavish imitation. Above all, the Trees' Kelmarsh was quietly elegant.

Nancy loved Kelmarsh. In 1948, after the failure of her marriage to Ronald Tree, she took as her third husband its owner, Claude Lancaster, and her friends were convinced that her emotional attachment was to Kelmarsh rather than its owner—an impression confirmed when this marriage also failed after only three years, and Lancaster was forced to cut off the electricity to Kelmarsh before Nancy would leave.*

But that was later. In 1933 Ronnie Tree was elected to Parliament as Conservative MP for Harborough in Leicestershire. That June the Trees were out driving in Oxfordshire when they came upon Ditchley Park, another Gibbs house but much larger and grander than Kelmarsh, with about thirty bedrooms and dressing rooms and seven reception rooms. They talked their way in to see it, ignoring the objections of an ancient butler in a red wig who protested that his master, the 17th Viscount Dillon, had just died.

What the interlopers saw, Ronnie recalled later, was "an unforgettable picture of magnificence and accumulated junk . . . a Sleeping

---

* Claude was a regular guest of the Trees in the 1930s. Ronald Tree's daughter by his second marriage later suggested he was Nancy's longtime lover and that this was the real reason why the Trees' marriage failed.

Beauty waiting to be called back to life."⁴ A week or two later the 18th Viscount put the Ditchley Park estate of 3,500 acres onto the market, together with its "stately mansion rich in historical associations."⁵

Ronnie bought it.

Like Kelmarsh, the refurbishing of Ditchley was a collaborative effort. Ronnie bought the grand pieces of furniture that he felt a stately home required and the good paintings, while his wife was responsible for the overall look, the choice of fabrics and the arrangement of the furniture. They made a great team, and long after their divorce, their son Michael recalled that "my parents, from a decorating point of view, were a marvellous pair."⁶ And there were other members of that team. Paul Phipps supervised the building work again, and again he installed decent lighting and bathrooms. (When the Trees took possession of Ditchley, there were no bathrooms at all, and they had to grope their way to their bedroom by the light of acetylene lamps.) Ethel Bethell had died in 1932, and Elden Ltd. was now being run by the Dutch decorator Herman Schrijver. The Trees didn't use him, perhaps considering him too modern, too flamboyant in his use of color. Instead, they bought chintzes and furnishings from a range of other London decorators.

They also employed the French interior designer Stéphane Boudin, director (and later president) of the prestigious Paris firm of Maison Jansen. After parting from her husband, Olive Wilson Filmer—or Lady Baillie as she now was—used Boudin to create a series of interiors at Leeds Castle that blended English and French eighteenth-century themes; and in 1935 the *ensemblier* designed an astonishing rococo dining room for Chips Channon's Belgrave Square house, based on the Hall of Mirrors in the Amalienburg near Munich. ("It will shimmer in blue and silver," wrote Channon in his diary. "It will shock and stagger London. And it will cost over £6,000."⁷). The project for which Boudin is best remembered today was still a long way in the future—his redecoration of the White House for the Kennedys in 1961–1963.

Ronnie and Nancy Tree weren't in the market for Bavarian rococo. They bought Ditchley Park in 1933 at a time when the so-called

New Georgian Age was flourishing in all its restrained elegance, even as George V, who had given his name to it, was nearing the end of his life. There had been a burst of enthusiasm for New Georgianism when the king came to the throne in 1910: Harrods opened a Georgian restaurant in 1911 and later a Georgian salon. Harold Monro and Edward Marsh published the first of their five anthologies of *Georgian Poetry* in 1912. Thomas Hardy talked of living "in neo-Georgian days."[8] Fashion commentators talked of the modern woman as a "Neo-Georgian [with] a boyish smile which matches her two-piece suit."[9] As the reign wore on and Modernist literature, art, and architecture fragmented and mystified, the gentler and more conservative New Georgians found themselves looking more and more to the Old Georgians for solace and for inspiration.

An indication of the long eighteenth century's popularity can be seen in the story of Sir Philip Sassoon's Royal Northern Hospital exhibitions. In 1928, Sassoon began to host a series of annual exhibitions in his Park Lane mansion in aid of the Royal Northern, where he was on the board. The first exhibition, *Early English Needlework and Furniture*, was an eclectic display, which included the veil worn by Mary Queen of Scots at her execution and William of Wykeham's mitre from New Hall, Oxford. But it raised £2,215 for the hospital. It was followed the next year by *Old English Plate*, which, like its predecessor, ran for two weeks and raised a similar amount, although it was a more professional affair—Sassoon borrowed warders from the National Gallery to supervise security and turnstiles from the Royal Albert Hall. The *Times* was enthusiastic, describing it as "the finest collection of plate that has ever been got together . . . The sheer mass of metal arranged in four rooms on the first floor exceeds anything that has been seen before."[10] Queen Mary, who had lent some George II tea caddies and seven silver boxes that had belonged to Princess Sophia, daughter of George III, visited and spent several hours admiring the displays.

The 1929 show wasn't confined to Georgian art objects. "I felt something like awe," wrote a breathless Mrs. Belloc-Lowndes, "when I gazed at the exquisite ivory vessel, richly mounted in silver-gilt, which is said to have been used, perhaps as a chalice, by Sir Thomas à Becket."[11] (Presumably she meant *Saint* Thomas.) But the Georgian pieces attracted a good deal of attention, and Sassoon's third Park Lane exhibition focused squarely on the eighteenth century. For *English Conversation Pieces*, which opened on March 4, 1930, he showed 152 paintings (6 from his own collection), including 9 Gainsboroughs, 18 Hogarths, and works by Reynolds, Stubbs, Arthur Devis, and the honorary Englishman Johann Zoffany. The only contemporary painting was Sir John Lavery's group of George V, Queen Mary, the Prince of Wales, and Princess Mary, lent by the Queen.

Serious shows of British art were rare at the time, and the exhibition, which was open every day from 11:00 a.m. until 7:00 p.m., at a hefty admission charge of five shillings, was so successful that Sassoon extended it for an extra week so that it ran until April 6. It led critics to acclaim and, in a sense, to reclaim eighteenth-century English fine art and "this peculiarly national side of British art," as Sir Robert Witt put it in a laudatory review.[12] Christopher Hussey announced that Zoffany was "the Jane Austen of English painting."[13] The conversation piece, said another critic, was "as native to the soil . . . as are the works of Giotto, Botticelli, Raphael and Titian to the soil of Italy."[14]

The year 1931 saw *The Four Georges*, which brought together paintings by Gainsborough, Reynolds, and Canaletto; furniture by William Kent, Thomas Chippendale, and Robert Adam; and silver, books, and artifacts, including fans from Queen Mary's collection at Windsor. The king and queen came to see the show, as did anyone who was anyone in London society: the Duke of Gloucester, Lady Caroline Paget, the Marquess of Londonderry, Sibyl Colefax, the Countess of Oxford, Polesden Lacey's Mrs. Greville, and the BBC's Sir John Reith. Charlie Chaplin was there and came back to visit the exhibition three times more. It was a huge success. "To walk from one room to another," wrote the *Times'* art critic, "is to be for the moment Georgian."[15]

Altogether, Sir Philip Sassoon held nine annual exhibitions at 25 Park Lane between 1929 and his death in 1939. They didn't deal exclusively with English art: the title for 1933 was *Three French Reigns: Louis XIV, XV & XVI.* Nor did they keep exclusively to the eighteenth century: 1932's *Age of Walnut* covered the period from the Restoration of Charles II in 1660 to the death of Queen Anne in 1714. Others had a much tighter focus: 1936 was *Thomas Gainsborough*, and 1937, *Sir Joshua Reynolds*. As they grew in impact and importance, the annual Park Lane exhibitions gave rise to books, to lectures at the Royal Academy, and to a flurry of critical praise both for Sassoon and for the long eighteenth century. And they confirmed a trend that had been gathering momentum ever since the beginning of the century, when the Wrenaissance of Edwardian baroque had begun to evolve into something a little quieter. In 1922 Margaret Jourdain published *English Decoration and Furniture of the Later XVIIIth Century, 1760–1820* and *English Interiors in Smaller Houses from the Restoration to the Regency* the following year. *Small Houses of the Late Georgian Period*, by Stanley Ramsey and J. D. M. Harvey, was published in two volumes in 1919 and 1923; Albert Richardson and Harold Eberlein's *Smaller English Houses of the Later Renaissance, 1660–1830* in 1925; and Tunstall Small's *Houses of the Wren and Early Georgian Periods* in 1928.

Publications like these helped to direct attention away from gleaming white modernism, away from the quaint last gasp of the Arts and Crafts movement, and above all away from the pomposities of Victorian revivalism and toward the country houses of Soane and Gibbs, the elegance of William Kent and Robert Adam, the England of the four Georges. It is no coincidence that 1937 saw the birth of the Georgian Group, an offshoot of the Society for the Protection of Ancient Buildings, which was dedicated to halting what the group called "a concerted attack" by speculators and developers on the best examples of Georgian domestic architecture in Britain.[16]

Ronald and Nancy Tree's remodeling of Ditchley Park formed part of this tradition, and like Sassoon's Park Lane exhibitions, the flood of publications on Georgian art and architecture, and the formation of the Georgian Group, it was both a cause and a consequence of it. Ditchley Park's history reads like a catalogue of Georgian genius: the house was designed by James Gibbs and decorated by Henry Flitcroft and William Kent. Its chimneypieces were carved by Henry Cheere and Peter Scheemakers. That may not have been

NEW GEORGIANISM AT DITCHLEY PARK. (Copyright: Country Life)

enough to guarantee a restoration that was in keeping with the spirit of the place—plenty of new owners of historic houses were happy to disregard such things—but in the Trees' case, it confirmed their taste and gave them an opportunity of displaying it.

The Dillons had left some seventeenth-century paintings behind, mostly of the Lee family who had owned the Ditchley estate from 1580 until 1776. They also left some furniture. There were half a dozen Georgian armchairs and a huge sofa, which the Trees thought might have been made by the house carpenter and re-covered in red leather; and three massive four-poster *lits à la polonaises*, which Ronald thought were by Hepplewhite. One was covered in a Regency or early Victorian blue-and-white chintz, which they kept; the other two had been draped in a heavy, red Victorian baize-like cloth. They had them both re-covered, one in a light flowered chintz, which probably came from Sibyl Colefax, the other in Indian muslin.

They brought some pieces with them from Kelmarsh: a pair of Kent side tables, for example, and a chandelier that they believed to be Russian. And they brought in pictures and furniture: a red-and-white carpet specially woven at the Wilton factory for the library and an oval Hepplewhite desk; an Aubusson carpet from Paris for one of the reception rooms; and "a set of chairs we found in Italy."[17] When the contents of Hartwell House near Aylesbury, another Lee family seat, were sold at Sotheby's in 1938, Ronald bid successfully for two Kent mirrors to match the side tables. He bought a pair of Tiepolos at Christies in 1936 for eighteen guineas and made a point of acquiring Lee family portraits as and when they came up at auction and returning them to the house.

Ditchley helped to confirm Georgian as *the* country-house style of the later 1930s and beyond. Not an authentic, museum-quality Georgian but a lived-in Georgian, a Georgian that had aged gracefully. The effect was one of quiet grandeur, opulence without pomp. Paintwork and gilding were cleaned but not restored. Brand-new damasks and velvets were bleached, or deliberately left to fade in the sunlight before being hung. Nancy "liked them to go shabby and live a life of their own," recalled her son Michael.[18] This shabbiness also gave Ditchley an artful aura of continuity, hinting that the life of the house in this particular incarnation stretched back two centuries rather than a year or so. Little wonder that other new owners of old country houses would try and achieve the same effect.

THE GREAT MAYFAIR DECORATORS WERE such accomplished self-publicists that it seems as if they completely dominated the 1920s and 1930s, as they vied with each other for the lucrative privilege of creating a new drawing room for David and Wallis, a new bedroom suite for this earl or that plutocrat. They didn't. Look around an English country house today, and you will see how pervasive was the taste of discerning amateurs Ronald and Nancy Tree.

But what about the legions of new brides and new chatelaines ordering willow-green silk damask from Waring & Gillow, finding fine old furniture in the corners of a saloon or long gallery? Their tastes in interior decoration, still surviving in hundreds of country houses around England, were gleaned from weekends at the homes of friends and neighbors and copies of *Vogue* or *Country Life*. Their contributions have passed almost unnoticed by historians of the decorative arts. But if any one group typified the country-house interior between the wars, it was them.

These less adventurous country-house owners, unashamedly wanting the "so-called good taste" dismissed by the experts as walls paneled with pine stripped from old discarded Georgian houses, all "limed to greyness, or waves to honey," might go to the department store ateliers. Maples, Harrods, and Waring & Gillow all ran perfectly competent decorating operations.[19] The vast majority of owners, however, spurned the off-the-shelf drawing room or boudoir and at the same time rejected the expense of engaging a firm like White, Allom or Syrie Ltd. Instead, they did it themselves—perhaps not with the flair and judgment of Nancy and Ronnie Tree but with enthusiasm.

When Loelia Ponsonby became the Duke of Westminster's third duchess in 1930 at the age of twenty-eight and moved into the vast Victorian pile that was Eaton Hall in Cheshire, she found a housekeeper in black bombazine with a bunch of keys chained to her waist who acted like Mrs. Danvers in *Rebecca*; a pack of inbred dachshunds who were not house-trained; and suits of armor on the grand staircase that were padded with pink leather that protruded obscenely between greave and cuisse. Her husband also kept a cartload of Himalayan monkeys on an ornamental island in the lake, and a Brazilian capybara (a kind of giant guinea pig and the largest rodent in the world) who ran loose in the gardens.

Bendor's two previous marriages had not been happy. None of his relationships were happy. Loelia, who was twenty-three years younger than her autocratic husband, came from a well-connected but poor background: although her father was keeper of the privy purse to George V with apartments in St. James's Palace and a medieval moated manor house in Surrey, she was used to making her own underclothes and at one point in her youth had to be taken out of school because her parents couldn't pay the fees. She was keen to put her own stamp on their private wing at Eaton, and Bendor, who could never be accused of numbering excessive thrift among his many faults, encouraged her to order anything she liked and to bring in pieces from the main state rooms of the house.

She didn't go to a Malacrida or a Sibyl or a Syrie. She didn't order up interiors from Maple's or distressed damasks from Harrods. Instead, she did it herself. Her bedroom was paneled and painted a pale fawn. There was an embroidered Queen Anne bedspread on the bed, green velvet bed curtains and pale pink sheets of crêpe de chine decorated in satin appliqué. She had a big dressing room of her own— Bendor slept in his own room, in a bed hung with blue taffeta that clashed with the blue walls—and a connecting bathroom with a bath of fawn-colored marble, which spouted water through a lion's mouth.

> My sitting-room was [she recalled] the most successful of all the rooms I decorated. On the walls loose, willow-green silk-damask hung in gentle folds above the pine skirting board. At one end a French armorial tapestry just fitted above a green velvet sofa. The carpet was a bronze-toned Aubusson, and the same colours were picked up in a painted leather screen, the greens and red-browns complementing each other perfectly. Between the windows was a magnificent pair of Chinoiserie lacquer cupboards and in the bay there was a Carlton House writing-table, with a semi-circle of little drawers surmounted by a gilt gallery. A Waterford glass chandelier glittered overhead, and the final touch was [an] enchanting Hogarth which we hung above the mantelpiece.[20]

Eaton Hall was scarcely sixty years old and a monument to Victorian Gothic revivalism to boot. That didn't stop Loelia reaching for the long eighteenth century. She was a New Georgian.

11

THE PRINCESS BRIDE
AND HER BROTHERS

ॐ ॐ

All of George V's children acquired country houses of their own between the wars, although some managed it sooner than others. And for all except the Prince of Wales, marriage was the catalyst.

Mary was the first. In 1922, when she was twenty-four, the Princess Royal married Henry, Viscount Lascelles, the forty-year-old son and heir of the Earl of Harewood. "I dread the idea of losing her," wrote the king, "but thank God she will live in England."[1] The newly-weds' London home was the Palladian Chesterfield House in South Audley Street, reckoned to have one of the finest marble staircases in London and one of the last surviving great mansions in the capital. But the Harewood estates were concentrated in Yorkshire, and besides the principal seat of Harewood House near Leeds, then still occupied by the princess's elderly father-in-law, the family owned Goldsborough Hall, a Jacobean house ten miles to the northeast and variously used as a dower house, a shooting box, and a convenient country home for the married heir-in-waiting.

Goldsborough had been let since the 1890s, but the longtime tenant, a Mrs. Lamb, obligingly vacated it for the couple, even giving the princess a brace of peacocks as a housewarming present. They moved in at the end of the year.

Goldsborough Hall was an attractive gabled pile of red brick on the main street of the little village that shared its name. It was big, with twenty-two bedrooms, four oak paneled reception rooms, and a striking oak staircase of the early seventeenth century that wound right up through the house. After an initial surge of publicity when the village was swamped with sightseers from Leeds and Mary refused to set foot outside for fear of being mobbed, she settled into the congenial life of a twentieth-century noblewoman—a life that offered the privileges of being royal without the responsibilities. She hadn't enjoyed her official public duties before her marriage, and now she slipped into the role of chatelaine, reveling in the relative independence it gave her. "She would have occupied a throne with distinction," wrote the anonymous author of a fawning 1929 biography, "but to be queen of her own household has more truly satisfied her ambitions."[2]

The same biography claimed to be "published with the approval of her royal highness" and gave a gushing account of a typical day for the princess at Goldsborough. It began with a visit to the nursery—the Lascelles had a son less than a year after their marriage and a second the following year—followed by breakfast with her husband. The rest of her morning was spent dealing with an avalanche of correspondence: begging letters, requests for advice or a job or a reference, invitations to open a fête or become a patron of something. Her lady-in-waiting usually sifted through all the letters first, "but every letter, unless of a wholly trivial nature, is brought to her notice."[3] After this, menus would be brought up for her approval, followed by a stroll in the gardens and then a quiet lunch. Afternoons were spent either paying calls or receiving visitors with her husband. If Lascelles was away, she sometimes went over to see her in-laws at Harewood. "The evenings were spent with books or music. The Princess is an excellent musician, with a taste for modern composers."[4]

It wasn't an arduous life. Nor was it a fair picture. In spite of her reluctance to play a big part in public life, Mary's royal rank and her position as the wife of Lord Lascelles meant that she was obliged to do rather more than inspect menus and play the latest composition by Elgar or Edward German. The newspapers of the 1920s show her giving out the annual prizes to nursing staff at Leeds General Infirmary one week and representing the Benevolent and Orphan Fund at a union conference the next; opening an exhibition of disabled soldiers' embroidery at Norfolk House and being guest of honor at a matinee in aid of the Waifs and Strays Society.

The Lascelles moved to Harewood House in 1930 after the death of the viscount's father. Goldsborough was rented furnished; Chesterfield House was sold. "The reason . . . it is assumed, is the need for economy, owing to the new increases in taxation," commented the press.[5] The couple was not as well-known at Harewood as one might have expected: when they opened the gardens to the public for charity shortly before they moved in, they arrived at the gate in their car to be asked for an admission charge of a shilling each and another shilling for parking.

Harewood was by far the most architecturally distinguished of all the houses occupied by George V's offspring. Designed in 1758 by John Carr of York, it had interiors by Robert Adam and his stable of craftsmen, a landscape by Capability Brown, and nineteenth-century alterations made by Sir Charles Barry, while he was taking a break from building the Houses of Parliament. But by 1930, it was coming to seem a little old-fashioned: there were only two bathrooms, for example. The earl and Princess Mary brought in the elderly Sir Herbert Baker, then in the middle of replacing Sir John Soane's Bank of England, an act described by Pevsner as "the worst individual loss suffered by London architecture in the first half of the 20th century."[6] Baker's work at Harewood was harder to take exception to: he modernized the private apartments and installed twenty new bathrooms, along with central heating and two elevators, one for staff and the other for guests. A nursery for the two boys was put in on the top floor of the east wing, and most of the main rooms were redecorated, under Princess Mary's personal supervision. Blue was the dominant color, according to press reports at the time.

Harewood was meant for entertaining, on a scale that hadn't been usual at Goldsborough. Every August Queen Mary spent ten days with her daughter on her way to Balmoral, as she had in the past, but now there was a stream of shooting parties, and Christmas parties, and parties for the races at Wetherby or York. Everything was planned with meticulous care. Before a big dinner, the butler, Slade, prepared a plan of the silver or gold to be used for the table decoration, and the head gardener, Hall, did the same with the flowers. The earl and princess went down to the plate room to approve Slade's scheme, and before they went up to dress for dinner, they came into Sir Charles Barry's spectacular State Dining Room to inspect the table. They kept an indoor staff of twenty-seven throughout the 1930s, but even that wasn't enough to cope with some of the dinners, so that extra servants had to be drafted in from the surrounding villages. With thirty or forty sitting down to eat, Slade superintended three service tables and nine people serving.

While Mary was settling down to motherhood and the life of an aristocratic landowner's wife, Prince George, the youngest of the princess royal's four brothers, showed no signs of settling down to anything. George spent most of the 1920s in the navy or in the arms of one of his many lovers, both male and female. At various times his name was linked romantically with Noel Coward, the art historian Anthony Blunt, and the musical actress Jessie Matthews. His most notorious relationship was with Kiki Preston, an American socialite and ex-cabaret performer known as "the girl with the silver syringe" because of her fondness for cocaine and morphine—a fondness that George came to share. In his memoirs, the Duke of Windsor recalled his brother as being "somewhat Bohemian by inclination," glossing discreetly over the fact that in the late 1920s he was charged with supervising George's rehab and that on at least one occasion he had to step in to save George from an unpleasant blackmail attempt that centered on some letters the prince had written to a young man in Paris.[7]

In 1934 Prince George was married to Princess Marina, third and youngest daughter of Prince Nicholas of Greece. (It was at their wedding in Westminster Abbey that George's niece, the eight-year-old Princess Elizabeth, first met her husband-to-be: Prince Philip was Marina's cousin.) The following year, George's aunt, Princess Victoria, died at The Coppins, the country house in Buckinghamshire she had bought when she was ejected from Sandringham on Queen Alexandra's death in 1925. The Coppins was an undistinguished two-storied house on 132 acres, with four reception rooms, a large music room, and fourteen bedrooms. Built in the middle of the nineteenth century by a successful theater manager named John Mitchell, it was all gables and high chimneys. It looked vaguely like York Cottage on the Sandringham Estate, in fact. There was also a model farm, with a pedigree herd and other livestock. And in her will, Princess Victoria left the lot to George.

The newlyweds, now the Duke and Duchess of Kent (the king had conferred the title on his youngest boy shortly before their wedding), spent the spring of 1936 renovating The Coppins inside and out. An important part of the work was the construction of a big nursery overlooking the gardens: they already had a son, Prince Edward, and the Duchess was expecting a second child. Princess Alexandra was born on Christmas Day 1936. They supervised the work themselves and often drove down from London to inspect progress, as did other members of the family. Queen Mary motored over from Windsor to see the house in April 1936, bringing Queen Victoria's granddaughter, Princess Alice.

"The district will expect much from [the Duke and Duchess]," predicted one press report when the legacy was first announced, "as the Princess Victoria had been Lady Bountiful there."[8] By the time they moved in on June 6, 1936, to the cheers of local villagers assembled at the gate, they had provided The Coppins with six bathrooms, electricity, water, central heating, and modern drainage. The ground-floor reception rooms were fitted out in an easy neo-Georgian style, and—one of the most talked-about improvements—they looked out onto modern flower gardens and lawns, which had taken the place of a dark and unkempt mass of laurel, yew, and holly.

For the next few years, Coppins (the Kents dropped the definite article) was often in the news. The Duke and Duchess celebrated their son's second birthday there, with a tea party and a two-tier birthday cake with pink icing created by the royal confectioner at Buckingham

Palace. Respectful visitors were photographed trooping across the lawns and resisting the temptation to press their noses against the windows when the gardens were opened in aid of the Queen's Institute of District Nursing. The duchess caused a stir when she popped over to Slough one Saturday and bought a toy kite at Woolworth's. "She had nearly completed her shopping before she was recognized," reported a breathless *Guardian*, going on to say that she also visited the haberdashery and food counters.[9]

To the twenty-first-century reader, cynically accustomed to the cynical manipulation of the media by everyone from royals and senior politicians to Z-list celebrities, stories like these smack of a deliberate attempt by the duke to put his awkward past behind him and reinvent himself as the head of an ordinary, if rather upper-class, family. That would be wrong. George had no need to recover his reputation, since in a period when the British press wouldn't dream of reporting any untoward behavior by a member of the royal family, that reputation was firmly intact, his various lapses remaining out of the public domain until decades after his death in a plane crash during the Second World War.

In the autumn of 1938, Buckingham Palace announced that George VI was sending his youngest brother to Australia as governor general in November 1939, for a tour of duty that was likely to last at least two or three years. The duchess was to go with him and their two children. The following spring the Kents put Coppins on the market "at a most moderate price," claimed the *Times*, without actually naming that price.[10] Even so, in that uncertain summer their "pleasing residence, most perfectly decorated and appointed and fitted with every modern improvement and convenience," with "exquisite gardens . . . renowned for their beauty" failed to sell, in spite of being advertised as the country home of the Duke of Kent. That turned out to be a blessing in disguise, since the outbreak of war in September put a stop to the Australian appointment, and the Kents remained at Coppins.[11]

Taking the four royal brothers in reverse order of birth, the next up was Prince Henry, two years older than Prince George and born with the century. In 1935 Henry, by then H. R. H. the Duke of

Gloucester, married Lady Alice Christabel Montagu Douglas Scott, daughter of the 7th Duke of Buccleuch.

A shy, retiring woman who was in her midthirties when she married (as was her husband), Alice's first year of marriage was difficult. Her father died less than three weeks before her wedding, and as a consequence, the planned ceremony at Westminster Abbey was called off and replaced by a quiet alternative in the private chapel at Buckingham Palace. Her new father-in-law, George V, died ten weeks later. She quickly became close to the widowed Queen Mary, only to find herself rather closer to the heart of the abdication crisis than she would have wished. She was staying with the queen at Marlborough House when Edward VIII came to tell his mother about Wallis Simpson. He later wrote of how sorry he was for her. "She had all unwittingly sat down at my mother's table only to find herself caught up in the opening scene of one of the most poignant episodes in the annals of the British Royal Family. Never loquacious, this evening she uttered not a word. And when at last we got up to leave the table she eagerly seized upon the interruption to protest that she was extremely tired and to ask that she be excused. After making her curtsy she almost fled from the room."[12]

The Duke and Duchess of Gloucester started their married life at York House, in the precincts of St. James's Palace. Their out-of-town home was the Royal Pavilion—not the famous Royal Pavilion at Brighton, George IV's magnificent Indo-Chinese folly, but one of the royal family's lesser-known residences: a curious wooden bungalow in Aldershot where Victoria and Albert used to stay when they were reviewing the army.

But they needed a conventional country seat, something more appealing than an oversized garden shed, and in 1938 they found one in Northamptonshire. At the dissolution of the monasteries, the duchess's ancestors, the Montagus, acquired the Barnwell estate from Henry VIII. It had at its heart a spectacular thirteenth-century castle with walls that were twelve feet thick and monumental round corner towers. The Montagus had reasons for buying up land in the county: they already had Boughton, ten miles away and destined to become their principal residence. But even in the unsettled years of the mid-sixteenth century, they had no use for a medieval castle, which they allowed to fall down in a most romantic way, building themselves a solid and attractive manor house next door. This was tinkered with by successive generations over the years—a room here, a bay window there, a whole new service wing in 1890—until 1913 when the duchess's grandfather sold it, along with the picturesque ruined castle and a four-thousand-acre estate, to a sugar broker named Horace Czarnikow.

Czarnikow made his own mark on Barnwell, laying out gardens and adding a new drawing room before putting it back on the market in 1920. It was bought by a Mrs. McGrath, and then in 1930 by a City financier, Colin Cooper, who added those vital adjuncts to a modern country house, a tennis court and a swimming pool. Cooper died suddenly on safari in Kenya in 1938, when he was only forty-six. In a rather modern gesture, his ashes were scattered over Barnwell woods from an airplane. It was this death that brought the estate onto the market for the fourth time in twenty-five years.

The Duke of Gloucester had been left some money by his father George V, and in the summer of 1938, he used the legacy to buy the manor house and the ruined castle, along with 2,100 acres, six farms, and twenty-one cottages. The Gloucesters commissioned the architect Sir Albert Richardson to remodel some of the interiors: his most interesting work at Barnwell involved designing new paneling for the drawing room, which was made to accommodate a group of five canvases from the 1740s depicting hunting scenes around Haddon Hall, the Duke of Rutland's Derbyshire seat.

It was a year before the Gloucesters moved into Barnwell—on August 5, 1939, to be precise, not a particularly auspicious moment in history with Britain preparing for war. They furnished the house with good Georgian and Regency mahogany, reflecting the ubiquitous and, by this stage, rather safe, neo-Georgian country-house look of the decade. But the layered look worked well: Tudor and Jacobean architecture blended artfully with the seventeenth-century paneling introduced by Mrs. McGrath or Colin Cooper, the Jacobethan additions of the late Victorian period, and the "real" Georgian and faux

THE DUKE AND DUCHESS OF YORK HONEYMOONING AT POLESDEN LACEY IN 1923. (Copyright: National Trust/Richard Holttum)

1930s work. And the Gloucesters had the lowering broken towers of Barnwell Castle for a backdrop to country living, a connection to an ancient past that was theirs not by pedigree but by purchase.

That leaves George V's two oldest boys, Bertie and David, both men who would be king. Bertie, who was created Duke of York in 1920, married Lady Elizabeth Bowes-Lyon in 1923, after she had twice turned down his proposals of marriage. Their courtship was conducted and consummated in a country-house world. Bertie began to woo the twenty-two-year-old, without much success, at Glamis Castle, one of the Bowes-Lyons's family seats. She was weekending with friends at Firle Place near Lewes in January 1923 when the *Daily News* ran a story that the daughter of "a well-known Scottish peer" was about to marry a prince—although to her mortification, journalists got the wrong prince and announced that her fiancé was the Prince of Wales. And it was at another country house, the Bowes-Lyons's St. Paul's Walden Bury in Hertfordshire, that she finally accepted Bertie's proposal of marriage a week later. He sent a telegram to his parents at Sandringham, saying simply "All right. Bertie."[13]

After their wedding at Westminster Abbey on April 26 that year, the newlywed Duke and Duchess of York began their honeymoon at Polesden Lacey, near Dorking, the Edwardian country home of the legendary society hostess Margaret Greville. Dame Margaret, the daughter of a Scottish brewer, had a startling ability to inspire dislike, even hatred, in her contemporaries. Harold Nicolson described her as "a fat slug filled with venom"; Cecil Beaton called her "a galumphing, greedy, snobbish old toad who watered at her chops at the sight of royalty"; and Leonie Leslie, Winston Churchill's aunt, said she would rather have an open sewer flowing through her drawing room than entertain Mrs. Greville.[14] The duke's acceptance of her offer of Polesden was quite a coup for her, and she discreetly kept out of the way at her Mayfair house so that the young couple could enjoy each other's company in relative privacy.

"Everything at Polesden Lacey has been perfectly arranged," reported *The Sketch*. "A little sunshine is all that is needed to turn it into a peaceful fairyland." But the couple's arrival at Polesden was anything but peaceful. Crowds gathered at Bookham station to catch a glimpse of them—ladies and local dignitaries on a reserved section of the platform, the rest, "mainly of the poorer class from the drab district surrounding the station," packed into the booking hall.[15] Hundreds of boy scouts, girl guides, and schoolchildren waved sprigs of hawthorn blossom. Cheering estate workers lined the route. Bouquets and illuminated addresses were presented at several points on the ten-minute drive from the station to the house. Eventually, the duke announced "in a brief but hearty response" that he and his bride were very tired.[16]

The fact that Princess Mary married a country house, Prince George was left one, and Prince Henry bought one with a legacy might suggest that their father didn't have much in the way of spare country property to bestow on his children. Quite the reverse. Besides the various lodges and cottages on the Sandringham estate, which were George V's personal property, there were literally hundreds of rural homes managed by the Commissioners of Woods, Forests and Land Revenues, who morphed in 1924 into the Commissioners of Crown Lands. Most of this property was let, or occupied by current and past members of the royal household. The eighteenth-century Thatched House Lodge in Richmond Park, for example, became the home of Sir Louis Greig in 1932, after he resigned as the Duke of York's equerry. Bagshot Park, a vast and ugly mansion built in 1877, was occupied by Queen Victoria's son, Prince Arthur, Duke of Connaught, from its completion until his death in 1942.

At Queen Mary's suggestion, the Yorks set up home at White Lodge, an early Palladian house in Richmond Park built as a hunting lodge for George II in 1727–1729. The queen had happy memories of the place—she and George V had started their married life there, and the Prince of Wales had been born there in 1894. And it was beautiful: designed by Roger Morris and, like his Marble Hill House in Twickenham, a model of early Palladianism, elegant and compact. (Although not too compact: there were sixteen or seventeen best bedrooms.)

But the Yorks didn't like it. The central heating was woefully inadequate, the electric lighting was dangerously unpredictable, the drains were suspect, and the only downstairs lavatory was in a secretary's office. Literally. The setting was too public for their taste: Sir Frederick Ponsonby passed on their complaints to the Office of Works, pointing out that "Richmond Park has been brought very near London by char a bancs and motor cars," so that at weekends the crowds of sightseers were so great that the duke and duchess hardly dared step outside.[17] Even on weekdays there was always a knot of people gathered at their gate. And the cost of keeping up the Lodge was prohibitive: £11,000 a year, according to the duke, and "the greater part of their income is spent in paying for quite unnecessary servants."[18] They couldn't go on living there, and they wanted a house in London instead.

Sir Lionel Earle, who as permanent secretary to the Office of Works was responsible for finding them somewhere else to live, was skeptical. He refused to believe that White Lodge cost so much to run and suspected that its distance from town was the real reason for the Yorks' unhappiness. "They are both passionately fond of dancing, and naturally wish to come to London practically every day for this purpose."[19]

It was four years before that wish was granted, when a lease on White Lodge was granted to Lord Lee of Fareham, and in return the Yorks moved to 145 Piccadilly, once the London home of the Marquesses of Northampton. Both before and after their move, the duke, who was an enthusiastic huntsman, rented country houses in the midlands for the hunting season, which implies that perhaps White Lodge was both too far from London and not far enough. In the first winter of their marriage, he took Guilsborough Hall in Northamptonshire, an exotic mixture of architectural styles. The exterior was long, low, and castellated; there was an Italian roof garden, a neo-Classical music room, and a Moorish bathroom with marble walls and something called "an electric light bath." The main attraction for the Yorks was that it boasted good stables and was only a couple of miles from the kennels of the Pytchley Hounds, and there were four days hunting a week to be had.

Guilsborough went up for sale in 1925. In the winters of 1928–1929 and 1929–1930, the Yorks took the eighteen-bedroomed Naseby Hall, also in the heart of Pytchley country and rather less exotic. Then in July 1931, Major Frederick Featherstonhaugh, the manager of the king's racing stables, died at the Royal Lodge, his residence in Windsor Great Park. The Royal Lodge was in the gift of the sovereign, and George V offered it to Bertie and Elizabeth.

Originally a *cottage ornée* designed as a refuge for the prince regent by John Nash, and extended by Sir Jeffry Wyatville, the Royal Lodge (and it was *the* Royal Lodge, "by which name it has been known ever since George IV built it," as the king was quick to point out to Bertie when he inadvertently referred to it simply as "Royal Lodge") was virtually demolished by Queen Adelaide in the 1830s, except for Wyatville's saloon, which was later partitioned into five separate rooms.[20] It was subsequently rebuilt as a big, rather bland block, with a whiff of the hotel or convalescent home about it.

But the duke and duchess were delighted. "It will suit us admirably," Bertie told his father, and they set to work to turn it into a home for them and their two daughters, Princess Elizabeth, born in 1926 at the Mayfair home of the duchess's father, the Earl of Strathmore;

and Margaret Rose, born at Glamis Castle in August 1930. The Yorks removed the partition walls to restore the Wyatville saloon to its original, magnificent proportions, forty-eight feet long and twenty feet high. They extended their private accommodation and redecorated the house throughout. The duke's bedroom was simple and austere; his wife's was a more opulent gray blue, with blue silk trimmed with lemon yellow for the bed and white applewood furniture.

The Yorks moved into the Royal Lodge in the early summer of 1932, and from the start, they were happy there, motoring down from 145 Piccadilly at weekends, staying for longer periods when they could. The duke took Princess Elizabeth out riding on her pony, and he and his wife became enthusiastic gardeners. Even after Bertie's income was cut along with his brothers' by their father, who set an example to his people in the Depression by lopping £50,000 off the expenses of the royal household, he stayed cheerful. He had to give up hunting and sell his six horses, but at least he had the Royal Lodge, his wife, and his daughters.

LIKE HIS BROTHER BERTIE, THE Prince of Wales rented a series of furnished country houses in the late 1920s, usually for a few months at a time. His requirements were simple. A rural retreat had to be reasonably private, it had to be fitted with modern conveniences, and, most important of all, it must be within easy reach of a golf course.

The prince's favorite golf links at Sunningdale in Berkshire offered plenty of suitable property, and by an odd coincidence, he rented three houses in a row designed by the same all-but-forgotten architect Walter Sand. The first was Middleton House, a stone's throw from the golf club, which he took for several summers in the late 1920s. When the lease on Middleton ran out in September 1929, he decided to stay on in the neighborhood, taking a two-month lease on Craigmyle, built in 1903 in a mixed Tudor, all half-timbering and gables on the outside and a cheery mixture of oak rafters and Adamesque decoration within.

Then for the last two months of 1929, the prince moved to Little Court, a neo-Georgian house overlooking the links, which Sand had built the previous year for an old soldier, Brigadier-General Basil

Buckley. *Country Life* immediately rushed out an article on Little Court, "a temporary residence of H.R.H. the Prince of Wales," which showed an attractive house whose newness had been tempered by the extensive use of old materials.[21] The roof was made of old tiles, the bricks came from a demolished eighteenth-century house in Twickenham, and Sand recycled all sorts of architectural details. The door to the garden came from a Georgian house in the Strand; an unusual triple Palladian window overlooking the rose garden, curved in plan, from the West Country; and the oak staircase, Queen Anne or very early Georgian, from a manor house in Norfolk. *Country Life* approved. "Mr Sand has shown in this house how comfortable 18th-century dispositions can be and how easily they can be brought into line with present-day requirements."[22]

Comfortable or not, the Prince of Wales had no intention of prolonging his stay into the New Year. He had already found a country house that he was going to call his own. Earlier in 1929 a shuffling of sinecures meant that Fort Belvedere in Windsor Great Park had fallen vacant. Like the Royal Lodge, the fort was George V's to dispose of as he pleased, and in the summer the prince went to his father and asked to live in it. "What could you possibly want that queer old place for?" asked the king. "Those damn week-ends, I suppose." But then he smiled and relented. "Well, if you want it you can have it."[23]

Fort Belvedere was a queer old place, with a queer old history. As its name suggests, it was built as a picturesque viewpoint, for the Duke of Cumberland, known to posterity as "Butcher" Cumberland for the merciless way he put down Bonny Prince Charlie's Jacobite Rising of 1745. Cumberland was ranger of Windsor Great Park from 1746 to 1757.

In its original incarnation, Fort Belvedere consisted of a triangular tower with turrets at each corner. Cumberland's architect was almost certainly Henry Flitcroft, who was paid over £2000 on account for works in the park in 1747–1748 and who also designed a triangular viewing tower on the Stourhead estate for Henry Hoare in 1765. Although sometimes described as a military lookout, it was clearly always intended as a toy fort, for the duke's private use. Mrs. Delany, who visited in 1757, described closets of blue and gold and green and

FORT BELVEDERE. "THE HALF-BURIED BEAUTY OF THE PLACE
LEAPED TO MY EYE," RECALLED THE DUKE OF WINDSOR. (Copyright:
Print Collector/Getty Images)

gold, painted stucco festoons of fruit and flowers, and a chandelier of
Chelsea china that cost £600. "Nothing can be finer than the prospects from all the windows," she wrote.[24] The prospect included a
faux Chinese barge painted with huge dragons, which the duke kept
moored on Virginia Water.

In 1827–1829, while Sir Jeffry Wyatville was remodeling parts of
Windsor Castle for George IV, he extended Fort Belvedere to create
a jumbled but undeniably picturesque collection of turrets and towers
of different heights, besides building a single-story octagonal drawing room and separate accommodation for staff. That staff included
a unit of bombardiers, whose duties involved firing royal salutes from
thirty-one brass cannon on a new terrace overlooking Virginia Water.
The last bombardier died in his cottage at the fort in 1910, aged ninety.

Although yet more changes had been made to the fort early on in
George V's reign, including the creation of a proper servants' wing, in
1929 Fort Belvedere was, said his son, a pseudo-Gothic hodgepodge,
kept in perpetual shadow by overgrown yew trees and surrounded by

wild and untended gardens. "But the half-buried beauty of the place leaped to my eye."[25]

Scaffolding went up that autumn. There were structural repairs, improvements to the plumbing, the installation of steel casement windows. The prince was adamant that he wanted the kind of modern conveniences he had enjoyed during visits to America: built-in cupboards, central heating, and plenty of bathrooms. In the basement he installed a Turkish bath and a shower; outside there was a new swimming pool and a hard tennis court. The gardens were laid out with lawns, and long borders were planted with roses, delphiniums, irises, and flowering shrubs to give color from June through November.

Around £21,000 was spent on the fort, most of it coming out of the prince's own pocket. It was ready for occupation by the end of April 1930, when he came back from a four-month safari to East Africa (on which, incidentally, he took a movie camera instead of a gun, observing that "vanity had betrayed my friends into defacing the rooms of their otherwise handsome homes with unsightly stuffed trophies").[26] In his own mind, whatever credit was due for the fort's reinvention was due to him. "Though I naturally sought professional advice," he recalled later, "the final result in the main represented my ideas."[27] And again, "Soon I came to love it as I loved no other material thing—perhaps because it was so much my own creation."[28]

Nevertheless, the list of professional advisors associated with Fort Belvedere is a distinguished one, although since very little survives from the 1930s, it isn't at all clear who contributed what. The flowering borders owed a lot to Norah Lindsay, the society garden consultant whose planting schemes graced Sir Philip Sassoon's gardens at Trent Park and Port Lympne, the Astors' at Cliveden, and the Marquess of Lothian's at Blickling Hall in Norfolk. At least three big names from the world of interior decoration were involved, or claimed to have been involved: Herman Schrijver, who also decorated York House for the prince, Sybil Colefax, and Syrie Maugham. The last two certainly supplied individual items of furniture for the fort.

To judge from the photographs and visitors' accounts of the time, the prince and his helpers achieved an easy air of informality.

The octagonal hall had a black-and-white marble floor and eight chairs upholstered in yellow leather. The drawing room, also octagonal, had curtains of yellow velvet, low modern sofas, and walls painted to look as though they were paneled in pine. There was a baby grand piano and a gramophone to which guests sometimes danced after dinner. Good pictures hung on the walls: Canalettos in the drawing room, a couple of Stubbs in the dining room. The prince's bedroom, which was on the ground floor, had white walls and red chintz curtains. The six guest rooms upstairs were named for either past or present associations— one was Prince George's Room because the prince's youngest brother stayed there when he came for the weekend, while another was The Queen's Room, although no one could quite remember why—or for their color schemes. Lady Diana Cooper stayed in The Pink Room, which lived up to its name: it was "pink-sheeted, pink Venetian-blinded, pink-soaped, white-telephoned and pink-and-white maided."[29]

Although the prince was understandably reluctant to publicize the fact, the ambience of the fort owed rather a lot to his mistresses, particularly Freda Dudley Ward, whom he had been seeing on and off since 1918. Freda, who was half-American, was the wife of William Dudley Ward, a minor courtier who led his own life and was content for her to lead hers. Philip Tilden once called at their Mayfair flat to be let in by Dudley Ward with the greeting, "Come in, there's nobody here but the Prince of Wales." The prince leapt up from an easy chair, and the four of them all went off house hunting in his car.[30]

Freda enjoyed buying houses to renovate and sell. "I doubt whether we were in any house longer than about two years," her daughter recalled.[31] As a result she was on good terms with fashionable Mayfair decorators: it was probably through her good offices that Herman Schrijver worked for the prince at both York House and the fort, and she was good friends with Syrie Maugham. Fêted by *Vogue* as one of "the Sophisticates of Mayfair," dressed by Cecil Beaton, and loathed by George V, who in references to her father's business as a Nottingham lace manufacturer called her "Freda Loom" or "the lace-maker's daughter," she was closely involved in the first stages of the renovation work at Fort Belvedere.

But she wasn't destined to enjoy weekends there. When the prince took up residence in the spring of 1930, he also took up with a new mistress, Thelma Furness, the twice-married American wife of a shipping magnate. They had begun to see each other the previous summer, and the relationship became more serious when she and her husband joined the prince's East Africa safari. So it was Thelma, rather than Freda, who acted as unofficial hostess at the first Fort Belvedere weekends.

They were relaxed, domestic occasions. "He puttered in the garden, pruned his trees, blew on his bagpipes," she remembered.[32] (The prince had learned the highland bagpipe as a young man and entertained guests with a tune after dinner, sometimes donning a kilt for the occasion.) There was no talk of politics. Bertie and the Duchess of York sometimes came over, and Prince George. They swam and played tennis and danced to the gramophone. One winter weekend they all went skating on Virginia Water. At other times Thelma's father, a retired US diplomat, came to stay. "If a visitor had come upon us on any of these occasions he would have witnessed an unexpected and old-fashioned scene of bourgeois bliss," Thelma wrote later, "the prince and I busy with our needlework [which he had learned from his mother, Queen Mary], and Papa sonorously reading to us from a novel by Scott or Dickens."[33]

The prince made no secret of his relationship, just as he had made no secret of his affair with Freda. In January 1932 some friends of Thelma's invited the couple to dine with them at their London flat. The friends were an Anglo-American shipping executive, Ernest Simpson, and his wife, Wallis. The dinner of black bean soup and fried chicken Maryland was a success; so much so that Thelma and the prince repaid the Simpsons' hospitality by inviting them to spend the following weekend at Fort Belvedere.

Subsequent events imposed an enormous and unlikely significance on this weekend. In 1934 Thelma Furness left for America to visit her twin sister, Gloria Vanderbilt, famously telling Wallis to look after the Prince of Wales for her while she was away. "It was later evident that Wallis took my advice all too literally," she wrote acidly.[34]

The latter's visits to Fort Belvedere, with and without her husband, were frequent, as she moved to occupy the center of what the Archbishop of Canterbury would later condemn as "a social circle whose standards and way of life are alien to all the best instincts and traditions of [the British] people."[35] Judging from the visitors' book kept at the fort in 1935 and 1936, the circle was quite mixed. Besides close friends of both Wallis and the prince, weekend guests included Dickie and Edwina Mountbatten, Duff and Diana Cooper, prominent antiappeasers like Anthony Eden and Robert Vansittart, minor diplomats from the American embassy, and major society hostesses such as Emerald Cunard and Sybil Colefax.

ONE THURSDAY AFTERNOON IN JANUARY 1936, the prince was out shooting in Windsor Great Park when a note came from his mother to say that "Papa is not very well." It wasn't a surprise: George V had been in poor health for several years. But this time was different.

Queen Mary asked the prince to suggest his coming up for the weekend, casually, so as not to alarm the king. But he decided not to wait. The next day he flew up to Sandringham—he kept his own De Havilland Puss Moth at an airfield ten minutes from the Fort—to find George V in his bedroom at the Big House, sitting in front of the fire in an old Tibetan dressing gown. The king was drifting in and out of consciousness and was clearly very ill indeed. Three days later, shortly before midnight on January 20, 1936, he died with his family at his bedside, his end hastened by a cocktail of morphine and cocaine administered by his doctor. Queen Mary immediately took her eldest son's hand and kissed it; the Duke of York followed suit. The man who had a moment before been the Prince of Wales was now King Edward VIII.

But not for long. Edward's determination to marry divorcee Wallis Simpson, his conviction that, as he told the nation in his abdication broadcast, "I have found it impossible to carry the heavy burden of responsibility and to discharge my duties as king as I would wish to do without the help and support of the woman I love," meant that his reign lasted a mere 326 days. In the last weeks before the abdication, Fort Belvedere, which was already a symbol of his suspect morals (especially among those who weren't invited to his house parties), loomed large in the nation's consciousness. "Events have made it a house of destiny," declared one newspaper.[36] As gossip about Wallis began to spread after her divorce hearing in Ipswich on October 27, 1936, she fled London and took up residence at the fort. It was there, on the terrace after dinner on the night of Wednesday December 2, that Edward told her about his crucial interview earlier in the day with Prime Minister Stanley Baldwin, at which Baldwin had told him the government and the nation wouldn't accept his marriage to a divorced woman and that he must either give her up or abdicate.

The next day, Edward packed Wallis off to the south of France, away from the gathering storm. Journalists descended in their hordes on Sunningdale, and Fort Belvedere became, in the king's words, "a battle headquarters, with telephones ringing constantly and despatch riders on motor-cycles bringing state papers from London."[37] Normal mail for the fort was usually brought by a postman on a bicycle: now the post office had to use a mail van to carry the sackfuls of private letters bringing support and accusation. Courtiers and lawyers and civil servants dashed back and forth. At one point Stanley Baldwin arrived with his suitcase. "Good God!" the king muttered. "Surely he doesn't intend to spend the night?"[38]

Harold Nicolson told his wife, Vita Sackville-West, a rather pathetic little piece of gossip he'd picked up from Baldwin's son on December 7. Apparently, the previous day the prime minister and the king had been pacing round and round the gardens at the fort trying to reach some kind of solution to the crisis until eventually they agreed that Edward must abdicate. Exhausted, they went into the library, and Baldwin asked if he might have a whisky and soda.

> The bell was rung: the footman came: the drink was produced. S. B. raised his glass and said . . . "Well Sir, whatever happens, my Mrs and I wish you happiness from the depths of our souls." At which the King burst into floods of tears. Then S. B. himself began to cry. What a strange conversation-piece, those two blubbering together on a sofa![39]

At ten o'clock on the morning of Thursday, December 10, Edward's three brothers arrived at the fort and were immediately shown into the octagonal drawing room. They found the king at his desk, a red dispatch box in front of him, and aides and advisers all around. Sitting at his desk and watched by the three princes, he signed the Instrument of Abdication and then stood for each of his brothers in turn to sign as witnesses. Then he left the room and stepped outside into the morning air.

The following night, Edward, now Prince Edward again, was taken by car from Fort Belvedere to Windsor Castle, where he was to make his now-famous abdication broadcast. From Windsor he would go to Portsmouth and across to France and exile.

As he drove down the hill, he caught a last glimpse of the fort. "In that moment I realised how heavy was the price I had paid . . . The Fort had been more than a home; it had been a way of life for me."[40]

He never saw Fort Belvedere again.

12

MY NEW-FOUND-LAND,
MY KINGDOM

The traditional explanation for the appearance of Americans in the great halls and long galleries of England is that the special relationship was transactional: that it was the result of an unholy alliance between the socially ambitious mothers of heiresses from New York or Chicago and unscrupulous but impoverished English aristocrats who were happy to offer a title in exchange for a hefty dollar dowry to save an estate encumbered with accumulated debt. The poster girl for that discordant Anglo-American *entente*, the archetypal heiress-bride, was Consuelo, the daughter of railway magnate William Kissam Vanderbilt.

In 1895 Consuelo was bullied into marrying Sunny Churchill, 9th Duke of Marlborough and the proud owner of Blenheim Palace in Oxfordshire, by her manipulative mother, Alva, who was determined to bag a duke. When Consuelo refused to go along with Alva's plans, she reacted badly. In fact she swore to shoot the girl's preferred suitor dead, then locked her daughter up in the family's Newport mansion, Marble House, while feigning a heart attack, which was caused, Consuelo was told, "by my callous indifference to her feelings."[1] Having secured her daughter's tearful acquiescence, Alva brought Sunny to propose in the Gothic Room at Marble House, "whose atmosphere was so propitious to sacrifice."[2] Consuelo cried all the way to the wedding. She cried again when her eleven-year-old brother told her Sunny was only marrying her for her money—as indeed he was. He received $2.5 million in railway stock as a dowry.

Consuelo spent eleven years lost in the marble halls of Blenheim Palace, surrounded by an army of blank-faced servants and condescending in-laws. The patronizing began on her honeymoon as her husband explained that there were two hundred families whose lineage and titles and relationship she must learn. In much the same way, the banker Lord Revelstoke's proposal of marriage to another American heiress was laced with pride: "Do you really think you could fill the position that would be required of my wife? You would have to meet Kings and Queens and entertain Ambassadors. Do you think you could do it?"[3] The object of Revelstoke's affections, Nancy Langhorne, decided she couldn't and married Waldorf Astor instead.

Consuelo's lessons in inferiority continued when the newlyweds arrived at Woodstock station, and the robed mayor greeted them on the platform with the announcement that Woodstock had a mayor and a corporation before America was discovered. They were still going on years later, when the formidable octogenarian Dowager Duchess of Abercorn, Sunny's great-aunt, decided to have her photograph taken with 130 descendants. Any pleasure Consuelo took in being included was tempered by the way in which family members queued up to tell her what an honor it was for her, since "I was the first American she had condescended to receive."[4]

The Marlboroughs' unhappy marriage has become the stuff of legend. Guides at Blenheim Palace today point out John Singer Sargent's magnificent portrait of the couple with their two boys—"the heir and the spare," they invariably say—and gleefully recount instances of their incompatibility. Their 1920 divorce, like their marriage, was played out on a public stage. Consuelo's one-sided and disingenuous autobiography, *The Glitter and the Gold*, stoked the flames with anecdotes of Sunny's odd behavior—he spoke so rarely at meals that she took up knitting to pass the time between courses—and her own bewildered naïveté: why were some of the Blenheim servants called "odd men" when there was nothing odd about them? Why, when she rang for the butler to set a match to the fire, did he send for a footman to do it?

Consuelo claimed that the enormous public interest in her wedding was due to the fact that "mine was the first international marriage that had taken place for some time."[5] That wasn't true. By crossing the Atlantic in search of an heiress-bride, Sunny Marlborough was taking a well-trodden path to wedlock for the British landed classes. (He was also following in his father's footsteps: the 8th Duke had married as his second wife a wealthy New York widow, the flames of his ardor stoked by her life interest in her first husband's $7 million fortune.) "It has been roughly estimated that English noblemen alone have captured by marriage with American women, in round numbers, $50,000,000 of enviable American cash," declared the *New York Times* in April 1893, listing forty-eight "of the more important international weddings between England and America" over the previous twenty-five years.[6] The same month, the 4th Earl of Craven married sixteen-year-old Cornelia Martin and her fortune, which was reputed to be $1 million dollars. Interest in that wedding was so great that when the doors of Grace Church on Broadway were opened after the ceremony for the bride and groom to pose on the steps, sightseers poured in, climbing over the pews and stripping the altar of its decorations in their rush for souvenirs. The police had to be called to clear the building. "One of the most disgusting exhibitions of American snobbery I have ever seen," wrote a senator's wife, describing the marriage as "a palpable sale."[7]

Between 1870 and 1914, 128 American women and three men married into the British nobility, although by no means all of the women—and of course none of the men—married titles or the heirs to titles. Thirty-nine baronets or their heirs married Americans in the same period, and in what can loosely be called the landed gentry, there were 176 Anglo-American marriages.[8]

The traditional view of the so-called American invasion is that its spur on this side of the Atlantic was the series of depressions that hit

British agriculture in the later nineteenth century, when falling rents and rising debts broke down the social barriers and snobbishness that had placed American brides beyond the pale. But it would be too cynical to suggest that money on one side and social ambition on the other were the only motives for the American invasion. For one thing, in the British landed classes legal wrangling over money was an integral part of courtship, no matter where the bride came from. And yes, George Nathaniel Curzon's marriage to Mary, daughter of retail emperor Levi Leiter, took place in 1895 only after lengthy negotiations about money between Leiter, Curzon, and Curzon's father. But those negotiations led up to a happy and loving marriage, and Curzon was distraught when his wife died, in his arms, after only eleven years together. In later life, he used to say he wasn't afraid of death because he would see Mary in heaven—a sentiment that perhaps contributed to the unhappiness of his second marriage, to another American, the diplomat's daughter Grace Duggan.

Curzon wasn't the only British nobleman to have two American wives. The 2nd Lord Leigh of Stoneleigh Abbey in Warwickshire married a New Yorker in 1890; in 1923, as a widower, he married another. The 5th Lord Decies of Leixlip Castle in Kildare lost his first wife, Helen, daughter of the railway magnate George Jay Gould, in 1931; five years later he married the widow Elizabeth Lehr, a member of the fabulously rich Drexel banking dynasty. In 1927 Decies's fellow Irishman, the 5th Earl of Gosford, deserted his ancestral seat of Gosford Castle in County Armagh, his wife, Mildred, the daughter of the US minister to Rumania, and his teenage son and went to New York, where he married a wealthy divorcee, set up a wine shop in Manhattan, and joined the NYPD.

After his own divorce, Sunny Marlborough immediately married again, and his second wife was also American. Gladys Deacon was a society beauty with a complicated past. Her father went to prison for shooting dead her mother's French lover in their suite at the Hotel Splendide in Cannes and then went mad. Her mother went off with an Italian nobleman. When Gladys was still a teenager, drifting around Europe, Proust and Rodin were captivated by her beauty. Bernard

Berenson and the Crown Prince of Prussia wanted to marry her. She later claimed she had slept with every prime minister in Europe and most kings.

In the 1890s, when she was sixteen, Gladys met Sunny, then just married to Consuelo, and decided that she wanted him. It took her nearly twenty-five years, but on June 25, 1921, she finally achieved her objective when the couple were married in Paris. Her bridal gown was "of gold tissue specially woven in Italy for the occasion," announced the *Times*. "The Court train is of gold tissue, and the veil, of old needlepoint lace, [is] arranged like a coronet."[9] That veil hid a slight but curious secret. Years before, Gladys had tried to improve on her considerable good looks by having paraffin wax injected in her nose. The procedure was not a success: the wax slipped and left her with a permanently bulky jaw.

The newlyweds settled in at Blenheim Palace and Carlton House Terrace, and Gladys took up the role of duchess with more ease than Consuelo had. There were house parties at Blenheim and receptions at Buckingham Palace. In 1923 she was presented to George V and Queen Alexandra, "wearing a classically draped dress of silver lamé with a ceinture of silver embroidered in diamante."[10]

Gladys was forty years old when she married, and Sunny was fifty. After spending several decades consorting with some of the world's most distinguished artists and politicians in the capitals and casinos of Europe, the new duchess soon began to tire of Blenheim Palace and country life, while three miscarriages in four years put an end to hopes of motherhood. She turned to breeding Blenheim spaniels with more success, until they overran the palace and drove the duke to distraction. This, coupled with Sunny's conversion to Catholicism and Gladys's dangerously erratic behavior—she once produced a revolver at dinner and, when one of her guests asked nervously what it was for, replied, "Oh, I don't know. I might just shoot Marlborough"—led to the breakup of the marriage.[11]

In 1931 Sunny fled Blenheim, and for several years Gladys and her spaniels had the place to themselves. But in 1933 he had the gas and electricity cut off. Gladys retreated to their London house, but he cut the power there, too, and then had her evicted. Only his sudden death the following year prevented their divorce.

WITH SO MANY OWNERS OF country estates unable to cope with rising taxes and falling rents, it wasn't surprising that the consolations of marriage to a wealthy American wife remained strong after the Armistice. But the tenor of the exchange was subtly different. Now, Americans brought glamour and dynamism, as well as money. When Iva Lawson bought Claude Lowther's Herstmonceux, undeterred by tales of ghostly gray ladies and a phantom giant drummer who walked the battlements, the British press was delighted. "Along Came a Brave American Girl Who Scoffs at Ghosts and Just Adores Haunted Rooms," ran one excited headline.[12] And sometimes glamour was enough without the fortune.

The Americanization of British culture was felt at the highest levels of society. One thinks of the young Earl of Jersey's film-star bride Virginia Cherrill "of Hollywood, U.S.A.," as *Debrett's Peerage* primly put it. In 1932 the 9th Duke of Devonshire's son married Broadway entertainer Adele Astaire, sister of Fred, who became Lady Charles Cavendish. George V and Queen Mary had private screenings of Hollywood blockbusters: in 1927 they watched Ben-Hur's legendary chariot race in the comfort of the Waterloo Chamber at Windsor Castle. The Prince of Wales, like many of his friends, used America as a yardstick by which to measure modern country-house conveniences: at Fort Belvedere he introduced "many of the creature conveniences that I had sampled and enjoyed in the New World—a bathroom to nearly every room, showers, a steam bath, built-in cupboards, central heating."[13] When as Edward VIII he left Windsor after his abdication speech, he drove into exile in a Buick.

But it wasn't just that America was becoming the dominant global culture. Post-Armistice Britain was a more cosmopolitan place, and some at least of the prewar social barriers were coming down. Before he found Virginia from Hollywood, the Earl of Jersey was married to Patricia from Cootamundra in New South Wales. Thelma Furness's husband, the Yorkshire shipbuilder, colliery owner, and iron and steel proprietor Marmaduke Furness, took as his first wife Daisy Hogg, who, like his mother, came from neighboring County Durham. She died in 1918, and in 1926 Duke Furness married Thelma. Her father was American, her mother was half Chilean and half Irish American. When Thelma's affair with Edward Prince of Wales (and others) brought that marriage to an end in 1933, the duke married the twice-widowed Enid Lindemann, an Australian whose first husband had been a New Yorker and whose second was an English brigadier general. The days had gone when marriage among the country-house-owning classes was confined to a British elite.

And Marmaduke married Thelma for love, not as a way of bailing out his finances or saving his country estate, which was draped around a well-maintained modern hunting box called Burrough Court near Melton Mowbray. In fact *he* tried hard to settle money on *her* and couldn't understand when she refused angrily on the grounds that it was un-American and amounted to "wife-buying."

The other side of the coin was an American admiration for the Old Country. This found expression in some unlikely ways. Antique and architectural fittings dealer Charles of London established an office on Fifth Avenue in 1904. White, Allom & Co. had showrooms in New York and Montreal; Syrie Maugham, in partnership with cosmetics queen Elizabeth Arden, had a shop on Michigan Boulevard in Chicago and another on East Fifty-Seventh Street in New York. Via dealers like these, stained glass from English country houses, fireplaces and plaster ceilings, even entire rooms, found their way across the Atlantic. When Cassiobury House in Hertfordshire, ancestral seat of the Earls of Essex, was demolished in 1922 after the 7th Earl's marriage to an American heiress had failed to restore the family fortunes, Edward Pearce's Restoration staircase was acquired by the Metropolitan Museum of Art; it is still there today, exquisitely beautiful but purposeless, leading up to nowhere. The Fifth Avenue apartment of Judge Irwin Untermeyer, a noted collector of English furniture, contained two paneled rooms from demolished country houses, complete with Elizabethan chimneypieces and overmantels and supplied by Charles of London.

THE SEVENTEENTH-CENTURY STAIRCASE FROM CASSIOBURY HOUSE, NOW IN NEW YORK'S METROPOLITAN MUSEUM OF ART.
(Copyright: Country Life)

In the 1920s firms like Charles of London, White, Allom & Co., and Robersons of Knightsbridge were packing up cartloads of fixtures and fittings from English historic houses and shipping them across the Atlantic. Robersons' list of "Some of the panelled rooms installed in America by Robersons of London" (c. 1926) mentions twenty clients, including Edsel Ford in Detroit, William Randolph Hearst, and Mrs. Childs Frick, daughter-in-law of art collector Henry Clay Frick. Among the items supplied were a "George I Painted Drawing Room," "late 17th Century Oak Room Christopher Wren period," "Fine Henry VIII Linenfold Room for Living Room, with Stained Glass in Windows," and "Pine Panelled Living Room, noted as from Stanwick Park."[14] Stanwick Hall in Yorkshire was one of five houses owned by the Dukes of Northumberland. It was sold to pay off death duties after the death of the 7th duke in 1918, and Robersons acquired at least four of the rooms.

AGECROFT HALL WAS DISMANTLED IN 1926 AND RE-ERECTED IN
VIRIGINIA. "THERE SEEMS TO BE A CRAZE IN THE UNITED STATES
AT THE MOMENT FOR THIS SORT OF THING," SAID THE SECRETARY
OF THE ANCIENT MONUMENTS SOCIETY. (Copyright: Country Life)

It was even possible for the American anglophile to acquire an
entire country house by mail order. The timber-framed Tudor Agecroft Hall in Lancashire was dismantled in 1926 and re-erected beside
the James River in Virginia. "There seems to be a craze in the United
States at the moment for this sort of thing," said the bewildered secretary of the Ancient Monuments Society. "No building of decent age
and character is safe from the danger of kidnapping," roared the *Manchester Guardian*.[15] Basildon Park, an elegant country house in Berkshire designed in 1777–1783 by Carr of York, was acquired in 1929 by a
property speculator named George Ferdinando, who offered to take it
down and re-erect it in any suitable position in America in return for a
million dollars. It would be left "ready for occupation as a Private Residence, or as a Museum, College Building, or Public Library," declared

the sales brochure. "Any patriotic American wishing to benefit his native State by presenting this imposing building is hardly likely to again meet with such an unique [sic] opportunity."[16] In the year of the Wall Street crash, Ferdinando's timing was bad. There were no takers, and he settled down with his wife and children to live in a wing of the house, although he sold some of the plasterwork to T. Crowther & Sons of the North End Road, and it found its way to the Waldorf Astoria in New York, which to this day boasts of its Basildon Room as having "spectacular panelling and a frescoed ceiling taken from the British estate, Basildon Hall, and beautifully offset by a Parisian marble fireplace."[17] British audiences who laughed at *The Ghost Goes West*, Alexander Korda's 1935 movie about an American businessman who reassembles a Scottish castle in Florida and finds that the castle phantom has come, too, tempered that laughter with the uneasy recognition that not everything about the film was fantasy.

ON BALANCE, A COUNTRY HOUSE is best left where it is. Fortunately, that was the line taken by most American purchasers. They bought. They rented. Very occasionally, they built. For the wealthy outsider, even in a comparatively diverse and cosmopolitan society that had outstripped its Victorian ancestry, a country house remained an essential adjunct to acceptability, a badge of access as much as of success.

The Wisconsin-born entrepreneur Harry Gordon Selfridge, who had settled in England in 1906 and opened his eponymous Oxford Street department store three years later, harbored dreams of grandeur. In the last days of 1920, he rented the Adam-designed Lansdowne House on Berkeley Square, home to four British prime ministers and described in the press as "the finest historical mansion in London."[18] Selfridge already had his country house: four years earlier he had taken a lease on Highcliffe Castle, a sprawling monster on the south coast near Bournemouth.

Highcliffe was an architectural curiosity. Essentially, a picturesque Gothic creation by the prolific but pedestrian architect W. J. Donthorne, it incorporated elements of an early sixteenth-century French chateau brought over by its then owner, Lord Stuart de

Rothesay, British ambassador at Paris between 1815 and 1824, and again from 1828 to 1831. The effect did not please the purists: Pugin ranted that "Mr Donthorn could not have had the slightest idea of Gothic architecture as he has . . . made a sad havoc of everything";[19] although the episode is a reminder that in removing bits and pieces from British country houses and shipping them overseas, Ferdinando and his like were following a tradition in trafficking that had been around for generations. Stuart de Rothesay was accused at the time of "Elginism," a reference to the 7th Earl of Elgin's recent looting of the Parthenon.

Selfridge liked Highcliffe's historical associations, which lent both romance and legitimacy to his tenure. He took the house furnished and proudly showed off the writing table that had belonged to Marie Antoinette and had been used by both Napoleon and, bizarrely enough, Kaiser Wilhelm II, who spent a holiday at Highcliffe in 1907 when he couldn't find anywhere to stay on the Isle of Wight. But Highcliffe didn't belong to Selfridge, and as his retail empire grew, he wanted a country house of his own.

A castle of his own, in fact, in the same way that Highcliffe was a castle—that is, not a castle at all. Selfridge was in love with the pseudo-Gothic, "the Walter Scott gothic, revived romantically through the influence of the Waverley novels," said Philip Tilden, who knew him well.[20] In 1921 Selfridge bought a two-and-a-half-mile stretch of coastline within sight of Highcliffe. It included Hengistbury Head outside Bournemouth, a beautiful promontory jutting out into the Channel, with views across to the Isle of Wight and the Needles. This headland was to be the site of Selfridge's castle.

Or more accurately, his castles. Selfridge commissioned Philip Tilden to design a Little Castle, which despite its name was to be the same size as Highcliffe, that would stand on the very edge of Hengistbury Head with only the sea beyond it. Above and behind it, a plateau encircled by four miles of turreted walls was the site of what Tilden labeled the Large Castle, and with good reason. It was to be the biggest castle in the world.

For Tilden this was a dream commission. "Things had been arranged so that I was untroubled in my designing by the thought of

GORDON SELFRIDGE'S PALACE OF DREAMS. (Copyright: RIBA Collections)

money or the means by which to live," he remembered artlessly, and with money no object, the only limits were imposed by the coastal site and his own imagination.[21] For more than a year, he paid monthly visits to Selfridge at Highcliffe or Lansdowne House, bringing drawing after drawing of what was to be "the most beautiful architectural effort of modern history."[22] As the palace grew, each new tower or gallery or saloon was greeted by Selfridge with the same uncritical approval, each disbelieving question from outsiders—"But how will you ever get it done?" "What on earth does he want to do it for?"—with the same unsmiling confidence, the same "cold, clear, blue and calculating eye."[23] And slowly, inexorably, Selfridge's palace of dreams edged further and further away from reality.

Tilden's vision began with a gateway that pierced the bastioned wall "like the gate to a Spanish city."[24] That was ambitious for Bournemouth, but it was only the start. From here, the main drive wound its way upward until it reached a piazza and a marble staircase hall with a dome almost as big as that of St. Paul's. The central vista, a thousand feet long, stretched out to either side of this hall, which opened into a cloistered garden with a vast *galerie des glaces* based on that at Versailles on one side, the entrance to Selfridge's own apartments, and an equally vast tapestry gallery on the other. There were 250 guest suites, dining chambers that would seat hundreds, a theater, tennis courts, picture galleries, and baths. Recitals would be held in a Gothic hall, "where the organ would reverberate through the stone lace of screen and vaulting." A winter garden led down through Piranesian archways to a covered lake fed with streams of clear water and filled with fountains that always played.

Dominating the palace was a great tower three hundred feet high, which contained suites of rooms, studios, laboratories, and observatories, culminating in a viewing platform on the roof. "From here," wrote Tilden with longing, "one could watch the great liners gliding up the Solent to their berths; here one could forget the labour that went to the making of all man-thought things, and remember and appreciate only the results that man could achieve; or through some giant telescope learn more of the eternal vastness of space."[25]

It was all bonkers, of course. A country house this size would take decades to build. (That was the reason for the Little Castle, which would be completed first so that Selfridge had somewhere to live during the years of construction work.) By 1923 Selfridge had given up Highcliffe Castle and abandoned his plans for a palace of dreams. He may never have taken the project seriously; he told *Building News* that it had always been meant as "an imaginative exercise" only, and he sold Hengistbury and the rest of his coastal holdings, seven hundred acres in all, in 1930 without a stone being laid.[26] Philip Tilden, who certainly meant it as more than an imaginative exercise, was astute enough to note that in the early days as news of the scheme spread, Selfridge's neighbors along the coast treated him with a new respect. And everyone enjoyed him- or herself. The palace of dreams was born out of a new optimism. "It was all a sign of the times," remembered Tilden, "a sign of hope that fear had been strangled, that culture was to be fostered, that men and women were to be happier."[27]

A COUPLE OF YEARS AFTER Harry Gordon Selfridge abandoned his dreams of an English castle by the sea, another American millionaire embarked on his. In the summer of 1925, Alice Head, editor and managing director of *Good Housekeeping* magazine, received a cablegram from her boss in California:

WANT BUY CASTLE IN ENGLAND
PLEASE FIND WHICH ONES AVAILABLE
STDONATS PERHAPS SATISFACTORY AT PROPER PRICE
BUT PRICE QUOTED SEEMS VERY HIGH
IF YOU CAN GET RIGHT PRICE ON STDONATS
OR ANY OTHER EQUALLY GOOD HEARST

Newspaper tycoon William Randolph Hearst was at the peak of his career and in the middle of a frenzy of building and collecting. He already owned a New York apartment reputed to be the biggest in the world, and a 250,000-acre estate at San Simeon on the California coast, halfway between Los Angeles and San Francisco. In the late 1920s he bought Sands Point, a castle on Long Island, for his wife Millicent; and built a 110-room "beach house" at Santa Monica for his mistress, the film actress Marion Davies. At Wyntoon in northern California, his architect Julia Morgan created an extraordinary group of brightly painted Hansel and Gretel cottages in a forest.

Hearst filled all these homes with precious things: Greek and Roman vases (he owned 450 of them); early Renaissance tapestries (he had the largest collection of important tapestries in private hands in the world); arms and armor; silver, paintings, manuscripts, and fine furniture. His rage to collect led his *New York Times* obituarist to make the astonishing claim that, at his peak, Hearst single-handedly accounted for a quarter of the world's art market.

Hearst began to think about renting or buying a country residence in Britain in the spring of 1925, and Alice Head, who acted as his London agent as well as managing the National Magazine Company, the British side of his publishing empire, went down to Kent to see Leeds Castle but reported that it was in a poor state without a single bath in the place. As the telegram suggests, the other leading contender was St. Donat's, an imposing medieval fortress dating back in parts to the twelfth century, overlooking the Bristol Channel and about twenty miles west of Cardiff (and hence in Wales, rather than England—a distinction that was lost on Hearst). Victorian Gothic Revival architects Bodley & Garner had renovated St. Donat's at the beginning of the century, leaving it in reasonable shape. It did at least have electricity from its own generator and three bathrooms. The owners, Lady Winifred Pennoyer and her American diplomat husband Richard, had bought it in 1922, but now they wanted to sell, opting instead to live at Ingestre Hall, the Staffordshire ancestral home of Lady Winifred's first husband, who had died in the war.

On August 16, 1925, a *New York Times* headline announced "Hearst Buys 12th Century Castle in Wales for a Residence When He Is Abroad."[28] Alice Head had managed to buy the castle and 111 acres for £27,000, although she used company funds, so that, strictly speaking, St. Donat's always belonged to the National Magazine Company rather than to Hearst personally.

Why did he want it? "Well," he told the press on his first visit (which didn't take place until 1928—he was in no hurry to see his new toy), "I had seen some of your great castles, such as Caernarfon and Conwy, and they made such an impression on my mind that I decided to acquire something in the same way, only smaller and more domestic, as it were."[29] That was only part of the story. He liked the idea of a place in the country where he and his mistress, Marion Davies, could entertain their friends, something that naturally didn't figure in his public pronouncements on St. Donat's: in 1928, and again in 1930, 1931, 1934, and 1936, they spent the summer touring Europe, sometimes starting and always ending their trip there. "We'd stay as long as we possibly could," Davies recalled, and "take life easy after the tour,"[30] Hearst's wife, Millicent, had visited the castle during a trip to Britain in 1926, but she and her husband never spent any time there together.

However, Hearst's real reason for buying an "English" castle, as he persisted in calling St. Donat's, had less to do with Marion Davies and rather more to do with finding the right setting for part of his growing collection of British and European art treasures. Before that happened, there was work to do to bring the castle up to American standards. Water mains and electrical lines were installed, and Hearst's architect, Sir Charles Allom of White, Allom & Co., demolished much of Bodley & Garner's recent work as not authentic enough. Allom created new bedroom suites and dozens of bathrooms,

an outdoor swimming pool on the site of an old tilt ground, and two
new halls, both of which made use of imported historic fittings. The
carved and gilded early Tudor ceiling of the banqueting hall was
bought by Allom after it had been removed from a church in Boston,
Lincolnshire—not, as Marion Davies rather sweetly misremembered,
from the Museum of Fine Arts in Boston, Massachusetts.

The second of Allom's great creations at St. Donat's was the
Bradenstoke Hall, so named because the timbers of its magnificent
fourteenth-century roof originally graced the Priory of Bradenstoke
in Wiltshire. In a separate purchase, Hearst also bought Bradenstoke
Tithe Barn for £3,600, unwittingly becoming embroiled in a national
scandal. When it emerged that the tithe barn was being dismantled
and removed from its site, reputedly for shipping to America, there
was a public outcry. "An historical building cannot be severed from
its site without destroying its spell," said the *Observer*. "In its new setting what it will most forcibly recall will be the misguided taste of its
uprooter."[31] Antiquarians wrote to the *Times* to complain about "this
stupid example of vandalism" and to mutter darkly that "the name of
a well-known American newspaper owner [was] associated with the
transaction."[32] The demolition was "an attack on the soul-life of our
people." Questions were asked in Parliament; Prime Minister Ramsay MacDonald was urged to "do something"; Americans in England
added their voices to the protests; and there were calls not only for the
British government to ban the export of such treasures but also for
the US Congress to ban their import.[33]

When it was finally confirmed in October 1930 that Hearst was
indeed the purchaser of the tithe barn and the priory buildings, but
that both were destined for St. Donat's rather than Fifth Avenue, the
Society for the Protection of Ancient Buildings, which had led the
campaign to save them, was decent enough to thank Hearst for providing a proper home in Britain for them and to recognize that "this
damage to our heritage is more the result of the action of our own
people than that of citizens of the United States of America."[34]

The introduction of historic elements into the castle was funda-
mental to Hearst's vision. "Need ancient atmosphere at St Donat's"

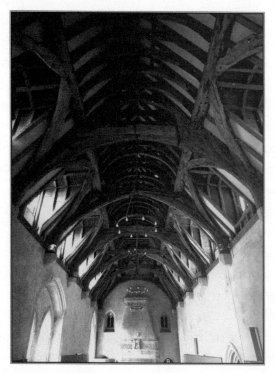

St. Donat's Castle: Hearst's Banqueting Hall. (Copyright: Country Life)

read one of his many telegrams to Alice Head.[35] On another occasion he urged her "always to add old things" rather than making new.[36] A stone chimneypiece and overmantel from Bradenstoke were installed in the Breakfast Room, and two sixteenth-century French chimneypieces in the Bradenstoke Hall. The Banqueting Hall had a Gothic screen, which had originally graced a West Country church but which Hearst's agents had found built into the wall of a house in Bridgwater. "We shall just increase [the castle's] historical interest," he told reporters in 1930, "by bringing tapestries, ceilings, panelling screens, pictures—every one of which will be genuinely antique."[37]

Some were more genuinely antique than others. Hearst's bed, for example, was said on rather slender evidence to have been the very one in which Charles I slept before his defeat at the Battle of Naseby. Other items were of more certain provenance but doubtful taste—thumbscrews, spiked collars, and other instruments of torture and an executioner's sword. But the majority of the contents amassed for St. Donat's were of the best quality and in the best taste: portraits by Zoffany and Sir Thomas Lawrence, furniture by Chippendale, Brussels tapestries, and neo-Classical sculpture. Of particular importance were the arms and armor, one of the greatest private collections in the world at the time, much of it acquired in Germany in the late 1920s and early 1930s. The highlight was a set of Milanese armor dating from the 1440s and now believed to be the earliest near-complete suit of plate armor in the world.

As well as masterminding the architectural renovations, Sir Charles Allom supplied hundreds of items. He understood Hearst's ambition from the outset. In 1930 he told the local press that "St Donat's is to become a great national museum, the repository of the most important objects gathered from all quarters . . . Mr Hearst is one of the world's most generous and most modest hosts. He will have learned societies to visit St Donat's in order to see the country's choice of historic treasures within its walls."[38] This was exactly the point. St. Donat's was a museum. Not a re-creation of a Welsh castle, nor even an English castle; not a Hollywood set—a museum.

Hearst left it to the native Welsh to turn his museum into a Hollywood set, a backdrop for a nonsensical piece of medieval make-believe. It was his custom to keep the castle fully staffed, with thirty to forty servants even in his absence, and to invite his friends to use it when he was away. In the summer of 1934, having celebrated the Fourth of July by floodlighting the castle and giving a fireworks display so spectacular that the authorities complained he was confusing shipping in the Bristol Channel, Hearst went off to Germany.* While he was away, he lent St. Donat's to ex–prime minister David Lloyd George, who was in the area to address the National Eisteddfod, the great annual festival of Welsh literature and music.

Lloyd George seized the opportunity to use the castle as a setting for an elaborate pageant to welcome 150 members of the Gorsedd, the Welsh community of bards. Everyone present wore either bardic or

---

*   It was on this visit to Germany that Hearst met Hitler and criticized his anti-Semitic policies. Hitler is supposed to have replied, "What about the American Indians?"

medieval costume, even the servants. Food was "as near 14th-century Welsh food as 20th-century stomachs can stand," reported the *Guardian*, "and mead will be among the drinks."[39] The Gorsedd arrived in procession with the archdruid; the heraldic bard rode at their head calling out to "halberdiers" patrolling the battlements to demand hospitality; and Lloyd George appeared in costume and announced that "in the name of the Castellan we welcome all to the Castle of St Donat's." The drawbridge was lowered, the portcullis was raised, and the procession trooped into the banqueting hall, where harpists in medieval costumes entertained the diners. Alice Head, also in costume, was there at the top table with Lloyd George, as was the old politician's wife, Dame Margaret, and their daughters, Olwen and Megan (both of whom resisted wearing medieval fancy dress, opting instead for Welsh national costume).

After dinner the company went out on the lawn to watch as a band of monks, actually members of a local choir, walked through the grounds carrying torches and chanting the *Nunc Dimittis* before "dawn" broke (the Fourth of July floodlighting was still in place, and it was put to good use), and the choristers reappeared as miners on their way home from a night shift, bringing the onlookers gently back to the modern day. It was all a far cry from the scenes that St. Donat's had grown used to over the past five or six years: Marion Davies and her Hollywood starlet friends lounging around the pool in pajamas while chefs imported from Claridges or the Ritz prepared their meals and Hearst sat in an Italianate teahouse on the grounds, speaking by phone to his office in Los Angeles or New York.

BESIDES THE BARTERED BRIDES AND business tycoons, there is another group of Americans who deserve a mention for their impact on the country-house world between the wars. We've already met some of them and their off-the-peg ancestral seats: Waldorf Astor at Cliveden, Ronnie Tree at Ditchley Park, Olive Wilson Filmer at Leeds Castle. Others circle the edges of the story: the diarist and MP Chips Channon, who bought the Georgian Kelvedon Hall in Essex in 1938 (cheaply, because during a spell as a boys' school in the early

1930s a string of drownings, fatal falls, and other accidents had given it a sinister reputation), and then quickly tired of playing the country squire; Major Lawrence Johnston, whose seventeenth-century country house, Hidcote Manor in Gloucestershire, will always be just a backdrop to the legendary gardens he created there.

What this eclectic group have in common is their anglophile Anglo-Americanism, the fact that they all had a foot on both sides of the Atlantic. All were products of the first wave of the American invasion of the turn of the century. Waldorf Astor's father became a British citizen in 1899 and sent his son to Eton and Oxford; Ronnie Tree was born of American parents but raised in England and sent to school at Winchester; Olive Wilson Filmer had an English nobleman for a father and a Whitney heiress for a mother. Chicago-born Channon reinvented himself as an upper-class English gentleman and gained a reputation for thoroughly English snobbery. Johnston, whose father was a Baltimore banker and whose mother was a New York heiress, was educated at Cambridge and fought on the western front as a major in the Northumberland Hussars.

Urban Huttleston Rogers Broughton, the owner of Anglesey Abbey in Cambridgeshire, was as much a product of Gilded Age America as a Newport mansion or a character in an Edith Wharton novel. Yet, he was also very British. His father, Urban Hanlon Broughton, was born in Worcestershire and trained at the Institute of Civil Engineers in London before going out to America in 1887 at the age of thirty to seek his fortune. He found it in love and sewerage. In 1895 the oil tycoon Henry Huttleston Rogers of Standard Oil employed Broughton to install a new sewerage system in his hometown of Fairhaven, Massachusetts. As the *New York Times* reported:

> At the Rogers home Mr Broughton met the financier's daughter, Cara, and as the trenches deepened where Mr Broughton superintended the work his love for the heiress also grew deeper. In his courtship the Englishman made even greater progress than in finishing his task for the young woman's father, with the result that the engagement was announced first.[40]

The marriage propelled Broughton into a world of very big business. Through Rogers's influence, he was placed in charge of a company that marketed all the copper produced by properties controlled by Standard Oil and that was the largest seller of copper in the world. By the time his father-in-law died in 1907, his name was being mentioned in the same breath as that of John D. Rockefeller as among "the younger men who are now looked upon as the real leaders of the affairs of the Standard Oil Company."[41] He had interests in mining and manufacturing, metal refining, railways, and finance.

But Broughton never became American. He was referred to in New York society as "The Englishman" for his constant championing of his home country; and it came as no surprise when in 1912 he announced that he was giving up his business interests and moving back to Britain with his wife and two young sons. He took a modern country house in leafy Surrey, not far from Windsor Great Park, and entered Parliament as a Conservative, although he didn't remain in the Commons for long, complaining that it was "tedious listening for hours on end to dull people making dull speeches."[42] He remained a good friend to the Conservative Party, however, and after Prime Minister Andrew Bonar Law's death, he was the main contributor to a Tory scheme in 1928 to buy Ashridge, the great James Wyatt–designed mansion in Hertfordshire, and turn it into the Ashridge Bonar Law Memorial College, with three objectives:

> To preserve for the national a historic site and a stately building; to establish a centre where all grades of Conservatives can find a curriculum suited to their requirements; and to give enjoyment to the public by admitting it to the gardens once a week.[43]

Broughton reaped the expected reward. Baldwin offered him a title, but he died in 1929 before he could take it up, and Huttleston, his elder son, was elevated to the peerage as the 1st Lord Fairhaven in his place.

Huttleston and his brother Henry both went to Harrow and Sandhurst and both served in Guards regiments in the war. In 1924 they bought a successful racing stud at Newmarket together and two years later the nearby estate of Anglesey Abbey, agreeing that whichever one of them married first would sell his share and leave the other in sole occupation. Huttleston never married, and after Henry's wedding and departure in 1932, he stayed on in the house alone. It remained his home until his death thirty-four years later.

When it came on the market in June 1923 in the first great wave of postwar country-house sales, Anglesey Abbey was described as "an exceptionally fine old manorial residence of moderate size, possession objects of great historical and architectural interest of early and Elizabethan date." It still failed to reach its reserve, perhaps because the agent's claim that it was "now adapted and equipped as a comfortable and modern country house" was unduly optimistic.[44] The abbey, founded by Augustinians in the twelfth century, was partly demolished after the dissolution of the monasteries, leaving the chapter house as the core of the house. It had slipped gently into decline over the years until by the time the Broughton boys bought it, it was little more than a run-down farmhouse, albeit one with some picturesque features of early, if not exactly Elizabethan, date.

The brothers set out to make the place more habitable, employing Sidney Parvin of the Mayfair firm of Turner Lord, Architects, Decorative Contractors, Cabinet Makers, and Upholsterers, to rearrange some of the rooms and install fireplaces and period paneling.[45] After Henry's departure, Huttleston turned again to Parvin to extend the house, adding a library wing in 1937 and a staircase hall two years later.

The main reason for the extension was Huttleston's growing mania for collecting. He liked to buy things, and he had the money to buy them—a happy combination. The result was a house filled with books and furniture and tapestries and paintings from different periods, brought together with a cheerful disregard for fashion. There were second-rate Victorian watercolors and Claude landscapes; carved Italian saints and exquisite giltwood side tables; Renaissance oak and George II walnut.

The entrance hall set the tone. A Bruges tapestry vied with Jacobean oak, Egyptian porphyry, and a pair of phoenixes from the

Summer Palace in Beijing, while seventeenth-century French walnut chairs and a sixteenth-century Italian carving of John the Baptist lurked in the background and the Fairhaven arms in a Bavarian giltwood cartouche supported by cherubs presided over the scene.

The 1st Lord Fairhaven enjoyed his wealth, and he enjoyed displaying it. He owned a fleet of Rolls Royces, one of which was driven into Cambridge every afternoon so that his valet could collect his copy of the *Cambridge Evening News*. There was a full complement of domestic staff, including a male chef, a pair of yellow-waistcoated footmen, and a butler in tails. Guests were said to have their shoelaces ironed before breakfast and noted with astonishment that, while lunch was being served, housemaids would brush the fitted carpets in the other rooms, so that when Fairhaven came out of the dining room "there was the room once again as if nobody had ever been in it." In the evenings, he listened to the BBC news on a wireless that was brought in on a silver salver.[46]

This opulence proved too much for many visitors, who found Fairhaven's transformation of Anglesey Abbey to be somehow un-English. "More a fake than not," was James Lees-Milne's verdict on the house after a visit in 1943, when he repaid Lord Fairhaven's hospitality by describing him as "a slightly absurd, vain man, egocentric, pontifical, and too much blessed with this world's goods."[47] Even the National Trust, which accepted Anglesey Abbey after Lord Fairhaven's death in 1966, was slightly nonplussed by the sheer exuberance and the variable quality of the contents. Staggering slightly under the weight of such riches, an early Trust guidebook led visitors out into the grounds—also Fairhaven's creation and justly famous—with relief, declaring that "not everyone will respond with the same enthusiasm to the rich interior of Anglesey."[48]

Reactions like these missed the point of Anglesey Abbey. Lord Fairhaven's tastes were, indeed, un-English, but that didn't make them bad. They were Gilded Age tastes, turn-of-the-century robber baron tastes, the tastes that Fairhaven's mother and Fairhaven himself grew up admiring in Long Island mansions and Fifth Avenue palaces.[49]

They are what makes Anglesey Abbey such an unusual example of the English country house between the wars, a fragment of an ancient religious house on the edge of the fens where two worlds met.

And Anglesey Abbey reminds us that America came to the English country house with more than just new bloodstock and a million dollars and an acquisitive admiration for the Old Country. It brought something of its own—a flamboyance and a joy in collecting.

13

A QUEER STREAK

F rom 1930 to 1945, society photographer Cecil Beaton rented Ashcombe, the surviving portion of a late-seventeenth-century mansion that once nestled in a remote valley on the Wiltshire Downs. Beaton's Ashcombe exemplifies a different side of country-house culture between the wars, one which has nothing to do with tweeds and guns and panting retrievers, but with the ABC of Art, Bohemia, and Culture, with masks and dressing up and playacting.

But the acts of reinvention and disguise that took place at Ashcombe hid an uncomfortable truth. Beaton's homosexuality, what he liked to call his "queer streak," made him an outsider in that most conservative of English milieus, landed society. He and his gay friends led double lives. They were welcome in some houses and not in others, tolerated as oddities, whispered about as being "artistic"—a common euphemism for homosexuality, just as "oriental" was code for Jewish. Some were outrageously camp, eager to shock. Siegfried Sassoon's lover, Stephen Tennant of Wilsford Manor in Wiltshire—part Peter Pan, part Dorian Gray, according to his biographer—caused outrage when he was photographed by Beaton in 1927 in the silver-foiled bedroom of his London house with makeup and marcelled hair, a flying jacket slung across his shoulders in a determinedly effeminate reminder of the masculinity that had been lost in the Great War.

Other gays were less flamboyant, more cautious, and with good reason. At the most visceral level, there was a threat of physical and verbal abuse, even in the politest of polite society. In August 1927, Beaton, whose affected voice and long hair weren't calculated to endear him to hearty young heterosexuals, was tossed into the river at Wilton by three of the other guests at a coming-of-age party for "Sid" Herbert, heir to the 15th Earl of Pembroke.

Throughout the 1930s, Beaton's Ashcombe was a place in the country rather than a fully fledged country house, a weekend retreat, although it was fully staffed all year-round by a tribe of servants called the Betteridges, who cooked and cleaned and managed the gardens and were portrayed in Beaton's memoirs, like most of the local population of that corner of Wiltshire, as picturesque country yokels.

Beaton drove down from London on Fridays in his Ford, often bringing hundreds of flowers acquired at Covent Garden market—a gross of hydrangeas or lilies, bright speckled carnations, and bunches of sweet-smelling sweet peas. The following day, his houseguests would arrive for the Saturday-to-Monday parties that were a feature of life at Ashcombe, their numbers supplemented by groups of friends who drove over for the evening, lured by the promise of lavish entertainments. Occasional visitors included earnest literary types—Clive Bell, Lady Ottoline Morrell, and H. G. Wells, for example—and politicians who weren't afraid to put their reputations on the line, like the Conservative MP and millionaire Alfred Beit, who came by plane, which he parked on the polo ground at nearby Ferne House, the country seat of the Duke and Duchess of Hamilton.

But most were drawn from the world that Beaton himself inhabited: actress Ruth Gordon, better known to my generation as the Maude of Hal Ashby's 1971 cult film *Harold and Maude*; the dancer Tilly Losch, between marriages to the surrealist Edward James and the 6th Earl of Carnarvon of Highclere Castle; exotics like the Marchesa Luisa Casati, of whom it was said that she kept albino blackbirds in her palazzo by the Grand Canal in Venice and had a pair of pet cheetahs. Casati was also reputed to have dipped her black servants in gold paint, with decorative but near-fatal results. When she stayed at Faringdon, Gerald Berners's country house, she brought with her a boa constrictor in a glass case. "Would it like something to eat?" asked Berners's mother. "No, it had a goat this morning."[1]

Unsurprisingly, considering Cecil Beaton's own sexuality and the milieu in which he moved, many of the Ashcombe guests were gay or bisexual, and Beaton took endless photographs of winsome youngish men leaning against trees in the Ashcombe gardens. Rex Whistler was a frequent visitor, as were Gerald Berners and his "Mad Boy," Robert Heber-Percy, and designer Oliver Messel and his own mad boy, the wealthy art collector (and unrequited love of Beaton's life) Peter Watson. Beaton never quite recovered from the hurt he felt after he invited Messel and Watson down to Ashcombe and, bringing them tea in the morning, found their bedroom door locked against him.

Games of all kinds were an important element in the Ashcombe weekends: "paper games, charades and impersonations," recalled Beaton, "burlesque operas and ballets."[2] There were compulsory sports on the lawn, with prizes awarded by Messel and filmmaker John Sutro in drag. A favorite trick of Sir Michael Duff-Assheton-Smith, later to be Lord Lieutenant of Caernarvonshire, was to dress up as Queen Mary and act out a royal visit to a hospital ward.

Fancy dress loomed large. At the first big party Beaton held at Ashcombe, guests were asked to come as their opposites. Doris, Viscountess Castlerosse, with whom Beaton was having a halfhearted affair as a way of establishing his heterosexual credentials or to get back at Peter Watson, came as a nun. Sutro made a film at the house, a dramatization of David Garnett's 1925 novel *The Sailor's Return*, with Lady Caroline Paget—soon to be Rex Whistler's lover and eventually to be Sir Michael Duff's wife—made up as Tulip, the black wife who is brought back to an English village by a sailor. Beaton played the sailor. The poet John Betjeman was the parson. "The result was quite a straightforward rendering of the story," claimed Beaton later, "with much pictorial beauty and delightful performances by some of the villagers."[3] The film was never finished.

The group of friends also played at interior decoration, extending their games until the edge between life and stage set was dangerously blurred. One wet Sunday afternoon in May 1932, Beaton's bedroom was transformed into an astonishingly garish circus, with flowered mirrors and murals executed by his guests:

> Rex Whistler painted a superb "fat woman," Lord Berners a Columbine with performing dogs (a very ungainly mastiff was caught in the agonising act of jumping through a paper hoop), Christopher Sykes [the biographer and orientalist] painted a tumbler, upside down, balancing, among other objects, a goldfish bowl on his feet. Oliver Messel created a small Negro, naked except for a pink flamingo ostrich feather worn on his head. Mme von Bismarck [Elsa von Reppert-Bismarck] pictured an equestrienne on a flower-dappled circus pony, and her husband [Jorg] decided to portray "the strong man of the Fair" with volute mustachios, tattoo marks, heavy ball-weights and chains.[4]

Whistler wasn't satisfied with Jorg Bismarck's panel. He "improved" it afterward, much to Beaton's embarrassment and Bismarck's annoyance when the latter next visited Ashcombe. The ensemble was completed when Beaton installed a four-poster with brass barley-sugar posts and a headboard depicting a half-naked Neptune lolling among cupids and sporting a suggestively erect trident. It was designed by Whistler and built by Savage's, a famous maker of fairground carousels at King's Lynn in Norfolk. "We were only disappointed," said Beaton, "that at any given moment, the bed could not be made to revolve to the accompaniment of steam music."[5]

The high point of the Ashcombe entertainments was reached in the summer of 1937, when Beaton and Sir Michael Duff cohosted an extravagant *fête champêtre* for several hundred of their friends and neighbors. The idea, all Watteau and dairymaids and contrived simplicity, had an obvious appeal to a decade in love with the eighteenth century. Beaton and Duff choreographed it with precision. Most of the guests would be weekending at other houses in the neighborhood, and each house party was allotted a theme, and if Beaton's memory can be relied on, even a set of drawings for the costumes they were to

CECIL BEATON AND MICHAEL DUFF PREPARING FOR THE ASH-COMBE *FÊTE CHAMPÊTRE*. BEATON WEARS HIS FAMOUS RABBIT COAT. (Copyright: ullstein bild/Getty Images)

wear. The Wilton group came as Greek gods and goddesses; guests staying with Lord Alington at nearby Crichel House were to be orientals. Mottisfont Abbey provided characters from Gay's *Beggar's Opera*; Longleat sent Arcadians. A group from Rockbourne, just over the border in Hampshire, came as Manet's *Déjeuner sur L'Herbe*, complete with bustles and brown bowler hats. The waiters wore sheep, goat, horse, and bird masks, "like Tenniel's illustrations from *Alice in Wonderland*."[6] Sir Michael was Adonis.

Beaton started out the evening in a jacket of his own design. His "rabbit coat" was so-called not because it was made of rabbit fur but because it was meant to depict a garden ravaged by a rabbit. The corduroy coat was decorated with muslin roses, woolen vegetables, and plastic eggshells and egg whites. "Broken eggs are as pretty as daffodils and much more unusual," Beaton informed the readers of *Vogue*.[7]

To complete the picture, he wore a rabbit mask, but not for long: he changed costumes at least three times in the course of the night, ending up in a flowered banyan. Even the supper tables wore fancy dress, in the shape of muslin tutus.

Everybody likes their party to go with a swing (although few would go as far as Chips Channon, who put Benzedrine in the cocktails at a formal dinner he gave for the queens of Spain and Rumania). Beaton provided nonstop entertainment, beginning long before his guests reached Ashcombe. As they converged on the valley where Ashcombe lay, they encountered gesticulating papier-mâché figures pointing them in the right direction; a bus that brought them in relays down the hill to the house was filled with libelous mock advertisements created by Gerald Berners. Villagers came to perform a rustic maypole dance, while the band from the Embassy Club in Old Bond Street were installed in the stables playing dance music. Local children dressed as gypsies wandered around, "pulling a baby in a goat-cart, or letting off fireworks in their hands."[8]

The highlight of the evening was a performance of *The Town Wench, or Chastity Rewarded*, a faux Restoration comedy written by John Sutro and starring Gerald Berners as the lecherous Sir Jonathan Mock-Twitchett. Against the backdrop of the house and flanked by tall lime trees, which glowed white in the arc lights, Mistress Sweet-meat, played by fashion model Olga Lynn in pink satin, did her best to resist Sir Jonathan's advances, to little avail:

> I will not listen to your threats nor prayers,
> You little West End baggage, come upstairs![9]

The party lasted all night, ending at 7:00 a.m., as a female guest dressed as a bacchante in a leopard skin tripped across the lawn and disappeared into the dawn.

SECTION II OF THE 1885 Criminal Law Amendment Act, usually known as the Labouchere Amendment after Henry Labouchere, the Liberal MP who presented it in the Commons, introduced a maximum penalty of two years in prison with hard labor for a man who procured, or attempted to procure, "any act of gross indecency with another male person." Section 11, which sent Oscar Wilde to Reading Gaol in 1895, criminalized any homosexual behavior, and in its vagueness it allowed considerable discretion to the police and the magistrates in deciding exactly what constituted an offense.

Prosecutions averaged around thirty a year, although the country-house-owning classes rarely figured. When they did, the consequences could be devastating. Sir Paul Latham Bt., the one-legged MP who took over the rescue of Herstmonceux Castle in Sussex in 1931, was ruined by a wartime scandal. While still an MP, he joined the Royal Artillery on the outbreak of war in 1939. Two years later, he was accused of indecent behavior with three of his men. He tried unsuccessfully to kill himself by riding his motorcycle into a tree; resigned his seat in Parliament; and was court-martialed, cashiered from the army, and sentenced to two years for "disgraceful conduct of an indecent kind." His wife divorced him and took their son to live in America.

More devastating than prison, particularly for a class whose status depended so much on social acceptance, was the disgrace. In the autumn of 1921 the Conservative politician Viscount "Loulou" Harcourt, whose nickname might have set alarm bells ringing in some quarters, attempted to seduce the thirteen-year-old Edward James, who with his mother was visiting Harcourt's country house, Nuneham Court in Oxfordshire. James, who may or may not have been the illegitimate son of Edward VII, fought him off and told his mother, who indignantly repeated the story to her friends. Polite society, which already knew or suspected much about Harcourt's proclivities, began to feel uneasy at turning a blind eye to them. On the morning of February 24, 1922, Harcourt, who was married with four children of his own, was found dead in bed at his London house, 69 Brook Street. He had taken a large dose of a sleeping draught prescribed for a heart condition.

It would be "grotesque" to suggest that Harcourt had committed suicide, announced the coroner at the ensuing inquest, recording a more kindly verdict of death by misadventure. Lord Esher, a friend whose son and daughter Harcourt had also assaulted—"It is so tiresome that Loulou is such an old roué," wrote Esher's daughter rather tolerantly, "[i]t is just ungovernable sex desire for both sexes"—quickly went through the viscount's personal papers and removed his child pornography collection, taking it off to his own house.[10]

The most notorious homosexual scandal of the 1930s concerned William Lygon, 7th Earl Beauchamp. That it is also one of the most well known is due to the fact that the Lygons of Madresfield Court in Worcestershire were used by Evelyn Waugh as models for the Marchmains of Brideshead. Sebastian was recognizable as Hugh Lygon, whom Waugh knew at Oxford and who like his literary offspring was a charming self-destructive drunk. The household chapel at Brideshead where Charles Ryder kneels to say a prayer, "an ancient, newly-learned form of words" in the final scene of Waugh's novel, is based on the Madresfield chapel, a riot of painted Arts and Crafts saints and metalwork that was created by Countess Beauchamp as a wedding present for her husband. And like Lord Marchmain, the head of the Lygon family lived in exile on the Continent, separated from his wife and children.

But whereas Marchmain's Venetian exile with his Italian mistress was of his own choosing, Earl Beauchamp's was not. The earl had a passion for male servants, which he indulged with reckless abandon throughout the 1920s. Harold Nicolson remembered a dinner at Madresfield where an astonished fellow guest turned to him and asked, "Did I hear Beauchamp whisper to the butler, 'Je t'adore'?" Quick as a flash, Nicolson, whose own homosexual affairs were pursued rather more discreetly, said, "Nonsense! He said, 'Shut the door.'"[11] Beauchamp openly slept with his young valet, George Roberts, during a visit to Australia in 1930—so openly, in fact, that when he was preparing to travel from Sydney to Canberra, his hosts there let it be known that the valet would not be welcome.

At Madresfield he was caught in flagrante with his doctor, and in London, with an anonymous boy in a public bath (by Hugh Walpole, who told Virginia Woolf). Invited to Walmer Castle in Kent, where the earl as Warden of the Cinque Ports had a household, Lady

Christabel Aberconway was surprised to be introduced to a handsome young "tennis coach" who didn't know how to hold a racquet. She was even more surprised to find the actor Ernest Thesiger, naked to the waist and wearing several strings of pearls. "He explained that he had the right type of skin to heal pearls."[12]

It was only a matter of time before the storm broke. Lettice, Beauchamp's wife and the mother of his seven children, seems not to have noticed his behavior; she wasn't altogether clear what homosexuality involved, in any case.* But her brother, the 2nd Duke of Westminster, was all too clear. Explanations of Bendor's motive for outing his brother-in-law vary: he was homophobic, he was jealous of Beauchamp's successful public life, he resented the fact that the earl had fathered three sons while *his* only son had died when he was four years old.

Whatever the reason, malice, jealousy, or moral indignation, in 1931 Bendor went to his sister and explained what her husband had been up to (with diagrams, according to one of the many legends that have grown up around the scandal). He then went to George V and told him that Earl Beauchamp, a senior politician, the Liberal Leader in the Lords, and a man who had carried the sword of state at his coronation and served as Steward of the Household, was homosexual and that he intended to expose him and have him arrested. The prospect appalled the king, who is supposed to have muttered to himself, "I thought men like that shot themselves."

Countess Beauchamp had a breakdown and ran to her brother, an act of betrayal that her children, who remained loyal to their father, never quite forgave. Bendor pressed his brother-in-law to agree to exile and a formal separation, but for several months Beauchamp tried to ride out the approaching storm, behaving, in public at least, as if nothing had happened. He hosted a coming-out party for his third daughter, Mary, at the family's London residence, Halkyn House in

---

* Or so the story goes. She later wrote to her children, confessing that "for many years, I had strongly suspected that (with Daddy) all was not as it should be—and that one side of his life and desires went contrary to everything that is right, normal and natural" (Paula Byrne, *Mad World: Evelyn Waugh and the Secrets of Brideshead* [London: HarperPress, 2009], 148).

Belgrave Square, and continued to fulfill official engagements, hosting political dinners and diplomatic receptions and speaking in the Lords. At the end of March, he held a weekend party at Madresfield; guests included Stanley Baldwin, then the Conservative Leader of the Opposition, and Cecil Beaton's cohost at the Ashcombe fête, Sir Michael Duff. Lady Beauchamp was conspicuous by her absence, which her husband explained as ill health.

The story still didn't break. Beauchamp's second daughter, Sibell, later claimed it was because she was sleeping with Lord Beaverbrook, and out of consideration for her, the press baron kept her father out of the papers. More likely it was due to George V, who was anxious to avoid public scandal. The king's bisexual fourth son, Prince George, had been romantically linked with Mary Lygon. He had stayed at Madresfield, and the thought that a prince of the realm might be called to give evidence in court horrified George V. In any case, the age was more discreet, more deferential. What would the papers have said, exactly?

But Bendor would not let it go. He wrote to Baldwin, suggesting it might not be appropriate for the politician to weekend at Madresfield in future and explaining why. He persuaded his sister to place an advertisement in the *Times* announcing that she was staying with him and that she "wishes her friends to know that she is very well and has been in good health for some time past."[13]

Most damaging of all, Bendor pressed his sister into filing for divorce. There was to be no collusion, no chance for the earl to spend an uncomfortable night in a Brighton hotel with an obliging woman while the private detectives kept watch in the corridor. The grounds were that he was "a man of perverted sexual practices" and that throughout their married life he "has committed acts of gross indecency with the male servants and other male persons and has been guilty of sodomy."[14]

Now Earl Beauchamp's reckless abandon came back to ruin him. The petition described in lurid detail the earl's sexual activities with ten men, nine of them named, at Madresfield, Walmer Castle, and Belgrave Square. The earliest instance, an encounter in the chauffeur's room at Halkyn House, dated back to 1909; the most recent, an act of sodomy committed in the library at Belgrave Square with an unknown male, was said to have taken place in November 1927.

Lady Beauchamp's petition was filed on May 14. The following day, a brief item appeared in the press to the effect that her husband "has been obliged on account of the unsatisfactory state of his health . . . considerably to curtail his engagements for the future."[15] He resigned his post as Liberal Leader in the Lords and retreated to Madresfield, where one evening at the beginning of June three senior peers arrived to tell him that the king wanted him to leave the country, hinting that if he did not do so immediately a warrant for his arrest would be issued. He crossed the Channel on June 9. Bendor sent him a charming little note: "Dear Bugger-in-law, you got what you deserved. Yours, Westminster."[16]

THE MORE OBVIOUSLY QUEER CULTURE espoused by Beaton and his set tended to be confined to safe artistic and theatrical circles where makeup and cross-dressing might raise an eyebrow but not a warrant for the victim's arrest; a world that was predominantly urban, metropolitan, at home backstage at a Cochran revue or listening to Ambrose's band in a Mayfair nightclub but not, perhaps, weekending in the country. Or so you'd think. But the acquisition of a place in the country was still seen by many as a desirable adjunct to success, especially among those from bourgeois roots.

Take just two iconic gays of the period. Ivor Novello celebrated a contract with Gainsborough Films in 1927 by buying Munro Lodge, near Maidenhead, which he renamed Redroofs and kept as his country residence for the rest of his life. And Noel Coward bought Goldenhurst, a beautiful seventeenth-century timber-framed house, barn, and cottage in Kent, tile hung and clad with ragstone.

Coward found Goldenhurst in 1926. He was twenty-six and buoyed up by the success on both sides of the Atlantic of *The Vortex*, his sharp depiction of decadent Mayfair society, he came back from America with a vintage Rolls Royce (which broke down so often that he reckoned it cost him as much as three brand-new Bentleys); a new business manager and lover, Jack Wilson; and a determination to find a place by the sea where he could move with an entourage that included Jack; his secretary, Lorn Lorraine; his father and mother (who were not always on speaking terms); his younger brother, Eric; and his Auntie Vida.

All the houses he looked at were "either too old and falling to pieces, or so new that they were horrible," he recalled.[17] Eventually a farmer, Mr. Body, contacted him to say his farmhouse was available to let with six acres for fifty pounds a year. Goldenhurst Farm was at Aldington in Kent, overlooking the Romney Marsh with views across to Dymchurch and the English Channel; on clear nights, the lights on the French coast sparkled on the edge of the horizon. But the house itself was poky with a Victorian feel to it, clad in red brick and filled with tiled fireplaces and awful wallpapers, surrounded by ponds and hedges and decrepit thatched barns, and boasting an eighteenth-century addition described by Coward as "a square edifice wearing perkily a pink corrugated tin roof and looking as though it had just dropped in on the way to the races."[18] No one was particularly impressed with the place, but at least it had electric light and a garage for the vintage Rolls; so the playwright decided to rent it while he scoured Kent for somewhere more suitable.

Coward lived at Goldenhurst for the next thirty years. When he and Jack found that behind the tiled fireplaces and awful wallpapers there lurked a rather lovely sixteenth- and seventeenth-century oak-beamed farmhouse, he bought it outright from Mr. Body; and between 1927 and 1930, they turned Goldenhurst into an attractive small country house, running together the farmhouse, the "square edifice," one of the barns, and an adjoining cottage. There were four reception rooms, six principal bedrooms, and a large studio or ballroom with a stage, the "Big Room," where Coward would entertain houseguests with performances of his latest works. It was at Goldenhurst that he wrote *Cavalcade*, the patriotic, jingoistic story of the Marryot family in the first thirty years of the twentieth century, which opened to huge acclaim in October 1931 and ran for 405 performances. ("It is sensational. It is staggering" was how the *Observer's* theater critic began his review.[19]) Well-known figures, including Cecil

Beaton and Joan Crawford, Somerset Maugham, Evelyn Waugh, and Ian Fleming, would motor down for the weekend. The village post-mistress went into shock one evening after putting through a call from Marlene Dietrich, phoning to congratulate Coward on his latest film.

Goldenhurst illustrates the blurred boundaries between farm-house, place in the country, and country house. When Coward found it in 1926, it was Goldenhurst Farm. (Although his mother, who could be difficult and didn't appreciate being moved from Coward's com-fortable townhouse in Ebury Street, referred to it dismissively as "the cottage.") Even after Coward and Jack Wilson had finished modern-izing the house, installing five bathrooms, a private electricity supply, garaging for four cars, and oil-fired central heating, it was still a farm-house. In 1937, when Coward's father died at the house, relegated to a lonely existence in a room above the garage, it was Goldenhurst Farm, and Coward himself referred to it as "a fine old 17th-century farm-house."[20] By 1956, however, when he put it on the market and moved to Jamaica, Goldenhurst had become a "country estate" with a "pic-turesque old manor house" and a "home farm." Its upwardly mobile metamorphosis was complete.

Neither Novello nor Coward were bred to country-house life. The former was the son of a Cardiff council rent collector; the lat-ter's father was a clerk. Beaton came from a more solidly middle-class background: his father was a timber merchant, although that scarcely equipped him for life in landed society.

By the time that Gerald Hugh Tyrwhitt-Wilson, 14th Baron Ber-ners, inherited Faringdon in 1931, he was nearly fifty. He was already well known as a minor composer—Diaghilev commissioned a ballet from him, *The Triumph of Neptune*, which was choreographed by Bal-anchine—and an even more minor painter and author. His homosex-uality was not a particular secret among his friends, but he was never as obvious as Beaton or as flamboyant as Stephen Tennant, perhaps because his sexual appetite was not particularly strong. His partner, Robert "Mad Dog" Heber-Percy, was bisexual, reckless, and nearly thirty years his junior. When they met at Sir Michael Duff's Welsh country house, Vaynol, in the early 1930s, Heber-Percy was only twenty-one but already had a checkered past, which included being asked to leave his cavalry regiment, working as an extra in Hollywood, and helping to run a dubious London night club. Heber-Percy is supposed to have gone to stay at Faringdon for the weekend after the Vaynol meeting, but things didn't go well in bed. On the Monday he asked Berners if he should go, and Berners simply said, "Don't leave. You make me laugh. I don't mind about the other."[21]

Stories of Berners's eccentricities at Faringdon are legion, as are examples of his jokey sense of humor. Every month he dyed the pigeons magenta, copper green, and ultramarine; fellow-composer Constant Lambert used to claim that they only mated with pigeons of the same color. He was also said to have experimented with dyeing the swans and a white poodle and suggested to neighboring farmers that they might like to dye their horses and cattle.

He entertained relentlessly. Visitors to Faringdon included Sacheverell and Georgia Sitwell, Harold Nicolson, Gertrude Stein and Alice B. Toklas, William Walton and Rex Whistler, and Winston Churchill and George Bernard Shaw. Penelope Betjeman used to bring her horse to tea. In the drawing room. Salvador Dali played the piano, having first had it moved into the ornamental lake. Sir Francis Rose, the theater designer, said that "odd large-beaked birds wandered through the Georgian silver on the Chippendale dining-table, pecked in one's plate or left squarking horribly on some guest's head."[22]

Such public eccentricities were one way of masking a deeper sense of otherness, of rendering it more harmless, less worthy of unwelcome comment. Another way was to live a lie. On his home ground in North Wales, Beaton's friend Sir Michael Duff was careful to avoid the flamboyant behavior that characterized his life in London and New York. While still in his twenties, he was made Mayor of Caernarvon—the youngest mayor in the country—and High Sheriff of Caernarvonshire. In 1935 he opened the Eisteddfod: "although he does not actually speak Welsh," reported the press, "he learned a speech in that language especially for the occasion."[23]

He even took a wife. In March 1935 Sir Michael married Joan Marjoribanks, daughter of Lord and Lady Tweedmouth, at St.

GERALD BERNERS PAINTING PENELOPE BETJEMAN AND HER HORSE AT FARINGDON. (Copyright: Hulton-Deutsch Collection/CORBIS)

Margaret's Westminster. The bride wore white satin and orange blossom; she was followed down the aisle by two bridesmaids, six pages, and seven small girls; and the glittering guest list included viscounts and brigadier generals, Astors and Churchills, Lady Diana Cooper and Megan Lloyd-George. (Also Gerald Berners and his Mad Boy.) The couple parted the following year, and Joan successfully petitioned for an annulment.

Each August Sir Michael entertained friends at Vaynol, his enormous eighteenth- and nineteenth-century family seat overlooking the Menai Strait in North Wales. In hot weather "meals on the terrace are generally served on red-checked tablecloths which were bought in Bangor hard by, and not on the Continent, as their appearance might suggest," gushed "Mayfair" in the *Sunday Times's* society column. "There is plenty to entertain the guests, and the big lake with its stately white swans is a pretty sight."[24] So was the herd of rare white Chillingham cattle, which the baronet kept as picturesque interest in the park.

In November or early December, Sir Michael usually held a three-day shoot, and every Christmas he invited a dozen or so friends to spend the holiday with him and stay until the New Year. The festivities were presided over either by his mother, Lady Juliet, or by his housekeeper, Nanny. Guests were a mixed bunch—socialites, peers and sons of peers, wealthy bankers. Guests at the 1937 party included Lord Charles Cavendish, alcoholic second son of the Duke of Devonshire, and his wife, Adele Astaire; "Baby" Jungman and her sister Zita, darlings of the gossip columnists in the 1920s and memorably described by Beaton as "a pair of decadent 18th-century angels made of wax";[25] and the soon-to-be baronet Charles Birkin, whose classic collection of horror stories, *Devil's Spawn*, had been published the previous year.

Christmas at Vaynol was almost too traditional, as though Sir Michael were playacting a Victorian country yuletide, just as he playacted marriage and the life of a country landowner. On Christmas Eve, carol singers, led by the local schoolmaster, came in to entertain the guests at dinner; the following morning presents were handed out at the breakfast table. A staff ball, attended by all the guests, was a fixture on Boxing Day; Sir Michael personally doled out plum puddings and beef to employees and tenants and provided a school treat for the children in Vaynol village.

Successful artists like Novello, Coward, and Beaton bought themselves small country houses and surrounded themselves with safe, like-minded friends. Long-lineaged landed gentry either led double lives like Sir Michael Duff—the hunting, shooting squire doling out plum puddings to the tenantry one moment, and the camp, cross-dressing Adonis the next—or hid behind a jokey, bemused façade like Berners. There weren't many who managed to bring these worlds together.

14

FIELD SPORTS

❦

The organized house party played to one of the country house's
great strengths: its role as a base for the elite's pursuit of leisure.
That role dated back centuries. Any number of country houses
started life as hunting lodges back in the Middle Ages, and the emer-
gence in the eighteenth century of foxhunting as a high-status sport
had strengthened the appeal of country sports for the gentry and the
nobility. But as the country house evolved into more of a retreat, a
place in the country rather than the administrative headquarters of a
great landed estate, leisure, and particularly field sports of all kinds,
came to occupy a central role.

In some parts of England, life revolved around the hunt. In
Gloucestershire, the Beaufort Hunt rode six days a week from the
middle of August through till the first of May in the 1920s, and there
were fifty horses kept in the stables at Badminton. In the Midlands,
where some of the country's most prestigious hunts met, the Meynell
and the Quorn and Pytchley and the Belvoir, there was a ready market in country houses to let for the hunting season. The day after the
invitation ball at Belvoir Castle that Chips Channon enjoyed so much
in January 1935, there was a special meeting of the Belvoir pack at the
castle purely for the convenience of the guests.

Edwina Mountbatten and the Duke of York, later George VI, shooting in Suffolk in 1920. (Copyright: PA Images)

Even so, when it came to organized country-house pastimes, the shoot was king, as it had been for three or four decades. So popular was the organized shooting party in the years before the First World War that it came to be *the* fashionable country activity. The numbers of birds killed in a single day, the Edwardians' marker of a successful shoot, could run into the hundreds. The all-time record belongs to a shooting party of seven men or "guns," which included George V and the nineteen-year-old Prince of Wales, hunting on the Hall Barn estate near Beaconsfield. On December 18, 1913, they killed 3,937 pheasants, three partridges, four rabbits—and one "other." Keen shots kept running totals of their kills. Looking back on his sporting life from the vantage point of the 1930s, the 6th Duke of Portland remembered with awe the prowess of the 2nd Marquess of Ripon, who died in 1923. Between 1867 and 1900, Ripon killed 370,728 creatures. The list included 142,343 pheasants, nearly 100,000 partridges, and 2 rhinoceroses, which Portland claimed to have seen him shoot dead, right and left, with a four-bore rifle from the back of an elephant in Nepal.[1] (*Are* there rhinos in the Himalayas?)

Portland recalled with relish other scenes from late-Victorian and Edwardian glory days, like the time when Winston Churchill's father, Lord Randolph Churchill, was shooting on the Marquess of Londonderry's Wynyard estate in the northeast of England and accidentally killed a fellow guest's pet dachshund. Anxious to make amends, Lord Randolph had the dog stuffed and presented it to its bereaved owner as a Christmas present. In a glass case.

The 9th Duke of Devonshire was notorious as an uncertain shot. There is a gate on the Chatsworth estate in Derbyshire that he would proudly show to friends as the place where he made a record bag with a single shot. A wounded cock pheasant was running past this gate, and he fired at it and killed it. With the same shot he also killed a retriever that was pursuing the bird, wounded the retriever's owner in the leg, and hit his own chef, who happened to be on the other side of the gate watching the action. My, how everyone must have laughed.

The size of the bag, in which dachshunds, chefs, and rhinos were mercifully rare, was due to both a steady improvement in the efficiency of firearms and also the growing popularity of battue shooting, in which streams of birds were driven toward the waiting guns, as opposed to rough shooting, where the sportsmen walked in a line across stubble or root fields to find their prey. Battue shooting required careful and intensive game management. On the famous twenty-three-thousand-acre Elveden estate in Suffolk, the Earl of Iveagh employed seventy men, and farming was subordinate to the all-important cultivation of birds. By 1911 there were around twenty-five thousand keepers employed on estates in England, Wales, and Scotland;[2] and the disadvantages to the tenant farmer of so much countryside—perhaps as much as 50 percent of all agricultural land—being devoted to game conservation was causing disquiet in official circles. A Land Enquiry Committee Report of 1913 complained that the preservation of game was one of the reasons why the land was not producing its full yield. Under the law, the owner of land could reserve the right to kill and take winged game and to let this right to whoever he or she chose; tenant farmers couldn't take game, and had to live with the damage done to their crops by pheasants and other birds. Many weren't even allowed to shoot rabbits on their farms, in case they disturbed the birds. Under the Agricultural Holdings Act of 1908, they did have a theoretical right to claim compensation, but few chose to go down that route, as one Norfolk farmer explained to the committee:

> We have legal redress, but not many care to put it in practice. Very few landlords will pay willingly for damage done by game, and when they are forced to do so generally find means of resenting it. Generally some excuse is found for getting rid of the tenant.[3]

The sun set on this golden age in 1914. Keepers went off to the war. The guns found the stubble fields of Norfolk and the Home Counties replaced by the mud of Flanders. The 1914 Defence of the Realm Act made it illegal to feed grain to birds, which in turn led to smaller bags when shoots were organized. There was a brief renaissance after 1918, but then the sale and break up of country estates began to take its toll. The stunning seventeenth-century Broome Park in Kent, once the home of Lord Kitchener but reduced piecemeal from 5,400 acres in 1908 to 650 acres in 1930, was still advertised in that latter year as having good shooting. But for those who preferred their sports bloodless, the advertisement for Broome Park also noted that there was golf at Deal and Sandwich and pointed out that the house boasted its own cricket pitch. Eighteen holes on the links and a summer afternoon listening to the crack of leather on willow were a good deal less expensive than maintaining a 5,000-acre shooting estate.

The fluid property market meant that some of the great game estates were let to syndicates, in a foretaste of the commercial shoots that are so common in the twenty-first century. The Duke of Portland looked at his Nottinghamshire neighbors in the 1930s and lamented the fact that at once-great houses like Clumber and Rufford, the shooting was either let or abandoned. At the same time there was a resurgence of interest in rough shooting as tenant-farmers, once barred by fear and feudal obligation, bought their farms and began to shoot on their own land—or to let it to new and enthusiastic sportsmen. "The breaking up of estates has made shooting possible for the multitude, and has increased its popularity enormously," wrote the author of a 1938 manual on rough shooting for the uninitiated. "Anyone who has a second-hand gun and thirty pounds to spare can take 'a bit of shooting' nowadays, and many who have no other qualifications do so."[4] The definition of rough shooting varied wildly, from a couple of fields, one man, a shotgun, and a dog to a highly organized affair with half a dozen guns or more and five or six beaters.

There was general disagreement about the best way to rear birds. The Euston system, named after the Duke of Grafton's Euston Hall estate in Norfolk where it was perfected at the beginning of the twentieth century, was popular but labor intensive. It involved taking eggs from game birds' nests in hedgerows, replacing them with dummies, and putting the real eggs under bantams to incubate, returning them to nests in the wild for hatching. This was a full-time job, fraught with difficulties in finding the nests and getting the timings right. The advantages were that it reduced the risk of eggs being taken by vermin and increased the stock of wild birds, thought to provide much superior sport to hand-reared birds. "In the main," wrote the author of *Rough Shooting*, "I have found that owners (i.e., those whose job it is to do the shooting and reap the rewards of their keepers' labours) are all for it, whilst the keepers themselves would rather leave it well alone, saying that it is a risky and unsatisfactory business at the best of times."[5]

It was also rather a difficult system to keep up, especially in the years after the First World War when the number of gamekeepers fell by around 30 percent from pre-1914 levels. This fall, coupled with a contraction in arable farming, led to a decline in game birds, particularly partridge. Fewer gamekeepers meant less management of the bird population and more damage from predators; while as arable fields were turned to pasture, they provided a less suitable habitat. By the 1930s the number of partridges shot per thousand acres had fallen by nearly half from prewar levels. Bad weather and disease also took their toll: a particularly wet summer and outbreaks of strongylosis, a disease caused by parasitic nematode worms, wreaked havoc in the partridge population in 1930–1931. The partridge bag at the Duke of

Portland's Welbeck in 1931 was 793, down dramatically from the previous year's 3,486. It fell again in 1932.

But other years told a different story. Driven partridges, "the acme of good sport" in the opinion of the Duke of Portland, were often in good supply. The annual partridge bag on the Welbeck estate topped 3,000 on ten out of sixteen years between 1919 and 1936. In the 1934–1935 season alone, 6,537 partridges were shot, along with 5,148 pheasants—all wild birds, since hand rearing had been abandoned several years previously. So it would be a mistake to think that after 1914 the grand battue and the large-scale organized shooting party were consigned entirely to history and corporate entertaining.

NOT EVERY COUNTRY-HOUSE OWNER INDULGED in field sports, of course, and even among those who did, there were wide variations. Some of the older and longer-established county families rode to hounds and shot because they were bred to it: such things were second nature. Newcomers did it because they thought it was expected of them, or because it would help them fit in. Some preferred tennis and bridge and to hell with what the neighbors thought.

The 2nd Duke of Westminster was one who took his sports very seriously indeed. He played tennis and golf. He owned racehorses and hosted house parties each year at Eaton Hall for the Grand National at nearby Aintree. He stalked deer in the Highlands and fished for salmon on his vast estate on the River Laxford in the far north of Scotland, or traveled to Mimizan, the lodge in the Landes between Bordeaux and Biarritz, which he used as a base to go after wild boar. He made fishing expeditions to Norway in his steam yacht, the *Cutty Sark*, or sailed up the Adriatic to Albania in his other yacht, the *Flying Cloud*, and roamed around desolate lakes in tweeds and Homburg hat, making friends with brigands and shooting snipe, woodcock, and teal. Then he would take himself off for several weeks each winter to St. Saens, the small château he kept in Normandy, for more boar hunting. Several times in Scotland he achieved the so-called triple crown, by shooting a stag and a brace of grouse and catching a salmon, all on the same day.

The annual autumn shoots on the Eaton Hall estate were major events, and long after the end of the First World War, they were still being conducted on an Edwardian scale and with Edwardian ritual and ceremony. There were about twenty keepers employed on the estate. On a shoot, they all wore bowler hats and fawn leggings, with the head keeper wearing a green velvet cutaway coat with brass buttons. His bowler hat was trimmed with gold braid to mark him out. Eighty estate workers acted as beaters, wearing wide-brimmed scarlet felt hats and calf-length white smocks. To see them emerging from the woods was like being in a Breughel painting.

Guests arrived at Eaton on a Thursday night and left on Sunday, in contrast to the normal practice at other country houses, where shoots were usually held on Tuesday, Wednesday, and Thursday. On the morning of a shoot, a horse-drawn wagon carried leather cartridge boxes to the stands, each marked with its owner's name, along with shooting sticks, extra coats, and cartridge bags. The stands were marked by up to twelve white numbered pegs driven into the ground, arranged in two staggered lines, one behind the other. The cartridge wagon was followed by a horse-drawn charabanc carrying the loaders, each with a pair of guns.

By the time Bendor and his guests arrived in chauffeur-driven motorcars at the pegs at nine thirty, the loaders had sorted out the equipment. One loader in each team of two carried a pouch containing two hundred cartridges, while the lad helping him carried another two pouches similarly filled. Pegs were assigned, everyone took their places, and at a shrill blow on a whistle from the head keeper, the Breughelesque beaters began driving the birds—pheasants, although there was also some limited partridge shooting on the estate—toward the guns.

A stand lasted for about thirty minutes, during which time each gun might get through two hundred cartridges. Then the cars and wagons appeared, and everyone climbed aboard and set off for the next stand, followed by an elaborately painted horse-drawn game cart with the day's bag so far. Three drives, and the guns were taken back to join the women for lunch at Eaton Hall. "The ladies find amusement in lawn-tennis, or in attending or assisting at some neighbouring bazaar or fancy fair," declared one etiquette manual—slightly misleadingly, because by the late 1920s women did shoot occasionally.[6] The Duchess of Bedford, who died in 1937 at the age of seventy-one when the plane she was flying crashed into the North Sea, is still reckoned by *The Field* to be one of the hundred best shots of all time.

In the afternoon the women usually joined the men as spectators for two more stands. That evening, game cards with the Grosvenor crest were placed in front of each gun's place at dinner, announcing the size of the bag. It wasn't uncommon for two thousand pheasants to be shot in a single day, or for 150 guests to be invited to dinner at Eaton Hall on one of the shoot nights.

In 1931, anxious that the Eaton woods were being shot out, the duke leased World's End, a remote valley near Llangollen, and introduced something like ten thousand pheasants. The site was spectacularly craggy, "like the background of a Wagnerian opera," remembered Loelia Ponsonby. "One would not have been surprised to see old Wotan perched on some boulder."[7] There was a timber-framed farmhouse, Plas Uchaf yn Eglwyseg, which had once belonged to the radical millenarian regicide John Jones, brother-in-law of Oliver Cromwell. Local legend said that in the sixteenth century Elizabeth I retreated here to have an illegitimate baby.

The autumn shoots continued as before. Only now they took place twenty miles from Eaton Hall. The guns, the carts, the 180 beaters and loaders and keepers and dog handlers, all trekked across the border into Denbighshire, bumping along in a procession of cars. Once they got there, the terrain was too rough for cars or carts to move the guns from one stand to another. They had to walk: Winston Churchill, who shot with Bendor at World's End in 1931, a few months after he had been knocked down by a car in New York, was provided with a donkey to take him from stand to stand. Cooks brought half-cooked dishes that were finished off in the ovens at Plas Uchaf yn Eglwyseg. "In these wonderfully wild surroundings," wrote Loelia, "we ate an entirely sophisticated lunch, washed down with mulled claret."[8]

Shooting parties on this Wagnerian scale were rare after the Great War. But then they were rare before the war, too. More common

was a grand battue—still big, but for seven or eight guns, with five
keepers supervising forty or fifty estate staff. Lunch would be brought
down to a keeper's house by the butler and a couple of footmen, con-
sisting of sandwiches or stews, usually with plenty of cider or beer to
wash it down. The opportunities to be shown up as an outsider were
numberless: talking too much; talking at all, in fact; tipping too little
(keepers' fees varied from ten shillings to five pounds, depending on
the number of days' shooting and the size of the bag—a sovereign to
the head gamekeeper was the going rate for a day's partridge shooting,
and as much as two sovereigns for a good day's pheasant shooting);
shooting a bird that rightfully belonged to another gun; bringing along
a badly behaved dog; wearing clothes that seemed just a little too new.
Even *Manners and Rules of Good Society*, that bible for the unconfident
nouveax riches, which was in its forty-first edition by 1920, hesitated at
the prospect of predicting all the perils and pitfalls that awaited the
inexperienced gun. "There are numberless other points relating to field
sports wherein the 'inexperienced sportsman' is apt to give offence," it
declared, "but [they] would take up too much space to enter into in a
work of this description."[9]

Cecil Beaton gave an atmospheric description of the shoots that
were arranged on the Ashcombe estate on the border of Wiltshire and
Dorset in the 1930s by his landlord, who until recently had also been
the landlord of the Grosvenor Arms in Shaftesbury. Alderman Robert Borley, JP, had made a point of buying up adjoining parcels of land
for shooting, and every autumn he held a big shoot for the county.
Beaton watched and listened to the sound of the beaters moving
through the undergrowth, pushing the birds on until they flew out to
meet the assembled guns. "Their squawks of fright were mingled with
the ghostly calls of the beaters, 'Over! Over!' the excited barks and
whines of the retrieving dogs and the echoes of the shots throughout
the valleys."[10] After the inevitably massive lunch at long tables with
starched white cloths—pies and joints and cheeses, all washed down
with wine and port—the party set off again for the afternoon drive
and the pheasants, "like some clumsy bomber," took to the air, only to
be brought down to earth in a flurry of feathers.

The beaters at these occasions were a motley crew, old men and boys in green frock coats, patched velvet breeches, and billycock hats. They seemed to come from another time, and they returned to it at the end of the shoot. "And as the years advanced and the shooting expeditions became poorer events, this strange army disappeared into the shades from which they seemed to come."[11]

EVEN AS THEY DISAPPEARED INTO the past, another strange army was coming to take the place of Beaton's beaters and their like, another motley crew in curious costumes whose shouts rang out from undergrowth and fields and lakesides on landed estates all over England.

Golfers.

In May 1931 the Prince of Wales flew from Hendon to Hamble Aerodrome in his De Havilland Puss Moth to inspect a new Canadian-Pacific liner, the *Empress of Britain*, at Southampton. Then he crossed Southampton Water in a speedboat to Hythe, where one of the new Imperial Airways flying boats was waiting for him. He took the pilot's controls and took off, roaring over the *Empress of Britain* as she steamed into the Solent, dipped low in salute, then handed over the controls to the pilot. Afterward he returned to Hamble in a speedboat and flew in his own machine to Hendon. He was speaking at a charity dinner in London that evening, but he sent a message to say that "I have been unavoidably delayed in the country, but I would ask that the dinner should proceed and I will join you in about half an hour."[12]

It later turned out that the unavoidable delay was caused by his touching down at Walton Heath Golf Club in Surrey so that he could play in a club competition.

In his youth, the prince was a keen steeplechaser. But in 1924, he fell at the first fence in a point-to-point and knocked himself out, ending up in bed for a month and causing Prime Minister Ramsay MacDonald to write from 10 Downing Street, urging him to be more careful. MacDonald's letter was followed by a less polite one from the king. "You have shown great courage & horsemanship which everyone appreciates," he told his son, "but the time has come when I must ask you to give up riding in the future in steeple chases & point to point races."[13]

The prince continued to hunt, but golf took the place of competitive riding. He had become captain of the Royal and Ancient Golf Club in 1922 with a fifteen handicap, and over the next few years, he accepted the captaincy of the Royal Mid-Surrey at Richmond and the Royal St. George's at Sandwich. He took lessons from professionals, including open champion Ted Ray, and in 1933 he reached the final of a parliamentary handicap tournament, being beaten after he lost his ball at the first hole in the final. When he came to the throne in 1936, headlines in the foreign press announced that "Golf Is Favourite Sport of Ruler."[14]

The prince's enthusiasm helped to position the sport in the pantheon of country-house pastimes. Proximity to a golf course or, even better, a golf course of one's own was now a sought-after adjunct to country-house life. The property pages in the *Times* extolled the virtues of this country house or that, claiming it was "practically adjoining golf course," or "adjoining the links" or offered "excellent golf." Tadworth Court in Surrey was put on the market in 1925 as "a genuine Queen Anne mansion . . . 1½ miles from Walton Heath Golf Course." (In the event the purchaser didn't have much use for the golf course—it was Great Ormond Street Hospital, which used Tadworth as a retreat for children with respiratory difficulties.) Nine years later, East Burnham Park in Buckinghamshire excited interest when it was offered for sale, partly because Mendelssohn and Jenny Lind had stayed at the house, partly because of the wealth of rare plants and trees, due to the fact that Sir Harry Veitch, the horticulturalist, had lived there—but mainly because "golf courses near the estate are Burnham Beeches, a mile, Stoke Poges, two miles, Beaconsfield, three miles, and Denham, five miles."[15]

Even better than living next door to a golf course was having one of your own. In 1926 the motor manufacturer William Morris, Lord Nuffield, bought the club in Oxfordshire where he played and ran it as sole proprietor until his death nearly forty years later. He moved into rooms over the clubhouse and lived there until 1933 when he was able to buy Nuffield Place, an Oswald Milne country house next door to the links. The Rocks, a nineteenth-century Gothic castle at Marshfield in Gloucestershire, boasted its own private golf course. Springfield, Lord and Lady Londonderry's ten-bedroom hunting box in Rutland, a mile from the kennels of the Cottesmore Hunt, was equipped with a nine-hole golf course for those moments when riding to hounds with the Cottesmore palled. At Meikleour in Perthshire, Lord Lansdowne created a nine-hole course in the park after his menservants, who had traditionally been allowed to use Meiklour's bowling green beside the local village pub, smelled of beer while waiting dinner after games of bowls.

Owners as disparate as the Duke of Portland and Sir Philip Sassoon built nine-hole courses in their grounds. Weekends at Sassoon's Trent Park went with a swing: on one occasion the house party trooped out after lunch to watch an exhibition of trick shots by the great Australian golfer Joe Kirkwood. Afternoon tea was followed by flights over the grounds in Sassoon's private airplane; and dinner, by a firework display over the lake better than anything seen in London during the social season. Even then, the entertainment wasn't over: as the moon rose over the gardens, everyone assembled on the terrace to hear songs from the Austrian tenor Richard Tauber.

Perhaps the finest country-house golf course was the work of Viscount Castlerosse, the *Sunday Express* gossip columnist and eldest son of the 5th Earl of Kenmare. Castlerosse, described by his biographer as "the best golfer who ever played the game without a right elbow" (he was badly wounded in France during the First World War), was a legend in the golf clubs of Kent, Sussex, and Surrey, not least because of his erratic behavior and the fact that he insisted on being accompanied on a round by a servant carrying a jug of whisky and helped himself to a tumblerful at each tee. During a competition at Deal, he buried his ball in a bunker: the crowd that gathered to see how he would extricate it watched as he cried to the skies, "Oh God, come down and help me with this shot. And don't send Jesus. This is no job for a boy."[16]

Castlerosse's family seat, Kenmare House in County Kerry, had burned down in 1913, and instead of rebuilding the vast Victorian mansion, his father had converted a surviving Georgian stable block into a house. In the late 1930s, Castlerosse resolved to create a full-size golf course at the western end of the park at Kenmare, on a stunning site overlooking the lakes of Killarney. He enlisted the advice of Henry Longhurst, golfing correspondent at the *Sunday Times*; the golf course designer Sir Guy Campbell; and, having decided on a whim that each hole must be associated with a different flowering plant, William Macdonald Campbell, the new curator of the Royal Botanic Gardens at Kew. "I am determined to call on the paintbox of heaven and draw a panorama of 150 acres in massed colours," said Castlerosse. "The thing is to be as loud and vulgar as God will let you . . . I am having three banks of one acre each of wild native flowers, then an Australian bank and also a New Zealand bank."[17]

The Kenmare course, one of the loveliest in the world, was opened with a blessing from the Bishop of Kerry in October 1939. Along with the banks of flowers and lake views from every green, Castlerosse hit on a plan to do away with the need for a servant to follow him with a jug. He set up a series of locked huts at strategic points around the course, each containing a bottle of whisky.

15

IN WHICH WE SERVE

A ny country house, *every* country house, relied for its smooth
running on a plentiful supply of cheap labor. Without servants,
who would cook and clean and wait at table? Who would make up the
fires and run the baths and raise the children? Who would answer the
bell when one rang? "No one will deny that servants are a necessity in
every home," wrote one commentator in 1906.[1]

So when in the years after 1918 the domestic service market
seemed poised on the edge of collapse, it sent a shiver through the
servant-keeping classes. The reasons for the crisis were many: women,
who made up the vast majority of indoor servants, found they enjoyed
the taste of freedom that war work had given them and were reluctant
to return to a rigidly controlled environment where their evenings,
and even their identities, weren't their own. Working-class women
had acquired a "restless desire for independence, which is a legacy
of the war," said the *Daily Mail*.[2] The rise of popular education widened their horizons. The high casualty rate among servicemen gave
them alternative job opportunities. And the social stigma, especially
among their peers, was becoming a powerful disincentive to service.
"I have suffered untold misery by the name 'only a servant,'" a parlor
maid reported to a government inquiry into the supply of domestic
servants. "Invitations start out, 'Be sure and don't let it be known you

are a domestic. We shouldn't like our friends to mix with servants.' It is the snobbery of our own class."[3]

The shortage of servants was serious enough in 1918 for the government to act—or at least, to set up a committee of inquiry. Weeks after the Armistice was declared, the Ministry of Reconstruction invited a Women's Advisory Committee to look into the problem. Their report, presented the following spring, highlighted a lack of training, a lack of status, and wide variation in pay and conditions.

Some of the committee's proposed solutions were quite innocuous: dispensing with caps, for example, and persuading employers not to call servants by their Christian names. This denial of identity was a common cause for complaint among female servants. Edith Lockwood's mistress called her Annie because she already had a friend called Edith. Gordon Grimmett went for a job as a second footman to be told by his employer, "If you come to me you'll be James, all my second footmen are called James, just as all my first footmen are called William."[4] When Florence David went into service as a kitchen maid, her employers called her Mary because that's what they called all their maids. They found it easier that way.

Other of the committee's proposals were more radical. It advocated "a substantial reduction of the length of the servant's working day, definite time allowances for meals and outings, the latter to comprise a half-day every Sunday, and one afternoon and evening each week; in addition, the provision of from two to 2½ hours free time each day, with the right to remain in or leave the house; also a fortnight's holiday in a year with board wages."[5]

The committee drew up a scale of weekly wages for different servants, ranging from twenty-five shillings a week with food for cook-housekeepers, down to a minimum of six shillings and sixpence for unskilled fourteen-year-olds. (Male servants didn't figure in this: the Women's Advisory Committee thought it wouldn't be appropriate to comment.) There were even suggestions that domestic staff should be paid overtime and eventually provided with a trade union of their own. This was too much for one committee member. The Marchioness of Londonderry, who hadn't actually attended any meetings, refused to sign sections of the report, explaining that "I regard any possibility of the introduction into the conditions of domestic service of the type of relations now obtainable between employers and workers in industrial life as extremely undesirable and liable to react in a disastrous manner on the whole foundation of home life."[6]

The irony was that while it was certainly true the supply of domestic servants was declining—had been declining since the beginning of the century, in fact—the Marchioness of Londonderry really didn't have very much to worry about. "The mistress of a small household will not be able to compete at all in the servant market" a correspondent to the *Times* pointed out in response to the Women's Advisory Committee's report. But "the position of the big house of the future will be better than it ever was."[7] The shortage of servants was making itself felt, not in the Londonderrys' Park Lane townhouse or in one of their four country seats, but in the middle-class suburban homes of bank managers and shopkeepers, doctors and lawyers. Even they would soon find temporary respite from the awful prospect of doing their own housework, when the Depression of the late 1920s drove women back into domestic service.

The main problem for servants with households that kept fewer staff was simple: there was more work to do. However, there was also a question of status. In 1924 Lucy McLelland, who was born with the century, went to the Duke of Rutland at Belvoir Castle as first kitchen maid. It was her seventh job since going into service at the age of sixteen. She quickly worked her way up to cook, with four girls under her and a total indoor staff of twenty or more.

Belvoir was a community of its own. When the Duke of Rutland invited the estate workers to a screening of a Charlie Chaplin film as a treat one Christmas, there were nearly a hundred people present. Lucy started walking out with the groom of chambers, an Ulsterman twenty years her senior, and in 1926 they married and took a place as cook and butler with the novelist Agatha Christie, then living in Sunningdale with her first husband, Archie. After working with a big staff at Belvoir, the Christies' house, Styles, was in Lucy's words, "a come down."[8] Apart from the McLellands there was a betweenmaid;

a nursemaid, who didn't do anything but look after the Christies' seven-year-old, Rosalind; and a gardener, whose wife was sometimes brought in to help. Agatha was fond of entertaining, "and poor me, I used to have to do the cooking and my own washing up," Lucy remembered.[9] Her husband had to wait at table and help her with clearing up afterward, and he had to clean and polish the dining room. They only stayed for four months.*

In contrast, a big country house with plenty of staff maintained strict lines of demarcation. At Belvoir, although Lucy ran the kitchen, with four kitchen maids under her, there were also two still-room maids who did the baking (the still room being a functional room where drinks and jams were made). "The kitchen never did toast. Never made no scones, no cakes, nothing of that. Tea, coffee—all came from the stillroom."[10] Charles Deane, who was underbutler to the 2nd Viscount Astor from 1922 to 1925, remembered that the division of labor was just as clear-cut at Cliveden. "Everything was separate," he said. "Nobody interfered. You couldn't dare to do other people's jobs as they would say, 'What the hell are you doing?' if you did something without asking."[11]

Cliveden, a palatial Italianate mansion overlooking the Thames, is a good example of how the bigger and wealthier country houses maintained a staff of Victorian proportions throughout the 1920s and 1930s.[12] It was designed in 1850–1851 by Sir Charles Barry, architect of the Houses of Parliament, for the Duke of Sutherland, after a previous house on the site had been destroyed by fire only a few months after Sutherland bought it. By the First World War, it belonged to the 2nd Viscount Astor, whose father William "Walled-Off" Astor presented it to him in 1906, a wedding present on his marriage to the wealthy Virginian divorcée Nancy Shaw.

The Astors' wealth, largely unconnected with land and so impervious to the agricultural depressions of the 1920s, meant that they were able to hold court at Cliveden in a style unaffected by the

---

* The Christies didn't stay much longer. Archie left his wife for another woman at the end of the year, at which Agatha famously disappeared, being found in a Harrogate hotel eleven days later.

vicissitudes and fluctuations of the market. They also owned a town-house, 4 St. James's Square, where they lived from Monday to Friday when Parliament was in session. Astor was MP for Plymouth until 1919, when his father's death sent him to the Lords as the 2nd Viscount Astor, and Nancy was elected in his stead, becoming the first woman to take her seat in the mother of parliaments.* The couple also had a fourteen-bedroom "cottage" at Sandwich in Kent, a house in Plymouth and Tarbert, and a shooting and fishing lodge on the Isle of Jura in the Hebrides.

The Astors used all five houses at different points during the year, but 4 St. James's Square and Cliveden were their main residences, with most of the domestic staff traveling back and forth between them—London during the week, the country at weekends. Lady Astor had what she called her town style and her country style. Town style at St. James's Square, where the majority of guests came from politics, was formal, with liveried footmen waiting at dinner and a reception for as many as a thousand people afterward. It was a big house.† The Astors were ardent teetotalers, and although there was usually wine with dinner, the receptions were sometimes rather dry affairs.

Country style weekends at Cliveden were more relaxed. The atmosphere was that of a grand hotel, with folk coming and going and gathering in small groups. (When the house actually became a grand hotel in the 1980s, there was remarkably little to do by way of conversion.) Visitors were a mixed but illustrious bag: writers like George Bernard Shaw and Sean O'Casey; fellow aristocrats like the Marquess of Lothian who, like Nancy Astor, was a committed Christian Scientist; visiting European royalty, friends from America, and film stars. Charlie Chaplin was a regular guest, as he seems to have been at most country houses between the wars. So was Lawrence of Arabia, by then known as Aircraftsman T. E. Shaw. On one occasion, Lawrence and Nancy

---

* But not the first woman to be elected. That honor went to Constance Gore-Booth, who as Constance Markiewicz was returned for Dublin St. Patrick's in the 1918 general election but who along with other Sinn Fein MPs refused to take her seat.

† The St. James's Square mansion is now the Naval and Military Club, better known as the In and Out.

suddenly leaped up from the Cliveden drawing room and ran outside. Nancy climbed on the back of Lawrence's Brough Superior, and the pair roared off down the drive in a cloud of dust. A few minutes later they were skidding back. "We did a hundred miles an hour," shrieked Nancy. Her husband turned and walked away, speechless with rage.

Sir Charles Barry's Cliveden was modified first for the 1st Duke of Westminster, who bought the house from the 3rd Duke of Sutherland, his brother-in-law, in 1869; and then again by the 1st Viscount Astor after he bought it from Westminster in 1893. By the time Astor handed it over to his son and daughter-in-law in 1906, Barry's Cliveden, although barely fifty years old, had acquired a clock tower and a *porte cochère*, and undergone some radical remodeling and redecoration. The house consisted of a main block nine bays wide, connected by curving corridors to flanking pavilions. This central section was dominated by a huge living hall, created for the 1st Viscount Astor by F. L. Pearson out of Sir Charles Barry's hall, morning room, and library. Next door there was the "French" dining room, so-called because the 1st Viscount had it fitted with Rococo paneling brought from the chateau of Asnières near Paris. A library and a drawing room completed the set of quasi-public rooms. Lord Astor's study and Lady Astor's boudoir were also on the ground floor. The main bedrooms above, for the family and important guests, were mostly named for flowers: the Rose, the Orange Flower, the Snowdrop, the Lavender. There were day and night nurseries on the top floor: by 1928, when the house was in its heyday, the Astors had five children aged from twenty-one to nine. Robert Gould Shaw, Nancy's troubled son by her first marriage, also put in occasional appearances.

The east wing contained guest rooms: when the house was full, there were as many as forty people staying at a time. The domestic offices and staff bedrooms were in the west wing, the basement of which housed the kitchens; the servants' hall; the china room and wine cellar; the butler's pantry, with its teak sinks for washing the silver; and the silver safe. There was an underground passage that connected the service wing to the guest wing, so that servants could come and go about their business without being observed by guests or family. Rosina Harrison, who came to the Astors in 1928 as lady's maid to their eighteen-year-old daughter, Phyllis, noticed that there were tramlines in the main kitchen passage, where food used to be wheeled along from the kitchen to a service lift. "This practice had stopped before I joined," she wrote, "and the food was carried by the odd men on butlers' trays to the lifts and transferred to the large hot-plate in the serving room next to the dining room."[13]

Cliveden was designed to be run by a small army of servants, and the Astors employed thirty-three staff in the 1920s: a butler, an underbutler, and three footmen; a valet for the viscount and two lady's maids for his wife and daughter; a housekeeper, four housemaids, two still-room maids, and two women who came in daily but lived out; a chef, three kitchen maids, a scullery maid, and another daily maid who helped in the kitchens; four laundry maids; two odd men and a hall boy; and a telephonist, a house carpenter, and a night watchman. And that was just the indoor staff. There were another seventy-odd estate workers, everything from gardeners and gamekeepers to electricians, a boatman, and a part-time clock winder.

The size of this army of labor fluctuated according to circumstance. When the children were young, for example, they were looked after by a nanny, Miss Gibbons, who ruled the day and night nurseries with a nursery maid to wait on her; there was also a succession of French or German governesses for the older children. The number of still-room maids, who baked the bread and cakes and made the breakfasts, had gone down from two to one by the later 1930s. There was a high turnover of staff, partly because Nancy Astor was a demanding employer, sometimes both mean and mean-spirited, but mainly because it was the nature of the domestic employment market for servants to move on, either to marry or to find a better place. And by the end of the 1930s, even big, prestigious country houses like Cliveden were starting to feel the winds of social change blowing through their servants' halls. Noel Wiseman, who went to the Astors as assistant estate agent in 1934, remembered that a younger generation was less prepared to accept the terms and conditions of employment that their elders had taken for granted:

It was alright when you got these older people who were willing to work these long hours, and happy in doing so, but once we'd lost that type and come out of that era, it was very difficult indeed to get people to stop.[14]

Theoretically, the responsibility for the management of the Astors' staff lay with their estate agent, H. J. Forster Smith. But as far as the indoor servants were concerned, they answered to one man, the Astors' formidable butler Edwin Lee, who had joined the staff as a footman in 1912 and worked his way up to the top job. Always immaculate, Lee was Lee or Mr. Lee to the family, and Sir to the other members of staff. "People have met him and thought it was Lord Astor," remembered one of his colleagues. "He acted like it."[15] He was a constant presence at Cliveden and the St. James's Square house, traveling between the two in a private car, separate from the other servants, who piled into a van. It was Lee who interviewed prospective staff, although Nancy Astor also gave them a perfunctory once-over; Lee who maintained discipline below stairs. When Nancy's son Bobby Shaw was jailed for homosexual offenses in 1931, Lee assembled the entire indoor staff in the servants' hall and explained in very general terms what had happened. Then he said, "After you leave the servants' hall no one will speak about the matter. Anyone heard or suspected of doing so in or out of the house will be instantly dismissed."[16]

Lee was the public face of the domestic machine, the primary point of contact with the family and their guests, greeting visitors during the day in a black alpaca jacket and bow tie, choreographing dinners in a dress livery of navy blue tailcoat, black knee breeches and stockings, and black pumps with gold buckles. And the Astors' dinners needed some choreography: at a dinner party and reception given in February 1922 to meet ex–prime minister Arthur Balfour, forty sat down at a table decorated with orange tulips in gilt plate. The diners included the current prime minister David Lloyd George, Winston and Clementine Churchill, the Duke and Duchess of Devonshire, the Marquess and Marchioness of Londonderry, the artist John Singer

Sargent, and a smattering of fashionable intellectuals. Eight hundred and fifty people came to the reception that followed.

Lee always supervised the table, ensuring that each diner was being attended to by the footmen, who were liveried in brown jackets, striped waistcoats, breeches, and white stockings and gloves. Until after the First World War, they also had powdered hair, an effect that they achieved with flour sent up from the kitchen. "It was not resented by the men even though it made the top of your head feel as if it was in plaster," Lee recalled.[17] He served the wines and brought in the port and liqueurs after dinner. As a teetotaler, Viscount Astor took no interest in the wines, leaving that side of things entirely to his butler. "It's as well to limit the choice of liqueurs," Lee believed, "otherwise if you leave it to personal preference, you can be bobbing backwards and forwards all the time."[18] He usually provided brandy, crème de menthe, and kümmel.

Lee was a hard master. On one occasion a footman dropped a plate of savories as he was about to take them into the dining room. Although the man pleaded afterward that the plate was scalding hot, Lee was not sympathetic: "You're hired to hold it and hold it you will in future, even if it burns you to the bone . . . Fingers heal, food doesn't."[19]

When the Astors held big receptions at St. James's Square, it was Lee who went round to the Vine Street police station to ask for police help in controlling the traffic, and Lee and his footmen who received guests and took their coats and cloaks. He didn't personally announce the guests at these receptions, feeling the business required a professional announcer; he usually engaged a Mr. Batley, who was noted for his clear voice and a delivery that "could make even a plain Mr and Mrs sound important."[20]

The cleaning was supervised by the Cliveden housekeeper, Mrs. Ford, who was paid forty-five pounds a year when she started with the Astors in 1936, plus a weekly allowance of half a crown for washing money, which in theory was to be spent on the regular laundering of aprons and other work-related clothes, and two shillings for beer money. She had two weeks' holiday a year and occasional weekends. Because she didn't travel up to London during the week like most of the other indoor servants, weekends were her busiest time. A day started at about eight thirty, after the servants' breakfast at eight, when she would patrol to make sure that the housemaids were working on the downstairs rooms. They started work early, at five in the 1920s and five thirty in the 1930s, since they had to be finished polishing, dusting, and laying fires by the time that guests started to surface. Then they would move upstairs to do the bedrooms. Interviewed in 1975, Mrs. Ford remembered some of her other duties:

> I had all the linen to see to, well, see that everything in the house, to start with, was alright, that all the work was done, that the rooms were ready for the visitors and that kind of thing. Then I had all the marmalades and jams and that to make while I was there . . . I had to do enough for Cliveden for weekend visitors and also the London house as well, and jam making was a big job in the summer [with] fruit from the garden, and then bottling as well.[21]

Not surprisingly, considering the size and complexity of its domestic staff, Cliveden maintained the old Victorian hierarchies. Edwin Lee and Mrs. Ford were the uppermost of the upper servants. Next in the pecking order, and still classed among the upper servants, were Arthur Bushell, Lord Astor's valet, and Rosina Harrison, Lady Astor's personal maid.

Bushell was the below stairs clown. Valets were traditionally regarded with mistrust by other staff, as were lady's maids, and for the same reason: they had privileged access to their employer and were suspected of reporting to them on inappropriate behavior in the servants' hall. At Cliveden, it was Bushell who was responsible for most of the inappropriate behavior, mimicking the Astors' guests, up to and including Queen Mary and George V, and often dressing up in drag to entertain the other servants. Like some medieval court jester, he pushed things to the limit and sometimes beyond. After the Astor children were invited to an evening party in the servants' hall and Bushell dressed up as a woman and told some rather adult jokes, their nanny told him she found his behavior left much to be desired. "Oh, Miss Gibbons," he replied, "what did it leave you desiring?"[22] Nor did he confine his antics to the servants. One Christmas he went to the Cliveden fancy dress dance as the music hall comedienne Nellie Wallace, and as he passed Nancy Astor, he lifted up his skirt to show green knickers emblazoned with a union jack and asked, "How do you like my greens, my lady?" "Arthur," she replied, "you're disgusting."[23]

Rose, who had been lady's maid to Lady Cranborne in London and Dorset before being poached by the Astors with an offer of sixty pounds a year to look after eighteen-year-old Phyllis Astor, soon moved up to acting as lady's maid to her mother and stayed with Nancy Astor until the latter's death in 1964.

As lady's maid, Rose's day was inextricably bound up with her mistress's activities. The day began at seven thirty when she went down to Nancy's dressing room to collect her clothes from the night before, for pressing later. She ate her breakfast at eight, and half an hour later took breakfast to Nancy and ran her a cold bath. At nine Nancy demanded solitude while she read her Bible lesson, after which she generally spent an hour or two with secretaries, correspondence, and phone calls. Then she changed for her morning exercise—squash, tennis, or golf—and again for lunch, for whatever she was doing in the afternoon, and for dinner. She usually got through five sets of clothes in a typical day:

> This required from me a deal of organizing, pressing, cleaning and repairing. Also there were perpetual messages to be run or delivered, shopping to be done either on my own or with her ladyship, and dressmaking or copying. I made many of her ladyship's things.[24]

A lady's maid led a relatively privileged life, in spite of being at someone else's beck and call round the clock. Rose had a big, comfortable bedroom of her own, well decorated and furnished with two easy chairs, a couch, and two wardrobes. She didn't have to wear a uniform. And she had opportunities to travel that most women of her generation and class could only dream of, with annual visits to Switzerland and the French Riviera and trips farther afield, to Bermuda, New York, and Istanbul. Once, in 1936, when Lord and Lady Astor arrived in Yugoslavia as guests of Queen Marie, widow of the assassinated King Alexander I, Rose and Arthur Bushell were provided with a chauffeur-driven limousine of their own to take them to their destination, a palace outside Belgrade. "Well, Rose, my queen, this is better than the bloody milk float," said Arthur.[25]

The downside of this privileged existence was having to deal with Nancy Astor's moods. By Rose's own account, her mistress was capricious, peremptory, and occasionally violent. During one tantrum, she tried to kick her maid. "Whenever I am hurtful, I mean it," she told her on another occasion, "and I enjoy it."[26]

The secret, as Rose found out, was to stand up to her. After one particularly bad spat, Nancy announced that the difference between them was "that I was born to command and have learned through experience how to deal with people." "The difference between us, my lady," countered Rose, "is that you have money. Money is power, and people respect money and power so they respect you for having it."[27] Their shouting matches became a byword at Cliveden: Lord Astor used to go his dressing room to listen in through the wall and have a good laugh, Rose found out later. And with the arguments came a closeness, an intimacy of sorts. When Nancy Astor's sister Phyllis Brand died of pneumonia in 1937, Nancy was distraught. But it wasn't her family she turned to for support. Rose remembered that the Brands' butler rushed in to her and said, "Go to Lady Astor. She needs you." She found her mistress screaming and crying and praying. "I took her in my arms and comforted her as best I could."[28]

IT IS ALWAYS RISKY TO generalize about domestic service, even at the grandest of houses. At Cliveden, the kitchens were controlled by the Astors' white-jacketed French chef, Monsieur Gilbert, who consulted closely with his mistress over the meals. The Duchess of Buccleuch at Boughton House in Northamptonshire left the ordering of the food and the menus entirely to her cook, who lived a strangely separate life, hardly ever coming out of the kitchen and eating alone in her own sitting room, served by the kitchen maids. At Croome Court in Worcestershire, the Earl and Countess of Coventry, who were finding it difficult to make ends meet, kept a cook-housekeeper, Winnie Sapsford, a thin, bird-like spinster in her late forties who was always referred to as Mrs. Sapsford. She wasn't particularly able: meals in the steward's room at Croome typically began with the butler, Mr. Latter, looking at his plate and asking sadly, "Winnie, Winnie, what have you done to this?"[29]

There were constants, however. At most big houses, the upper servants—butler, housekeeper, valet, and lady's maid—signaled their status by eating the main meal of the day apart from the other staff. In some households, the upper servants ate their meals in a separate room entirely, the stewards' room perhaps, while the cook and her staff ate in the kitchens, the nanny was waited on in the nursery by the hall boy, and the governess ate in her own room or in the schoolroom. Oliver Messel's sister Anne recalled that when she went to Birr Castle as the new Countess of Rosse in 1935, there were six different lunches in six different rooms every day. At Cliveden there were two tables in the servants' hall, the upper table and the second table. Lee presided over the one, and his immediate subordinate, Charles Dean the underbutler, looked after the other.

Dean was underbutler at Cliveden from 1922 until 1925, when he left to become butler to Lady Astor's niece Alice and her new husband, the divorced Russian émigré Sergei Obolensky. ("Prince Obolensky was a near-penniless Russian exile, so Alice Astor's millions came in useful," observed Rose waspishly.[30]) Dean described his duties at Cliveden:

My first job was getting up at 6.30 to 7.00 a.m. If there was a weekend party . . . it was my job to get everything ready to go up to the dining room as soon as the footman came along to lay the table [for lunch]. It was the footman's job to lay the table but my job to see that everything they wanted was there, like silver and things. It was my job to lay the dining room table for dinner; that was

nothing to do with the footman or the butler, it was the underbutler's job. When there was a big crowd naturally other people
helped you but in general it was your job to get everything ready
so that they did not have to run around looking for a few knives or
forks or salt or pepper or what have you. The butler would inspect
everything . . .[31]

And, Dean added, Lee would invariably move a few things just to
make a point, before putting them back exactly where they were.

The Astors acquired their servants through informal word-of-
mouth recruitment and also through the conventional London agen-
cies that specialized in domestic servants. Although Rose's move came
about after a casual conversation while on a visit to Cliveden with
her mistress Lady Cranborne, she had found the job with the Cran-
bornes through Masseys of Baker Street, established in 1845 and one
of the best known of all servants' registries, along with Mrs. Hunt of
Marylebone. There was also a more shadowy and entirely informal
recruitment network, generally run by tradespeople. Lucy MacLel-
land found her first post through Masseys, but as she moved up the
career ladder, she used to find her jobs "through the desk" at Jackson's of Piccadilly, the famous teahouse and grocery store. She got to
know the staff at Jackson's on regular visits to collect coffee from the
shop; when a chef or a cook came in and asked if the staff knew anyone looking for a kitchen job, they might recommend her. She had a
similar arrangement at Fortnum & Mason.

Charles Dean found his job as underbutler with the Astors
through the Mayfair Servants' Agency in North Audley Street, an
agency that specialized in butlers, valets, and footmen and that was
used regularly by the Astors (or more accurately, by Edwin Lee, who
was in charge of recruiting the male servants). Their window was full
of cards showing different jobs, and men servants in the area would
keep an eye on that window even if they weren't looking for a change
of job. "It kept you in touch with the market price for men servants,"
said Gordon Grimmett, who joined the Astor household as second
footman in the early 1920s. Grimmett was seen initially by Lee and

then interviewed by Lady Astor, if their brief conversation can be described as such:

> "He looks a big strong boy, Lee. Where is your home, Gordon, and have you a mother and father?"
>
> "I have a mother and father and my home is in Ascot in Berkshire, your ladyship," I replied.
>
> "Well now, isn't that nice. We have a country house at Cliveden, near Taplow in Buckinghamshire. You will be able to go home to your parents regularly." Then she sped towards the door.
>
> "How soon can you join us? We want you in one week's time. Good-bye, I must fly to the House of Commons." And out she went.[32]

Lee was left to tell Grimmett his terms and conditions of employment—thirty-two pounds a year with half a crown for beer and laundry money—and to arrange for him to be measured for suits and livery at the Astors' Mayfair tailors.[*]

Like the butler, footmen were public servants, operating at the interface between family, guests, and staff. They must look athletic— the Portlands made the Welbeck Abbey footmen do calisthenics to stay trim—and they were often matched for height, although this didn't happen at Cliveden, because Lee harbored a sad memory of once being turned down for a job because "they wanted to match one of their footmen and I was an inch and a half too short."[33] At Flete in Devon, the Mildmays' butler refused to have footmen who were taller than him. Fortunately, he was six foot three, so new footmen had to be taller than six foot and not more than six foot two. One of their odder duties at Flete was to remove the electric lamps from the tables every morning and bring them in again in the evening, a relic of the time when oil lamps were taken down to the lamp room to be trimmed and filled each day. "I can see them now," recalled Lord

---

[*] These tailors often cheated their servant-keeping clients, if Grimmett is to be believed. They charged the Astors for a pair of long woolen pants to go under his livery trousers and quietly offered him a glass of whisky not to take them.

Mildmay's daughter Helen, "groping about under the big table in the library on their hands and knees, plugging in these lamps."[34]

At Cliveden, there were three footmen, occasionally four. They had their own room in the basement of the west wing, near the servants' hall. The footmen greeted guests and served drinks before dinner and waited at table; they answered the bell and carried and fetched as needed. They may have acted as valets to the older Astor boys, who didn't have valets of their own, and they were required to valet visitors who came without their own servants.

The heavier work of the household was done by the two odd men who, as their title suggests, did odd jobs about the place, anything that wasn't the specific duty of another servant, from carrying luggage up and down to bedrooms and heavy trays from the kitchen to the serving room, to cleaning below stairs and helping out behind the scenes at receptions. The odd man was someone who hadn't quite made the grade and never would. "Some of them were not as other men are," wrote Rose Harrison. "By that I mean they were often lacking in brain power and had little ambition . . . Their interests were mostly limited to beer and baccy. I never knew one who was married."[35] Lee used to say he could always recognize an odd man by the way he walked, as though he were carrying a heavy burden.

THE NETWORK OF SUPPORT THAT enabled the Astors to live as they did extended far beyond the basements and corridors of Cliveden. There was Ann Kindersley, variously described as the controller and Viscount Astor's head secretary. There were seven more secretaries, three accountants, and resident housekeepers at the Astors' houses in Plymouth and Sandwich.

Five chauffeurs maintained their cars and drove them from place to place: one each for Lord and Lady Astor, and neither allowed to encroach on the other's duties; a horse-box driver, and two driver-mechanics, who also looked after the mowers. A married couple, Mr. and Mrs. MacIntyre, looked after the Astors' lodge up on the Isle of Jura. On the Cliveden estate itself, there were farm managers and cowmen, grooms both for the horses that the Astor family rode recreationally and for Viscount Astor's 450-acre stud farm; and of course a platoon of gardeners, more than twenty of them. It was their job to maintain the kitchen gardens and greenhouses and the breathtaking Thames-side pleasure grounds with their miles of walks and woodland rides.

One of the workers who crossed the divide between indoors and outdoors was Nancy Astor's decorator, whose job it was to provide and arrange the flowers at Cliveden and St. James's Square. Frank Copcutt came to Cliveden as a gardener in 1928 from the Rothchilds' Waddesdon Manor, thirty miles north, and worked initially in the greenhouses until Nancy's existing decorator, George, moved on and he got the place. (For more than a year afterward Nancy Astor called him George, and he didn't dare to correct her.) His day started at 7:00 a.m. when he walked up to the house to water, replace, and arrange the flowers downstairs and then, when guests came downstairs, in the bedrooms. The rest of the morning was spent in the greenhouses, before he returned to the house to do the lunch flowers. The process was repeated in the evening, when he would put out fresh flowers on the dining-room table. If there was a party or a reception, the procedure was more complicated:

> The first thing to be thought about when decorating for a party [Copcutt said] was the general area: the hall, the staircase and the ballroom. These were large areas and could be set off with shrubs, forsythia, almonds, cherries, laburnum and wisteria, things of that kind. Standard fuchsias and standard geraniums were also useful and colourful. Planted around these would be primroses, polyanthus, forget-me-nots, the smaller border plants. These would be forced in the greenhouse. If I could get her ladyship marigolds at Christmas-time she was more pleased than if they'd been orchids. Medium-sized flowers we put in "coffins," containers which are miniatures of the real thing. They were packed in with clay and overlaid with moss.[36]

Copcutt liked to use orange trees as decoration, although it was difficult to have them in blossom and in fruit at the same time. He hit on a simple solution—wire the oranges to the branches. No one noticed, not even Lord Astor.

THE DOMESTIC STAFF AT CLIVEDEN seem to have been quite content with their lot, although most of the recollections of below-stairs life with the Astors come from the upper servants, who carved out careers at Cliveden and came to identify strongly with their employers and their employers' values. Not much is known about the attitudes of the more lowly members of the team, the kitchen maids and scullery maids and odd men. But there is no doubt that the Astors were good employers. They did their best to create a model estate community at Cliveden between the wars, with a clubhouse that served alcohol, in spite of their commitment to teetotalism, and football and cricket teams for the staff. Indoor and outdoor servants had the use of a bowling alley and a gymnasium, and there were staff dances every two weeks. "There would be a staff sports day," remembered Tom Spuggard, whose father was a woodman on the estate, "and they would have the Maidenhead town band up here, playing all the afternoon . . . And Lord and Lady Astor were amongst it enjoying it, really enjoying it."[37]

The paternalism is hard to ignore and difficult to swallow today, but in the hard Depression years of the late 1920s and 1930s there were plenty who would gladly have swapped places with Edwin Lee and Rose Harrison and the rest. The view from the country house, even the country-house basement, was still a good deal more attractive than the view from the dole queue.

16

THE POLITICAL HOUSE

There are country houses that earn a place in political history as discreet venues for the great and the good to decide the fate of nations over port or on the grouse moor. There are country houses whose fame rests on the distinguished political reputation of their owner—Chartwell and Churchill, or Hughenden and Disraeli. And there are houses whose owners, while never big players in the Great Game, earn a place in the pantheon as ideological extremists.

Wallington Hall in Northumberland belongs in this last camp. Visitors to Wallington in the 1930s quickly realized that its owner was not a conventional member of the landed classes. On one gatepost was the royal cipher, a reminder that Sir Charles Trevelyan, Bt., was Lord Lieutenant of Northumberland and, as such, the king's personal representative in the county.

The other gatepost was emblazoned with a hammer and sickle.

The thirteen-thousand-acre Wallington estate had been in the Trevelyan family since an ancestor's advantageous marriage in the eighteenth century. When Sir Charles inherited, in 1928, he was in his late fifties and a serving Labour MP with a reputation for radicalism and experience as a minister for education in Ramsay MacDonald's short-lived minority government of 1924. He was known for his pro-Soviet sympathies, and his socialism had earned him the slightly uncertain praise of the British left and accusations of class betrayal by his fellow landed gentry, led by his own father.

Sir Charles and his wife, Lady Molly, took possession of Wallington in 1928, and they found the place in a poor state, after more than a decade of neglect. But contrary to the conventional country-house narrative of crisis and decline, this neglect was not the result of poverty. The Trevelyans were really very rich. It was because Sir Charles's elderly father had combined an inability to manage the estate efficiently with a determination that his dangerously radical son should have nothing to do with the running of it as long as he was alive.

When the 2nd Baronet died, at the age of ninety, Sir Charles and Lady Molly immediately embarked on a huge program of repairs. They modernized dilapidated estate cottages, improved farms, mended outbuildings and restored Wallington Hall itself, an attractive house of the seventeenth and eighteenth centuries with a Victorian central hall that was filled with vast Pre-Raphaelite murals by William Bell Scott. "Builders, electricians, water engineers and plumbers possess our house," Sir Charles told tenants who had gathered at the Hall in the spring of 1929, and in the midst of the renovation work, to celebrate the Trevelyans' silver wedding anniversary.[1]

This was no ordinary tenants' ball, held to provide an opportunity for loyal addresses and the tugging of forelocks; and the building works at Wallington were not, or at least not solely, for the benefit of the family. If the tenants didn't know that already, Sir Charles spelled it out for them:

> You are all aware that I am no friend of the system which by pure chance makes me rich and a thousand others poor for life . . . I want you to know that I regard myself not as the owner of Wallington and the people of Wallington, but as a trustee of property which under wiser and humaner laws would belong to the community . . . I want you to feel that to come and see Wallington is on your part not an intrusion but a right . . . We would like to think that the pictures, the china, the books, the woods, the garden, are possessions for all the people round here to cherish or to use.[2]

A POLITICAL RALLY HELD AT WALLINGTON IN 1933. (Copyright: National Trust/Trustees of the Trevelyan family)

He ended by announcing that he intended to pay generous child allowances to every family on the estate.

That summer, the Trevelyans opened Wallington to visitors, free of charge, every weekend and on public holidays. The stables were turned into a youth hostel: Sir Charles's younger brother, the historian G. M. Trevelyan, was first president of the Youth Hostels Association. Adult education classes were held in the house; the People's Theatre of Newcastle was invited to regard Wallington as its second home.

Trevelyan's politics didn't pass without remark. After he lost his parliamentary seat in the 1931 election, the Lord Lieutenant's flag was stolen from its flagpole in the grounds, and statues in front of the house were tarred and feathered by midnight raiders who were thought to have driven up from Newcastle, although it was never clear exactly what these raiders were protesting about. All the time Sir Charles pushed for new ways to reconcile his politics with his pedigree. "I still am not nearly content with the use we make of Wallington," he told Molly in 1934. "I want to try more definitely to make it a resort for socialist and international minded people."[3]

In the summer of 1936 he found a solution. At a garden party for estate workers and their families that August, he announced that he was bequeathing Wallington to the National Trust, lock, stock, and barrel—the house, its contents, and thirteen thousand acres of farms and moorland.

His motives were mixed. He didn't believe in private ownership of land, and he wanted to ensure that Wallington would always be available to the community and the wider public. He also acknowledged that the system of taxation, which he supported, made the continued existence in its traditional form of the country house difficult, if not impossible. And with commendable honesty, he confessed that he wanted a way in which the Trevelyans could maintain their connection with Wallington: under the terms of the bequest to the National Trust, his wife, and then their children, would continue to live there as tenants, a desire that "will be understood by many who have no sympathy with my Socialism."[4]

Trevelyan's decision met with widespread approval. Other answers to the country-house problem were being aired at the time. In France, La Demeure Historique had pioneered a public-benefit-for-public-funds option by which owners of historic houses opened their homes to the public in return for state grants toward their upkeep; and closer to home, the Marquess of Lothian, who was struggling to maintain his own ancestral seat, Blickling Hall in Norfolk, was busy advocating an annual grant from the state to the National Trust, enabling the Trust to buy endangered mansions and gardens and keep on the ex-owners as tenants. But Sir Charles's honesty appealed. As a good Socialist, said the *Times*, he wanted the people to get all the benefit of Wallington. "As a Trevelyan, he yields to a sadly unproletarian weakness for his family tradition."[5] With a stroke of the pen, he had made the best of both worlds.[*]

---

[*] Sir Charles Trevelyan was a visionary, but he was no saint. His refusal to consult with his eldest son over the disposal of Wallington led to disquiet in the family, as did his close relationship with some of his tenants (he fathered a child by one of them when he was in his seventies) and his habit of walking naked on the Northumberland moors.

ALTHOUGH IN THE LEAD-UP TO the First World War it was hard to find a member of the British government without a country estate and a house to go with it, after 1918, it seemed that the country house had less of a role to play in a more democratic world, where it was possible to climb to the top of the greasy pole without the validation of status, pedigree, and economic worth, which ownership of a landed estate brought with it. In 1922 Lord Curzon, with a string of country houses (one of which, Kedleston Hall in Derbyshire, had been in his family since the thirteenth century), was beaten to the job of prime minister by Andrew Bonar Law, who owned no country house at all and was born in New Brunswick, the son of a minister in the Free Church of Scotland.

But the country house continued to hold its own as a power base and, more important, as a congenial setting for the making of strategy and the breaking of political alliances. And still, despite the rise of the Independent Labour Party, the breakup of big estates, and the Depression, throughout the 1920s and 1930s the country house as a political salon enjoyed something of a renaissance. Leading the way here, as in so many things, was Sir Philip Sassoon at Port Lympne and Trent Park.

Sassoon had served as private secretary to Douglas Haig for most of the war, and in 1919 it was he who went to London to negotiate directly with Lloyd George over his boss's earldom, which the field marshal would only accept if it came with a hefty pension. It did, and Sassoon returned to Haig's G.H.Q. in France, as his friend Viscount Esher told him, "with the plumes of Talleyrand and Metternich flowing from your red hat."[6] His handling of the negotiations impressed Lloyd George, and the young man was careful to cultivate both the prime minister and, crucially, the prime minister's personal secretary and mistress, Frances Stevenson. "Philip Sassoon dropped in for a chat," wrote Stevenson in her diary in December 1919. "He has become very attentive lately."[7] And later that month, after Sassoon and Lloyd George had played golf together, she noted again how he singled her out. "He seems to be fabulously rich, but is clever also," she wrote, "and can be most amusing. But one of the worst gossips I have ever come across."[8]

In February 1920, after Sassoon had entertained Lloyd George and Frances Stevenson, this time at Trent Park, he was appointed as the prime minister's parliamentary private secretary (PPS). The move led to predictable sniping about Sassoon's Jewishness. The Fascist leader Oswald Mosley, whose anti-Semitism in the early 1920s was of the common or garden-variety British sort rather than the virulent race hate it would become in the 1930s, criticized Lloyd George's habit of retreating to Port Lympne to consider affairs of state, with a side-swipe at Sassoon's origins. "No longer are the abrasions of controversy to be soothed by a liberal application of precious ointment from the voluptuous Orient."⁹

In fact just *because* he remained an outsider, Sassoon was per-fectly placed to act as facilitator, hosting a gathering of international figures at Port Lympne or Trent Park; inviting the right combina-tion of statesmen, financiers, and industrialists to a discreet week-end house party; sometimes simply handing over one of his mansions to the prime minister for the day and leaving him to make his own arrangements. Mosley, who got on surprisingly well with Sassoon on a personal level (he first met his future wife, Diana, at Sassoon's Park Lane mansion), wrote that Sassoon's "amiable idiosyncrasy was to entertain the great, the bright and the fashionable."¹⁰

Within weeks of Sassoon's appointment as the prime minister's PPS, the press was announcing that Port Lympne was to be the venue for a weekend summit between Lloyd George and the French prime minister, Alexandre Millerand. The summit was to be held in a mar-quee in the garden if the weather was good enough; in the event it wasn't, the two premiers and their ministers would retreat inside to the drawing room with its apt black-and-gold Sert allegory of France triumphing over German elephants, recently modified by Philip Til-den with gold-streaked walls and high mirrors of black-and-oyster-colored glass. The *Times*' correspondent reported, slightly hesitantly and not at all accurately, that "the house itself is a modern antique, scarcely finished, in the rambling Old English style of architecture."¹¹

The object of the so-called First Hythe Conference, to agree on an Anglo-French position on German war reparations, wasn't achieved. But Port Lympne was established as a perfect meeting point for the two premiers. The French delegation crossed the Channel in a destroyer and was met at Folkestone Pier by Sassoon and driven the seven miles to the house in a matter of minutes. The premiers walked in the gardens arm in arm; Sassoon motored over to Canterbury Cathedral with them, where Millerand was shown the tombs by the dean, and an enterprising schoolmistress persuaded Millerand and Lloyd George to pose for a photograph with fifty schoolchildren she happened to be shepherding round at the time of their visit.

As its name suggests, the First Hythe Conference was quickly followed by a second, five weeks later, and once again at Port Lympne. In a group photograph taken beneath the colonnade at Port Lympne, Sassoon lounges to one side of Lloyd George, Millerand, and the others, his hands in his pockets, smiling but apart. His pet chow, Herbert, is less diffident, standing full center in front of the British prime minister and staring straight at the camera.

Lloyd George holidayed at Port Lympne in March 1921 and presided over a third Anglo-French Hythe Conference there in April. "The members of the Conference were entertained after dinner on Saturday night at a kinematograph performance," reported the press, "and much laughter was evoked by the antics of Charlie Chaplin in the trenches."[12]

"Sir Philip Sassoon's villa," as Port Lympne was usually called in the papers, became a recognized venue for political weekends, often in its owner's absence. Lloyd George regularly used it when he was still prime minister, whether Sassoon was present or not. Frances Stevenson recalled a jolly evening in 1921 when she was staying there with her lover, and he summoned Rufus Isaacs, lord chief justice, and Gordon Hewart, the attorney general, to tell them his plans for a minor government reshuffle. He wanted Isaacs to go out to India as the new viceroy and Hewart to take his place as lord chief justice. The news pleased both men. They stayed on to dinner, and afterward, Frances played the piano while Isaacs sang sea shanties and Hewart did a turn singing a comic song from the music halls. It would be rather hard to imagine senior figures in a twenty-first-century British government behaving with quite that abandon.

Sassoon didn't share in Lloyd George's fall from power in 1922. By 1924 he was serving as undersecretary of state for air in Stanley Baldwin's government. It wasn't a cabinet post, but it was important enough, especially at a time when the role of air power in any future war was being keenly debated. Churchill wrote to congratulate him, telling him how well situated he was at Port Lympne to keep an eye on the various south coast air stations. "I think you must have built your house there upon a prophetic inspiration."[13]

THE WEEKENDS AT PORT LYMPNE gave Lloyd George a taste for a country house of his own within striking distance of Westminster. He found one, or rather a site for one, in the summer of 1921. That September Lord Ashcombe, the same Lord Ashcombe who once owned Bodiam Castle and who was the great-grandfather of the present Duchess of Cornwall, put his two-thousand-acre Churt estate in Surrey on the market. Among the lots were sixty acres on a slope of the Downs near Hindhead, with glorious views across the Surrey hills, and, so the story goes, the prime minister sent Frances Stevenson down to assess the site's potential.

She liked what she saw and reported as much when she got back to Downing Street. Lloyd George wanted sun, and he wanted the view: when he asked Frances which way the slope faced, she said "south." Only after he had bought the site did they both realize she had made a mistake: the view faced due north. According to their granddaughter, Frances was close to tears, but Lloyd George merely laughed and said, "We'll call it Bron-y-de," which in Welsh means "slope of the south."[14]

Lloyd George already had his architect. He had met Philip Tilden at Port Lympne during the Hythe conferences, and Tilden worshipped him. (It is a sign of a less formal age that Sassoon's architect could still be wandering around Lympne in the middle of an international summit, and no one seemed to mind.) "Druidical and elemental . . . the most arresting figure of his time," wrote Tilden, who was fascinated to find that in the flesh the prime minister lived up completely to his public image—dynamic, dramatic, and filled with a passionate empathy for the countryside and his fellow human beings.[15]

Initially Bron-y-de was to be little more than what Tilden called "a picnic home"—a country retreat for the weekend, although Lloyd George planted orchards with a view to doing a little gentle farming. He was still prime minister, and Tilden put a long army hut hidden away in the trees where the detectives who provided his personal security could sleep, unobtrusive but essential in the aftermath of Irish partition, when there were fears that Sinn Fein was poised to bring a campaign of bombing and shooting to the British mainland. (The fears were well founded: in June 1922 Field Marshal Sir Henry Wilson, one of the British army's senior staff officers, was shot dead on the doorstep of his house in Eaton Square by two IRA men.)

Almost as soon as it was built, Lloyd George outgrew Bron-y-de, and within the year, Tilden was brought back to create additional accommodation, bigger kitchens, and garage space for more cars. Furniture, chosen by Tilden and Frances Stevenson, wasn't grand: it was mostly good solid oak, with bright curtains and comfortable beds. And from the first, Lloyd George loved being there. "The centre of the political universe was moved from London," wrote Tilden. "Cars came and went, important people made long journeys, secretaries stayed in hotels, and a thousand inconveniences took place so that Lloyd George could smell the pine needles in the morning and wander out last thing to see the sun set behind the heathered hills."[16] Frances Stevenson, ignored by Margaret Lloyd George but loathed by the prime minister's children, had to move out whenever the family arrived. To begin with, she converted Old Barn, a disused farm building nearby. Then in 1935 Anthony Chitty, a founder member of Tecton, England's leading firm of modernist architects, designed for her a timber bungalow overlooking the orchards of Bron-y-de. She called it Avalon and installed her illegitimate five-year-old daughter by Lloyd George, Jennifer, with a nanny and a pair of discreet Scottish servants.

Lloyd George's coalition government collapsed in November 1922. He retreated to Bron-y-de with Frances to write his memoirs and dream of the day when the country would come to its senses and call on him again. (Is that why Frances named her new house Avalon, because she saw her lover as an aging King Arthur?) That never happened, but he still sat as an MP, and Bron-y-de remained, if not the center of the political universe, then at least one of its distant moons. Lloyd George held court there until almost the end of the Second World War. He summoned John Maynard Keynes to confer with him on industrial conditions; offered advice to progressive young Conservatives who came to find out how to win the next election; and talked privately with Arthur Henderson, leader of the Labour Party, about his prospects if he should desert the Liberals and come over to them. Factions from all parties in Parliament still came to solicit support or sound him out on their plans for palace revolution. As Frances confided to her diary in 1934, her lover and employer "now sits at Churt and welcomes all and sundry, and in this way gets a very fair account of all that is happening in the outside world whilst remaining far from it."[17]

Lloyd George played the part of gentleman farmer at Bron-y-de with enthusiasm, installing modern irrigation systems and bringing in a giant mechanical gyro-tiller on caterpillar tracks to turn parts on the farm into a market garden. He went for long walks with Frances, hunting for holly in the woods near Christmas time. Occasionally, the gardens were opened to the public for charity: one year Edward Fitzroy, Speaker of the House of Commons, came down to discuss the political situation and found he had to pay a shilling admission to come in.

PHILIP TILDEN CORNERED THE MARKET in politicians' country houses. In the spring of 1922, with Port Lympne and Bron-y-de still unfinished, he was commissioned to repair and remodel a rambling patchwork of a house, tumbling down with leaking roofs and dry rot, which stood on eighty acres outside the little Kent village of Westerham. The house was called Chartwell Manor, and Tilden's client was the forty-eight-year-old secretary for the colonies in Lloyd George's government. His name was Winston Churchill.

Churchill had fallen in love with Chartwell, an awkward Victorian concoction, all high gables and ivy, in the spring of 1921, and he tried and failed to buy the house when it came up for auction that July. He persisted, without telling his wife, Clementine, and in September 1922, his offer of £5,000 was accepted.

Churchill had already consulted Tilden, who had come to know him, as he came to know everybody, while working for Philip Sassoon at Port Lympne. Sassoon tried to persuade the politician to take Bellevue, a small early eighteenth-century country house at Lympne, which he also owned, but Clementine turned it down because it felt cluttered and contained too many antiques. Even before the sale of Chartwell went through in November 1922, Churchill was pressing the vendor for permission to start building work, estimating with wild optimism that the house could be remodeled and brought up to a decent standard for £7,000 or £8,000.

Over the next eighteen months, Tilden virtually rebuilt Chartwell. It wasn't his finest hour. He added a new east wing, which juts out awkwardly overlooking a valley, and introduced crow-stepped gables for no good reason. With neither the flamboyance of Port Lympne nor the easy informality of Bron-y-de, and no vision of what the finished work would look like, the house suffered from a piecemeal approach to remodeling. Any enthusiasm that Clementine Churchill may have had soon waned, although she retained a severely practical interest, commenting on the provision of servants' bedrooms, the balance between living-in and living-out staff (the Churchills' employed both at Chartwell), the height of the new kitchen ceiling. And she was cross with Tilden for ordering the domestic arrangements without consulting her, as when he ordered a fitted kitchen range without asking her first. After the Japan earthquake of September 1923, she suggested he might emigrate there, where he would be better employed in rebuilding Tokyo.

As Chartwell grew—at one stage the plan was for six reception rooms, twenty-two bedrooms, seven bathrooms, and a servants' wing—so did the cost. Like many architect's clients before and since, Churchill's reaction to burgeoning bills was to look for reasons not to pay them. And he found them. When the family moved in just after Christmas 1923, they discovered that their new home was still plagued by dry rot and leaking roofs. There was damp, and plaster fell off the ceilings. The windows let in water. The timber was unseasoned. The newly installed electrical system was dangerously faulty. In September 1926, a glass chandelier fell down in the drawing room, "fortunately not killing anyone," reported Churchill.[18] The tale of Chartwell's rebirth ended in a flurry of threats and solicitors' letters, with Tilden saying plaintively (and disingenuously) how sorry he was "for Mr Churchill that Chartwell has proved so unlucky to him for I hope and wished it to be a really beautiful and well-built house."[19]

Client, contractors, and architect reached a settlement at the end of 1927. By then, the Churchills were talking seriously of letting the house, or shutting it up and laying off most of the servants. They didn't, and for all its faults, Chartwell Manor, as it was still being called, became what they had always wanted it to be: a comfortable family home in the country for their four children and a setting for discreet weekend gatherings of leading figures in the political establishment, men like Philip Sassoon and Arthur Balfour and Lloyd George.

Chartwell also became a sanctuary. For ten years, from the fall of Baldwin's second ministry in June 1929 until the outbreak of the Second World War, Churchill held no ministerial office. One of the ways he filled these wilderness years was by tinkering with his country seat. He created a heated swimming pool in the grounds, built an aviary, and planned a butterfly house (the construction of which was interrupted by war). He acquired a parrot, an African gray called Mr. Parrot (or, according to the Churchills' daughter Mary, Polly), who lived in a cage in the dining room and pecked anyone who ventured within range of its beak.* There were cranes and geese and budgerigars. Clementine brought home two black swans from a cruise to Australia and threatened to introduce an opossum and a brace of wallabies. In the intervals between enthusiasms, Winston toyed with the idea of selling up, going as far as to put Chartwell on the market in 1937. A couple of prospective purchasers came to view the house, but

---

* In 2004 the owner of a Surrey garden center claimed that his aged macaw, which shouted anti-Nazi insults, was 104 years old and was the very bird that had once belonged to Churchill. The story proved to be unfounded.

THE CHURCHILLS BREAKFASTING AT CHARTWELL, 1927. (Copyright:
National Trust/Anthony Lambert)

within a few months, he thought better of it, and the family stayed
put in their Kentish country house. It took a war to force them out.
Chartwell was too close to the south coast and the threat of German
invasion, and it was shut up for the duration.

IN 1909 A CONSERVATIVE MP and his American wife, Arthur and
Ruth Lee, acquired a life tenancy of Chequers in Buckinghamshire.
The owner, Henry Delaval Astley, died in a flying accident three years
later, and with the aid of Ruth's substantial inheritance (she was the
daughter of a New York banker), the Lees bought the estate outright
from his widow, a musical comedy actress with no interest in running
a country house.

At its heart, Chequers was an attractive redbrick Elizabethan
manor house, although it had been heavily medievalized in the nineteenth century. When the Lees took possession, some of the later
accretions—battlements and finials and pointed windows—had
already been stripped away by the architect Sir Reginald Blomfield.
Others, including a porch that Arthur Lee described as "a spurious

Gothic and battlemented atrocity," still remained, and internally the house was "an orgy of Victorian Gothic" (Lee again), with little evidence from the earlier period still surviving.[20] Although the sale of the estate didn't go through until 1917, the terms of their tenancy allowed the Lees to remodel the house, and this they did with Blomfield's help, introducing paneling, staircases, plasterwork, and fireplaces.

The Lees had no children, and almost as soon as the house was theirs, they began to plan for the future. In October 1917, the press announced that Sir Arthur Lee, as he now was, had presented Chequers to the nation along with fifteen hundred acres, a capital endowment, and many of the contents. There were paintings by Rembrandt, Reynolds, and Constable; a library of five thousand books, mostly dating from the sixteenth, seventeenth, and eighteenth centuries; and a collection of Cromwell memorabilia belonging with the house, which Astley had pawned and Lee had retrieved. This included the sword that Oliver carried at Marston Moor, his slippers, a life mask, and a fine collection of Cromwell family portraits by the English miniaturist Samuel Cooper. (The Russells, eighteenth-century owners of Chequers, had connections with the Cromwells: one Russell ancestor had married Oliver's son and another his daughter, hence the relics.) The Lees also gave manuscripts by Tennyson and Robert Louis Stevenson and a collection of documents and letters of Napoleon I, together with a lock of the French emperor's hair and "the key of the room in which he was born."[21]

The Lees were both in their forties, and they planned to live out the rest of their lives at Chequers. Their idea was that after their deaths, the house would become the official country residence of British prime ministers, a sanctuary from the cares of state. Their reasoning says a lot about changing social structures, and about contemporary concerns over what that might mean:

> It is not possible to foresee or foretell from what classes or conditions of life the future wielders of power in this country will be drawn. Some may be, as in the past, men of wealth and famous descent; some may belong to the world of trade and business;

others may spring from the ranks of the manual toilers. To none of these, in the midst of their strenuous and responsible labours, could the spirit and anodyne of Chequers do anything but good. To the City-bred man especially, the periodic contact with the most typically rural life would create and preserve a just sense of proportion between the claims of town and country. To the revolutionary statesman the antiquity and calm tenacity of Chequers and its annals might suggest some saving virtues in the continuity of English history and exercise a check upon too hasty upheavals.[22]

At the beginning of the twentieth century, the prime minister, the 3rd Marquess of Salisbury, could point to ancestors who had served in government since the days of Queen Elizabeth I and to not one but two country seats, Hatfield and Cranborne. Then, it was almost unthinkable that the leader of the greatest nation on earth might spring from the ranks of the manual toilers. The Lees' conviction that a future prime minister might not have a country house of his own was evidence that the rise of the Labour Party and the declining constitutional role of the House of Lords had changed all that. Just as interesting was their claim that time spent at Chequers would connect metropolitan politicians with rural values, and Socialist firebrands with the past.

They also saw the bequest as a means of preserving Chequers itself from harm, from what they described as the kind of "outrages inflicted upon it by late Georgian Goths and vandals." One of the stipulations in the deed of trust transferring ownership of the estate was that "no alteration, mutilation, addition, or subtraction shall be made to the principal features of the house."[23] Another was that the name should remain the same: when there was talk a few years later of it becoming The Chequers, Lee was swift to write to the *Times* pointing out that this would be a breach of the deed of trust. In spite of such conditions, it was a generous gift, and David Lloyd George wrote publicly to say that "future generations of prime ministers will think with gratitude of the impulse which has thus prompted you so generously to place this beautiful mansion at their disposal."[24]

Critics hinted that Lee was trying to buy himself a title, and the sniping intensified in July 1918 when he was raised to the peerage as Lord Lee of Fareham. It wasn't altogether fair, since the barony was awarded primarily for his war work as director-general of food production in Lloyd George's coalition government. The following year the Lees decided to bring their plan forward and hand over Chequers as soon as possible, as a memorial to victory over the Germans; but the handover, which took place at the beginning of 1921, was marred by Lord Lee's sense of grievance over Lloyd George's failure to support his efforts to force a new Agriculture Act through Parliament. "To think," wrote Lady Lee in her diary, "that in two weeks' time we are handing over to them our dear Chequers, with more than half of our whole fortune, and all the things that we love most in the world."[25]

On January 8, 1921, after hosting a dinner for Lloyd George, the Lees signed the deed of settlement and drove away, leaving a poignant little note in the visitors' book:

> Tonight we leave this dear place, with a sense of loss which cannot be measured, but content and happy in our faith that Chequers has a great part to play in the moulding of the future and that in freeing it for this high task we are doing the best service to our country that it is in our power to render.[26]

Lloyd George liked his new official country residence. In fact, he liked it so much that he wouldn't leave. Over the coming days, news of official appointments was issued from Chequers. The press was full of rumors that Lloyd George was plotting a cabinet reshuffle—at Chequers. The servants were being worked so hard that they threatened to walk out, and there was talk that the Prince of Wales, who was scheduled to meet with the prime minister at Downing Street, would have to come to Chequers instead.

Lloyd George finally tore himself away to preside over his cabinet a week after the Lees had left. He was back again three days later, celebrating his birthday. And the following week, taking a break from the Paris peace conference, and again a couple of weeks after that, entertaining the prime minister of France. When the coalition government collapsed in 1922 and he left Downing Street for the last time, his daughter Megan's verdict on events was uncomplicated: "Damn," she wrote. "There goes Chequers."[27]

IN SPITE OF THE LEES' forebodings, and a general feeling that British politics was no longer the preserve of the landed classes, two-thirds of the cabinet in Neville Chamberlain's National Ministry of 1937–1939 had their own country house. The prime minister himself wasn't one of them: although his predecessor, Stanley Baldwin, had owned a modest Victorian country house in his home county of Worcestershire since before the First World War, Chamberlain was content to use Chequers, regularly escaping for a weekend without the panoply of office.

His ministers' country homes ranged from a modest but charming Gloucestershire manor house belonging to William Morrison, his minister of agriculture, to Chevening, the magnificent seventeenth-century seat of the Stanhope family near Sevenoaks in Kent, which Lord Stanhope, the president of the board of education, would eventually bequeath to the nation. The home secretary, Sir Samuel Hoare, owned Sidestrand Hall in Norfolk; although as we saw in Chapter 8, he disposed of it and built himself something more manageable, the Palladian Petit Trianon that was Templewood.

Lord Hailsham, the lord chancellor, lived in the picturesquely named Carter's Corner Place in Sussex, an Elizabethan house on fifty-six acres, which he had enlarged in 1920 and which had been the scene of a minor cause célèbre in 1932 when Hailsham's stepson Edward Majoribanks, MP for Eastbourne, was found shot dead in the billiard room. The secretary of state for the colonies, William Ormsby-Gore, had two country houses, the Greek Revival Brogyntyn Hall in Shropshire and Glyn Cywarch, a big gentry house of 1616 in Gwynedd; Chamberlain's secretary of state for India, Lord Zetland, had three.

Some politicians were born into the country-house world. Witherslack Hall in Kendal had been in the family of Oliver Stanley, president of the board of trade, since 1485, although the current house was less than seventy years old. Others were newcomers. Sir Kingsley Wood was the son of a Wesleyan minister who had made good in local politics and the law before entering the Commons at the end of the war. The Minister for Health and then Secretary of State for Air in Chamberlain's government, he only joined the ranks of the landed classes in 1927, when he bought Broomhill Bank, a big Victorian pile near Tunbridge Wells.

One of the most distinguished members of Chamberlain's pre-war government, Edward Wood, 3rd Viscount Halifax, was born at Powderham Castle in Devon, home of his maternal grandfather the Earl of Devon, and at birth he had a silver spoon in his mouth and the front door keys to two ancestral seats in his hand.[*] Chamberlain's Lord President of the Council and then foreign secretary, known by friends and enemies as the "holy fox" on account of his devout Anglo-Catholicism and his lifelong passion for hunting, was born into a prominent Yorkshire landowning family whose principal seat for the past hundred years had been Hickleton Hall, a Georgian country house near Doncaster with a park that his father, a whimsical man who was prone to seeing ghosts and building secret passages in his houses, stocked with yaks, emus, and kangaroos. In 1904 when Halifax was in his early twenties, an aunt died and left him Temple Newsam, a glorious Tudor house near Leeds known as "the Hampton Court of the North." In 1923 he sold the estate for £35,000, a good deal less than its market value, to Leeds Corporation, which opened it to the public. "The house has now ceased to be a home of famous families and has become the heritage of the democracy," declared the *Guardian*, reporting a speech at the opening ceremony by the Minister of Labour, Sir Montague Barlow, who hoped "that Temple Newsam might in some degree restore a sensitiveness to beauty which English people seemed to him to be losing."[28]

Halifax didn't need Temple Newsam because his father had already handed him Garrowby Hall, a family shooting box in the East

---

[*] Almost, anyway. Edward was the fourth son, but before his tenth birthday, his three elder brothers had all died, leaving him as heir to his father's fortune.

Riding that had been vastly extended in the last years of the nineteenth century. Garrowby was Halifax's spiritual home: inviting Stanley Baldwin to stay in 1937, he wrote, "Let us walk over a Yorkshire wold and smell the east wind and watch the gulls in from the sea following the plough on the bleak tops!"[29]

Garrowby was never a political salon. The East Riding of Yorkshire was too far from London for that. But with other cabinet members disappearing up to their Yorkshire estates for shooting or for the Christmas holidays, it was natural that every now and then friends and colleagues would gather there for the weekend. Chamberlain was a regular visitor, as Baldwin was before him, and he only had to be in the same county as Halifax for the rumors of secret meetings and plots to begin. Halifax was known to be sympathetic to the cause of appeasement: Lord Birkenhead recalled a weekend at Garrowby where his host said Hitler "reminded him of Gandhi."[30] At the end of 1938, when Chamberlain was staying on the Yorkshire estate of another of his ministers, Lord Swinton, the press began to report that the holy fox was to play host at Garrowby to a meeting between the prime minister and an emissary from Hitler. Both men were forced to issue denials: "These rumours are absurd," Halifax told reporters.[31]

There were other political houses. The Marquis and Marchioness of Londonderry, eager to further the cause of Anglo-German friendship, invited Ribbentrop, then the German ambassador to Britain, to spend Whitsun 1936 with them at Mount Stewart, their country house on the banks of Strangford Lough in County Down. The visit wasn't a success: Ribbentrop arrived in an airplane supplied by Goering, with an escort of noisy SS men who upset everybody. When the Londonderrys took him sailing on the lough, he fell overboard.

AT THE END OF APRIL 1938, the writer and politician Philip Kerr, 11th Marquess of Lothian, spoke out publicly against rumors that he was part of a pro-Fascist clique that met at Waldorf Astor's Buckinghamshire country house, Cliveden. A week later Astor himself sent an angry letter to the Times. "For years," he wrote, "my wife and I have entertained in the country members of all parties (including Communists), members of all faiths, of all countries, and of all interests. To link our weekends with any particular clique is as absurd as is the allegation that those of us who desire to establish better relations with Germany or with Italy are pro-Nazis or pro-Fascists."[32]

Many of the regular guests at Cliveden were journalists: Geoffrey Dawson, editor of the *Times*; James Garvin, editor of the *Observer* (which Astor owned); Robert Barrington-Ward, chief leader-writer on the *Times*. But active politicians also came along to enjoy the Astors' lavish hospitality. In June Harold Nicolson, his own flirtation with the ultra-right firmly behind him, spent a weekend at Cliveden in June 1936 and found himself in the company of the foreign secretary, the Speaker of the House of Commons, an Oxford professor of political theory, a Liberal MP, a Conservative peer, the Canadian High Commissioner, Winston Churchill's aunt, and a gaggle of forlorn Americans, Astor relations, and assorted hangers-on.

History doesn't record what the house party talked about—the impending Berlin Olympics, perhaps, or Mussolini's annexation of Ethiopia. Nicolson remarked on the "great groups of delphiniums and tuberoses, great bowers of oleander,"[33] the work of the Astors' decorator Frank Copcutt. But apart from the flowers, Cliveden wasn't to Nicolson's taste. "I simply do not want a house like this where nothing is really yours, but belongs to servants and gardeners," he reported to Vita. "There is a ghastly unreality about it all . . . I enjoy seeing it. But to own it, to live here, would be like living on the stage of the Scala theatre in Milan."[34]

Sections of the press saw the Astors and their friends as leading players in the horror that was unfolding across Europe in the late 1930s. When Lothian and Astor made their denials in the spring of 1938, they were responding to what Nancy Astor tried to dismiss as "a false and stupid story published in a Communist rag."[35] For months a small-circulation paper called *The Week*, edited by the left-wing journalist Claud Cockburn, had been suggesting that a group of pro-Germans in positions of power were using their influence to move the government toward an alliance with Hitler and Mussolini, allowing

Germany to achieve its territorial ambitions in Eastern Europe. It was this group, the Cliveden set, that had forced the resignation of Foreign Secretary Anthony Eden, who was opposed to Mussolini's expansionist policies; this group that had engineered his replacement by the pro-Hitler Lord Halifax; this group that was pushing Chamberlain into appeasing the Nazis.

The campaign gained strength over the winter of 1937–1938. When Chamberlain spent a weekend at Cliveden, the Labour politician Sir Stafford Cripps declared that "the Cliveden set . . . are the people who are running policy today behind Neville Chamberlain and they are the people who would like to see Great Britain a Fascist State as well."[36] In the *Evening Standard* cartoonist David Low portrayed Nancy Astor, Lothian, and Geoffrey Dawson of the *Times* as the "Shiver Sisters," dancing as they held high a placard reading "Any Sort of Peace at Any Sort of Price." The set was lampooned on the stage and in the press. US ambassador to Britain Joseph Kennedy, back in New York to report to Roosevelt on Germany's anti-Semitism, was quizzed by reporters about his sympathy with them. "I have never met any of that set," he told the *New York Tribune*.[37] When George VI dined at the American embassy and was served Virginia ham and Georgia pickled peaches, the *New York Times* jokingly put the menu down to the malign influence of the Astors, who were on the guest list. "The chief engineer of the Cliveden set has been pulling the string again," it reported. "It is a well-known fact that Nancy Astor of Virginia gets in her deadliest work around the dinner table. This time she has been rigging things for her native Southland."[38]

Less amusing was the hate mail. "You blasted American whore of a chorus-girl," ran one example. "Go back to your own country." Another accused Nancy of having Hitler's bastard child. When she was finally introduced to Claud Cockburn in the lobby of the Commons, she spat at him.

There are two questions to ask about the Cliveden set. Perhaps the easiest is, Was Cliveden really a hotbed of appeasers and pro-Nazis? Nancy and Waldorf welcomed all sorts to their weekends. George Bernard Shaw, then pro-Stalin and a self-styled Communist, dismissed the furor about the set as "senseless," pointing out that "I could prove that Cliveden is a nest of Bolshevism, or indeed of any other bee in the world's bonnet."[39] Astor's valet said the story was a pack of lies. "Whoever invented them ought to come and work here for a week as a housemaid. They'd find no Nazis under Cliveden beds."[40] But Lothian, Dawson, Garvin, Nancy Astor, and others of their friends *were* pro-German and remained so long after it was obvious that Hitler was a very bad thing indeed. Nancy was an outspoken and bigoted anti-Semite. At different times and in different degrees, members of the set believed that the Treaty of Versailles had left Germany with legitimate grievances; that what Hitler did in pursuit of Lebensraum in eastern Europe was no business of Britain's; that the Nazis would prove a formidable bulwark against the creeping Bolshevism of the Soviet Union; and that another world war must be avoided at all costs.

A lot of people in Britain believed these things. A lot of people envied Germany its strong leadership and disliked the Jews and cheered when Chamberlain sold Czechoslovakia down the river and promised peace in our time. This raises the second question. Did the set really wield much power? Did those country-house weekends make a difference to British policy? And here the answer is a qualified no. Individual members of the set had some little impact, particularly Dawson, who kept the *Times* to a pro-German line for far too long. But they just weren't that important. Prime Minister Chamberlain and Foreign Secretary Halifax needed no encouragement in their appeasement of Hitler, and when they saw there was no help for it and that war would come, they disregarded calls to give up on Poland and sue for peace at any price.

Harold Nicolson put his finger on the hubristic heart of the Cliveden set in the spring of 1939. As war loomed, he railed at Nancy Astor for being one of those "silly selfish hostesses" who do immense damage by giving the impression "that foreign policy is decided in their own drawing-rooms."[41] By now, most of the set was revising its opinions. Lothian read *Mein Kampf* and belatedly decided that Hitler was "a fanatical gangster who will stop at nothing."[42] Astor stood up in the Lords and urged Chamberlain to think about negotiating with Stalin. "I think," he said, "we should be big enough to admit that during the past year or two each of us and all of us as individuals and as parties have probably made some mistakes."[43]

The last of the Cliveden political weekends, and one of the last great country-house parties of the decade, took place at the beginning of June 1939. The Astors had thirty-odd guests, including Halifax, Lothian, and Dawson. They had gathered to meet Adam von Trott, a German diplomat who was in England to rally support for a strategy to avoid war. Trott was no friend to the Nazis, but his proposals didn't go far enough to satisfy most of the Cliveden set, now firmly opposed to appeasement. He went back to Germany. And Britain went to war.

17

THE OLD ORDER DOOMED

O n June 16, 1939, an announcement appeared in the letter columns of the *Times*. It was from Lord Derwent, chairman of the Georgian Group. Owing to the great kindness of Lord Jersey, he wrote, the Georgian Group planned to hold its first annual ball at Osterley Park in Middlesex. This would be a Georgian-themed *fête champêtre*, and it promised to be the event of the season.

Osterley had been in the news a lot over recent weeks, the result of the Earl of Jersey's decision to open the family's Adam mansion to the general public for three days a week, at sixpence for admittance to the grounds, and another shilling to see the house. When asked why he was doing it, Jersey said "it was sufficient answer that he did not live in it and that many others wished to see it."[1]

So they did. Twelve thousand visitors came in the first month, and the papers were full of praise for both the owner and his house. An exhibition of work by contemporary English artists from Augustus John to Duncan Grant and Charles Cundall was an added attraction. "In these days, when the great country houses which once surrounded London are for the most part empty, pulled down, or turned into institutions," said the *Times*, "it is highly satisfactory to know that the public will be able to see a country house of Middlesex not only in all its glory but in its natural setting."[2]

At twenty-five shillings a head "including buffet, beer and cup," the *fête champêtre* was a more exclusive affair, a fundraiser with profits going toward the Georgian Group's work of preserving the architecture of the eighteenth century. Guests were invited to come in costume. The film star Countess of Jersey (Virginia from Hollywood) wore a pale blue lavender and rose net gown designed for her by Oliver Messel, who did most of the organizing and was also in charge of decorating a vast lakeside pavilion for the ball. She had a diamond tiara in her powdered gray hair and a diamond bracelet on her wrist, although she had managed to lose the £250 bracelet by the time the sun came up, "a dramatic climax," wrote one society columnist, "to a season which has been remarkable for the mysterious 'disappearances' of jewels and furs at almost every function."[3]

Oliver Messel's sister, the Countess of Rosse, wore aquamarines at her throat and blue-dyed hair piled high, like Madame Pompadour. Diana Cooper wore a wimple. Actor and director Peter Glenville spurned the eighteenth-century theme altogether and came as the Trojan prince Paris in another Messel costume designed seven years earlier for a production of Offenbach's *La Belle Helene*. Cecil Beaton wore a coat of tapestry, and Lord Antrim, a Northern Ireland protestant, chose the bright red robes of a cardinal.

Footmen greeted the thousand or so guests on the steps of the floodlit portico wearing powdered wigs and period livery. There were fireworks across the lake, which was floodlit in a purplish green for the night; an eighteenth-century beer garden; and displays of open-air wrestling. An orchestra dressed as eighteenth-century peasants played sprightly minuets, "to which the guests, instead of dancing, listened with religious solemnity," before retiring to Messel's pavilion, where they danced till dawn to a modern swing band.[4]

That day, the government distributed fifteen million leaflets to households all over the country: "Your Gas Mask: How to Keep and Use It."

As the world shambled toward war that summer, the stately homes of England kept calm and carried on. Nancy Astor hosted the annual

rally of the local branch of the National British Women's Total Absti-
nence Union at Cliveden. The tea arrangements, reported the local
press, "were carried out to the satisfaction of all."[5] The guest of honor
at Blenheim Palace's annual garden fête was Sir John Simon, the chancellor of the exchequer. War may never come, he told the crowd. The
strong heart and cool head of the British people would "see this business
through."[6] Ginie Courtauld entertained members of the Anglo-French
Art and Travel Society at Eltham Palace, while four huge barrage bal-
loons hung in the sky above them. At Harewood House, the Princess
Royal's two teenage sons receive a reprimand from the War Office after
the *Harewood News*, a news sheet they produced on a typewriter in the
school holidays, described an antiaircraft battery in too much detail.

Three hundred guests danced in the ballroom of Castle Howard to celebrate the coming-of-age of Mark Howard, "tenants rubbing
shoulders with titled persons."[7] Major Mark Howard of the Coldstream Guards died in Normandy five years later, a few months before
his younger brother, a bomber pilot, was killed in a daylight raid over
the Rhine. At Chatsworth, the Duke of Devonshire threw a garden
party for 2,800 people to mark the coming-of-age of his son and heir,
Billy Cavendish, with troupes of circus ponies performing for their
entertainment. As darkness fell, Chatsworth was floodlit, and hundreds of cars were parked along the lanes overlooking the park to
catch a glimpse of the spectacle. Billy Cavendish was shot and killed
by a sniper in Belgium in 1944.

The octogenarian Duke of Portland and his duchess celebrated
their golden wedding that hot, humid August with a pageant at Welbeck Abbey involving eight hundred of the duke's estate workers in
costume, enacting scenes from the abbey's past. Robin Hood and his
merry men put in an appearance, as did two kings: Charles I, who
visited the abbey in 1633 and William of Orange, who came in 1695.
There was a ballet and an elaborate prologue in which local women
represented the three Fates spinning the web of life, and schoolchildren from the surrounding villages playing the part of the threads.
The Archbishop of Canterbury came to watch.

A STATE ROOM AT BLENHEIM BECOMES A SCHOOL DORMITORY. (Copyright: Country Life)

Country houses were in the news that summer for other reasons. Schools were poised to occupy empty mansions in an emergency, preparations were made to set up camps for evacuees in their grounds. Big companies were buying up country houses as out-of-London accommodation if the worst came to the worst. Milton Hill House in Oxfordshire became Esso House; Chesterton Lodge, an enormous Italianate mansion outside Bicester, was bought by the Royal Exchange Assurance Corporation; the early Georgian Alresford Place near Winchester was sold to the Provident Mutual to serve as their headquarters in the event of war.

Sensitive to criticism that owners like the Jerseys were playing at dressing-up games while Europe stood on the brink of Armageddon, *Country Life* was protective about the Osterley *fête champêtre*, suggesting that it was just such events that we were about to be called upon to defend, "for a great country house ball on a July night is, in a sense, the fine flower of one aspect of civilization."[8] At the same time, the magazine began to carry advertisements that offered advice on air raid precautions "for fire protection of country mansions."[9]

And advice was coming thick and fast, as the government instructed the population on everything from how to black out windows to procedures for the evacuation of children, expectant mothers, and "adult blind persons who can be moved."[10] Incendiary bombs were considered to be a major threat to country houses, and owners were urged to clear junk out of attics and roof spaces, where a fire from an incendiary was most likely to start, and to keep firefighting gear—buckets of water and sand, a hand pump, and a bath or tank of water to replenish the buckets—on the top floor. "If you throw a bucket of water on a burning incendiary bomb it will explode and throw burning fragments in all directions. You may be able to smother it with sand or dry earth."[11]

The Air Ministry announced plans to turn part of the Stourhead estate into an airdrome, then abandoned them. Enterprising firms marketed concrete air raid shelters with outer walls of wattle hurdles; circular and domed, it was claimed that they might be mistaken for a rustic garden temple. In fact they looked more like public conveniences.

War was declared on the morning of Sunday, September 3. Harold Nicolson, now an MP, drove down from Westminster to Sissinghurst that afternoon, passing convoys of lorries filled with evacuees from the East End. He was shocked when an old lady in one of the trucks shook her fist at his passing car and yelled that the war was all the fault of the rich. When he reached Sissinghurst on a day redolent with omens, he found that the Sackville flag, which flew from the top of the tower, had been taken down.

Almost before Neville Chamberlain had come to the end of his famous radio broadcast to the nation at 11:15 a.m. that morning—"It is the evil things that we shall be fighting against—brute force, injustice, oppression and persecution—and against them I am certain that the right will prevail"—country houses were being put to new uses. By the end of the month, Blenheim Palace and Attingham Park, the Marquess of Lansdowne's Bowood and Lord Methuen's Corsham Court

**THE COUNTESS OF CARNARVON PLAYING WITH EVACUEES FROM
THE EAST END OF LONDON ON THE LAWN AT HIGHCLERE CASTLE.**
(Copyright: Country Life)

were all playing host to boarding schools. The Earl of Harewood offered Harewood House for use as a hospital, an example followed by many owners of large mansions. Donington Hall in Leicestershire was set up as a prisoner of war camp, although there were as yet no prisoners of war. The Earl and Countess of Pembroke took in forty nursery school evacuees at Wilton: Cecil Beaton, still at Ashcombe, came over and photographed them, beaming and bewildered, huddled together on Wilton's Palladian Bridge.

"The most unmanageable white elephant of a mansion is now securely harnessed to the war-time machine," commented *Country Life*. "Indeed, the more rooms and wings and outhouses a residence possesses the more desirable it has seemed."[12]

HOW HAD THE COUNTRY HOUSE changed in the years between the Somme and the Second World War?

For one thing, it had changed its purpose. In 1944 Robert Lutyens reckoned there would be no more ancestral houses after the war was over. "Fluctuations of income between generations, and extensive recruitment to the possessing classes, on the one hand, and the gradual dispossession of the territorial families on the other," meant that this time the Old Order really was doomed.[13]

That didn't mean the country house was doomed as well. As we've seen, the dismantling of traditional bonds between family, mansion, and local community, the breaking up of estates and the sales of houses and their contents often led simply to a change of ownership and a less traditional approach to life in the country house. But the perception of doom was there, and the late 1930s and early 1940s were dominated by the quest to find a future for historic mansions that were no longer financially viable. At the 1934 annual general meeting of the National Trust, the Marquess of Lothian called on the Trust as a private charity to extend its protection, until then confined to areas of countryside and smaller historic buildings, to "another part of our national treasure now threatened with potential destruction—the historic dwelling houses of this country."[14] He told his audience that English country houses were under sentence of death and that the axe that was destroying them was taxation. They cheered.

Lothian proposed that the National Trust should take on a number of furnished historic mansions. (It currently owned two, Montacute and Barrington Court, both in Somerset, and it wasn't at all sure what to do with them.) He also urged that historic houses should be exempted from death duties unless they were sold; that the Treasury should allow all maintenance claims for sums spent on upkeep and restoration; and that country houses could be exempt from death duties even if they were sold, providing that house, garden, and contents were preserved as a whole, and provision made for public access from time to time.

Lothian's remarks struck a chord. Three months later, at the national conference of the Council for the Preservation of Rural England, the pioneering town planner William Harding Thompson called for the setting up of an owners' association to lobby for the "remission of duties in approved cases in exchange for regulated public access at specified times." And the National Trust's Chairman, Lord Zetland, proposed that in return for an undertaking by owners to open their houses to sightseers, "the Government should be asked to make easier the upkeep and preservation of the houses by remitting some of the taxation that now burdens them."[15]

The government wasn't about to give these kinds of concessions to the owners of country houses, particularly in the middle of a depression; but the notion of public money for public benefit was one that would eventually come to inform the entire stately home business in Britain. In the meantime the National Trust lobbied Parliament to pass new legislation that would allow the owners of historic houses to hand them over to the Trust while continuing to live in them—something prohibited by charity law. In the summer of 1937, the National Trust Act passed into law, and the Trust launched its Country Houses Scheme.

> The essence of the scheme [reported the *Observer*] is that owners will be able to transfer the ownership of approved country houses to the National Trust while retaining the right for themselves, and for their families and successors, to continue in occupation as long as may be desired. Places so transferred will be preserved for all time, not as dusty museums but as inhabited houses with their rooms and contents in constant use, possibly by the families who have been associated with them for centuries.[16]

Prominent figures lined up to promote the scheme. There was no alternative, said Vita Sackville-West, whose romantic ruined tower at Sissinghurst would come to the Trust thirty years later. Owners might feel "that they could not bear to do it, but what else was there for them to do when upkeep alone cost a fortune?"[17] Lord Lothian, whose 1934 speech started it all, left Blickling Hall to the Trust when he died in 1940. Sir Charles Trevelyan handed over Wallington in 1942, and in the same year the Astors gave Cliveden, along with a large endowment. Sir Henry and Lady Alda Hoare, whose son Harry had died so tragically in Palestine in the First World War, began negotiations over Stourhead during the second. The house and garden finally came to the Trust in 1946. Sir Henry and Lady Alda died a year later, on the same day.

There had never been a proper national survey of country houses, but at the time conservationists reckoned there were 57 "great mansions" and 550 to 600 smaller country houses "which are worthy of preservation for their historic or architectural interest or their natural beauty."[18] That was a wild underestimate, no matter how one defined "worthy." In any case, even when the trickle of mansions that came to the Trust before the Second World War turned into a flood after 1945, the Country Houses Scheme could only account for a fraction of the whole. By the early 1950s, the Trust opened a total of 98 houses and gardens to the public. That left several thousand in private hands.

Many country-house owners continued in the 1940s as they had for decades. They stayed put or sold up. Some hung on by getting rid of yet another "outlying parcel of land" or some rare books or a portrait of an ancestor; others took the place of those families who had gone and bought themselves a past and a place in country society. They installed electricity plants and bought labor-saving devices to help them cope with the shortage of servants. They complained about taxes and cursed the government and took in evacuees and sent their sons off to die for their country.

On the outbreak of war, smart owners were quick to offer up their mansions for the war effort. There was a feeling that being able to choose one's tenant gave a degree of control: better a girl's boarding school than an army camp. And they were right: it has been estimated that more than one thousand country houses were demolished in the decade after 1945 as a direct result of wartime mistreatment. Classical garden statues were smashed by servicemen who couldn't care less about what Lothian had called "the national treasure." Rococo paneling was defaced; baroque staircases were broken up for firewood. Port Lympne, which Philip Sassoon had left to his cousin Hannah Gubbay on his death in 1939, was requisitioned as accommodation for British and foreign airmen, who vandalized it comprehensively. Tyneham

House in Dorset was requisitioned for gunnery training by the Ministry of Defence and never given back to its owners. The forecourt at Lowther Castle, where Loelia Ponsonby had been regaled with stories of Arctic expeditions by the Yellow Earl, was peppered with concrete pillboxes; its elaborate gardens vanished under a wilderness of weeds, "with just the faintest outline of the one-time paths and rides, and here and there a pagoda or a summer-house as a pathetic relic of the romantic past."[19]

More serious for many country houses were six years of neglect, so that by the time the Second World War was over and the Ministry of Defence began to hand back requisitioned mansions, leaking water pipes and sagging roofs and dry rot had achieved the kind of destruction only dreamed of by Hitler's bombers. Many owners never occupied their homes again.

Their fate is all the more ironic because all through the war the government exploited the idea of the country house as the epitome of British values, ancient and romantic and ivy covered—in contrast to the hard, mechanized inhumanity of the enemy. These were the values that featured in dozens of wartime films from *Mrs. Miniver* to *The Tawny Pipit*. They portrayed Britain—or rather England, and a quiet, Cotswolds-type of England at that—as quintessentially rural, individualistic to the point of eccentricity, above all humane and rooted in the past. The country house, moated and timber framed or stately and magnificent, was an emblem of this particular brand of Englishness, a symbol of what the historian G. M. Trevelyan eulogized in 1945 as "the rural and agricultural life and the natural and historic beauty of England."[20] It was precious, and it seemed to represent a common cause. A war widow told Christopher Hussey that before her husband's death in North Africa he had found a copy of *Country Life* and written to her "that it was so lovely to read what one was fighting for."[21]

There is an echo of this in the story told by novelist Elizabeth Bowen, who was staying with Gerald Berners and Robert Heber-Percy at Faringdon when Allied victory in Europe was declared in May 1945. After lunch they all went out and stood on the terrace, overlooking the fountain that had been turned off at the beginning of the war and, beyond it, an impossibly long vista across the rolling English landscape:

> Robert did something to the fountain; there was a breathless pause, then a jet of water, at first a little rusty, hesitated up into the air, wobbled then separated into four curved features of water. It was so beautiful and so sublimely symbolic—with the long view, the miles of England, stretching away behind it, that I found myself weeping.[22]

Sir George Vernon of Hanbury Hall was the last in a long line of country squires. His ancestor, Richard Vernon, had been rector of Hanbury in Worcestershire before the time of the Spanish Armada. In the reign of Queen Anne, Thomas Vernon, a successful chancery barrister, marked that success by building Hanbury Hall, an exquisite essay in red brick with dormers and white sash windows, its interiors filled with murals by the court painter Sir James Thornhill. Victorian Vernons added to the estates, and by the 1920s Sir George owned and managed five thousand acres of good Worcestershire farmland.

He was of his class and of his time. He served as a local magistrate for thirty-five years, resigning because he thought his colleagues on the bench were too lenient with speeding motorists. He was a leading figure in the National Farmers' Union, and like so many country-house owners, he did his duty and opened the gardens at Hanbury Hall once a year in aid of the Queen's Institute of District Nursing. He wrote angry letters to the papers complaining about the punitive effects of taxation on farmers, he protected his tenants when times were hard, and every now and then he discreetly sold off the odd pieces of jewelry and family silver, or a few books and manuscripts from the Hanbury Hall library to keep things ticking over.

In so many ways Sir George Vernon was the archetypal English squire—irascible, always grumbling that the country was going to rack and ruin, while he struggled to keep his ancestral seat and his place on the creaking boughs of a family tree that stretched back for hundreds of years and was rooted in community and country.

In other ways Sir George was less typical. In 1905 at the age of forty, he had married Doris Allan, the twenty-two-year-old daughter of a neighbor. But the marriage wasn't a success. There were no children, and in the 1920s, Doris moved out of Hanbury and went to live in the couple's townhouse in Chelsea. Sir George was left alone in his Queen Anne mansion.

One day in 1928 he walked into the house of his estate manager, Edward Powick, and announced that he wanted to borrow the man's daughter for six months. "Things are in a mess at the Hall," he told him. So sixteen-year-old Ruth Powick went to live with the baronet as his secretary.

She never left. Ten years later, Sir George changed his will in her favor, and Ruth changed her name to Vernon. Among those who weren't aware of their real relationship, the couple passed her off as his daughter.

In the mid-1930s Sir George took up the cause of the Tithe Campaigners, who were protesting against the fact that the established church was able by law to extract tithes from many farmers, payments that were unrelated to their profits. He attacked the Church of England in print and on platforms, telling his audiences that he refused to be buried in consecrated ground: "No snivelling parson is going to read any service over me."[23] And in common with other landowners and farmers across the country, he refused to pay his tithes. In June 1935, in front of hundreds of supporters, he stood on the steps of Hanbury Hall as bailiffs carried out a distress sale of furniture from the Hall. Afterward, he addressed the crowd, telling them that "we English have always regarded it as our most sacred duty to resist oppression and injustice from whatever quarter it comes."[24]

Sir Oswald Mosley and the British Union of Fascists also embraced the Tithe Campaign, with Blackshirts disrupting sales and barricading farms against bailiffs and the police. This brought the baronet into contact with Mosley, and when the latter wanted to put up a local man as a Fascist candidate to oppose Stanley Baldwin in his Worcestershire constituency, Sir George approved the plan and told Mosley he would use his influence to help the movement. He never joined the BUF, but he flirted with Fascism, which proved a good fit with his own highly individual brand of right-wing politics.

Then came the war. In the last week of May 1940 Mosley and hundreds more Fascist sympathizers were rounded up and arrested under Defence Regulation 18B. In the days that followed, Sir George worried that his prewar links with the Fascists, insubstantial though they were, might be enough to bring Special Branch detectives to Hanbury Hall. He was also depressed about a heart condition and convinced he had not long to live.

At noon on June 14, 1940, Ruth heard the crack of a pistol shot from a small room leading off Sir George's bedchamber. She dashed in and found him lying dead, his revolver next to his body, and a letter that read: "My heart is causing me great and increasing trouble at night, so instead of enduring what can only be two or three weeks' more misery, I take the short cut."[25]

There were other things to claim the attention of the public that June. The demoralized remnants of the British Expeditionary Force had just been evacuated from Dunkirk. Paris and Norway had fallen to the Germans. Chamberlain had gone, and Churchill was standing defiant in his place and telling the Commons that "we shall never surrender." The suicide of a seventy-four-year-old baronet didn't merit much coverage in the press.

But the death can serve for other endings. There was no place any more for Blimpish country squires like Sir George Vernon. With this new war, the old order, whose demise had been so confidently predicted at the end of the last, really would fade away, quietly and without protest.

There was no sniveling parson to stand over Sir George at his burial. On Monday, June 22, his coffin, draped in a Union Jack, was taken from Hanbury and placed on the back of a farm lorry. The makeshift cortege drove to a clearing in nearby woodland, the site of an old summerhouse, and he was buried there without any ceremony.

Ruth was the only mourner. And whether she knew it or not, she mourned for more than a lover, more than an irascible country squire. She mourned for a past. For a way of life. She mourned for an England. The long weekend was over.

ACKNOWLEDGMENTS

I have had so much help in the writing of this book—from friends, from colleagues, and from complete strangers who commented with kindness on items in my sporadic Long Weekend blog or offered ideas and enthusiasm at country houses and archives and libraries all over the United Kingdom. I can't mention them all by name: indeed, there are many whose names I don't even know, like the members of the staff at Bath Central Library, who retrieved endless quantities of heavy-bound volumes of *Country Life* from deep in the stacks for me, staggering under the weight with unfailing cheerfulness. But they all have a place in my heart. I am grateful to them.

I do want to thank by name Jean Appleton, Felicity Bryan, Gavin Johns, Patricia Lankester, George Lucas, Katherine Ponganis, and Nerys Watts. They know why.

And I want to thank Helen. She knows why, too.

BATH, OCTOBER 2015

NOTES

CHAPTER 1: **The House Party**

1. John Galsworthy, *Maid in Waiting* (Di Lernia, 2010), Kindle edition, chap. 11; first published 1931 by Heinemann (London).

2. Henry Channon, *Chips: The Diaries of Sir Henry Channon*, ed. R. R. James (London: Weidenfeld & Nicolson, 1967), 21.

3. Vita Sackville-West and Harold Nicolson, *Vita and Harold: The Letters of Vita Sackville-West and Harold Nicolson, 1910–1962*, ed. Nigel Nicolson (London: Weidenfeld & Nicolson, 1992), 285.

4. Channon, *Chips*, 21.

5. Clement T. Gwynne, "Week-end," *Notes & Queries*, series 5, vol. 12, no. 309 (November 29, 1879): 428.

6. Quoted in Merlin Waterson, *The Country House Remembered: Recollections of Life Between the Wars* (London: Routledge & Kegan Paul, 1985), 77.

7. Loelia Lindsay, *Grace and Favour: The Memoirs of Loelia, Duchess of Westminster* (London: Weidenfeld & Nicolson, 1961), 90.

8. Maud C. Cooke, *Social Etiquette: or Manners and Customs of Polite Society* (London: McDermid & Logan, 1896), 83.

9. Colefax Papers, MS Eng. C.3170, fols. 46–61, Bodleian Library, University of Oxford, UK.

10. Lady Troubridge, *Etiquette and Entertaining* (London: Amalgamated Press, 1939), 11.

11. Ibid., 9.

12. Waterson, *The Country House Remembered*, 58, 59.

13. Lindsay, *Grace and Favour*, 148, 149.

14. Troubridge, *Etiquette and Entertaining*, 134.

15. Channon, *Chips*, 37.

16. Waterson, *The Country House Remembered*, 58.

17. The Duchess of Windsor, *The Heart Has Its Reasons* (New York: David McKay, 1956), 174.

18. Ibid., 175.

19. Ibid., 177.

20. "The Cocktail Habit," *Manchester Guardian*, December 17, 1928, 6.

21. A Member of the Aristocracy (anonymous author), *Manners and Rules of Good Society*, 38th ed. (London: Frederick Warne, 1916), 47.

22. Elizabeth Craig, *Entertaining with Elizabeth Craig* (London: Collins, 1933), 8.

23. Waterson, *The Country House Remembered*, 63.

24. Member, *Manners and Rules of Good Society*, 119, 121.

25. Ibid., 119, 216.

26. Lindsay, *Grace and Favour*, 149.

27. Quoted in Waterson, *The Country House Remembered*, 80.

28. *Manchester Guardian*, April 9, 1928, 6.

29. Waterson, *The Country House Remembered*, 69.

30. Member, *Manners and Rules of Good Society*, 213–214.

31. Lindsay, *Grace and Favour*, 91–2.

32. Philip Tilden, *True Remembrances: The Memoirs of an Architect* (London: Country Life, 1954), 48.

33. Frances Stevenson, *Lloyd George: A Diary by Frances Stevenson*, ed. A. J. P. Taylor (New York: Harper & Row, 1971), 217.

34. Quoted in Peter Stansky, *Sassoon: The Worlds of Philip and Sybil* (New Haven, CT: Yale University Press, 2003), 163.

35. Waterson, *The Country House Remembered*, 132.

36. *Country Life*, March 21, 1931, 369.

37. Waterson, *The Country House Remembered*, 92.

38. Rosina Harrison, *Rose: My Life in Service* (London: Book Club Associates, 1975), 31.

39. *Dundee Evening Telegraph*, November 12, 1926, 4.

40. Ibid.

41. Troubridge, *Etiquette and Entertaining*, 186.

CHAPTER 2: **Everyone Sang**

1. Lady Alda Hoare, Stourhead Annals, MSS NT 3027141, Stourhead, Wiltshire, UK.

2. Sir Henry Hoare, Stourhead Annals, MSS NT 3027141, Stourhead, Wiltshire, UK.

3. Alda Hoare, Stourhead Annals.

4. Henry Hoare, Stourhead Annals.

5. Alda Hoare, Stourhead Annals.

6. Nicholas Mosley, *Julian Grenfell: His Life and the Times of His Death 1888–1915* (New York: Holt, Rinehart and Winston, 1976), 265.

7. *Times* (London), November 12, 1920, 15.

8. Lady Angela Forbes, *Memories and Base Details* (New York: George H. Doran, 1923), 130.

9. John Buchan, *Memory Hold-the-Door: The Autobiography of John Buchan* (London: Hodder & Stoughton, 1940), http://gutenberg.net.au/ebooks12/1201761h.html #chap12, accessed November 17, 2015.

10. Ibid.

11. C. P., "A Revelation of the Pity of War," *Manchester Guardian*, December 29, 1920.

CHAPTER 3: **It Is Ours**

1. Vita Sackville-West and Harold Nicolson, *Vita and Harold: The Letters of Vita Sackville-West and Harold Nicolson*, ed., Nigel Nicolson (London: Weidenfeld & Nicolson, 1992), 67, 113–114.

2. Horace Walpole, *The Letters of Horace Walpole, Earl of Orford* (London: R. Bentley, 1840, 6 volumes), vol. 2, 445.

3. Sackville-West and Nicolson, *Vita and Harold*, 227.

4. Ibid.

5. Harold Nicolson, *Diaries and Letters: 1930–1939*, ed. Nigel Nicolson (London: Collins, 1966), 47.

6. Ibid., 48.

7. Ibid., 247.

8. Ibid., 311.

9. *Country Life*, August 9, 1930, 190.

10. Ibid. The paneling has since been reinstated in the Great Chamber. Sections of the long gallery are now at the Bowes Museum, Barnard Castle, County Durham.

11. *Country Life*, July 19, 1930, 94.

12. The Duke of Montrose, "The Future of the Landowner I," *Country Life*, April 12, 1930, 541.

13. Ibid.

14. *Country Life*, December 28, 1918, 614.

15. *Country Life*, January 10, 1920, 58.

16. *Times* (London), December 31, 1919, 4.

17. *Country Life*, January 4, 1919, 24.

18. *Country Life*, January 11, 1919, 50.

19. *Country Life*, March 8, 1919, 264.

20. *Times Literary Supplement* (London), May 28, 1925, 372.

21. *Times* (London), August 5, 1925, 10.

22. *Times* (London), May 10, 1927, 17.

23. *Times* (London), November 8, 1919, 7.

24. Quoted in John Harris, *Moving Rooms: The Trade in Architectural Salvages* (New Haven, CT, and London: Yale University Press, 2007), 252.

25. *Times* (London), October 1, 1927, 20; October 15, 1927, 23.

26. *Nottingham Evening News*, August 1, 1929.

27. *Montgomery Express and Radnor Times*, August 9, 1921.

28. Quoted in Peter Somerville-Large, *The Irish Country House: A Social History* (London: Sinclair-Stevenson, 1995), 356.

29. *Manchester Guardian*, August 26, 1926, 16.

30. *Manchester Guardian*, January 25, 1926, 5.

31. *Manchester Guardian*, August 30, 1929, 9.

32. *Manchester Guardian*, September 1, 1929.

33. *Manchester Guardian*, February 24, 1928, 7 (referring to Lupton House, Devon); September 15, 1926, 8 (referring to Summerford Park, Cheshire); January 18, 1926, 7 (referring to Rolleston Hall, Staffordshire).

CHAPTER 4: **The King's Houses**

1. *Times*, June 15, 1927, 16.

2. Edward Windsor, *A King's Story: The Memoirs of the Duke of Windsor* (London: Cassell and Company, 1951), 186.

3. Ibid.

4. W. A. R., "Autobiographical Passages in the Life of Mr. Nash," *The Mechanics' Magazine*, 1836, 27.

5. Ibid.

6. *Builder*, August 28, 1847, 405.

7. Lord Stamfordham to Lionel Earle, November 10, 1912, PRO WORK 19/52; in Ian Dungavell, *The Architectural Career of St. Aston Webb (1849–1930)*, PhD thesis, University of London, 1999, 279.

8. *Times* (London), November 12, 1918, 11.

9. Sir John Fortescue, *Author and Curator* (Edinburgh: Blackwood, 1933), 97–98; quoted in Kenneth Rose, *King George V* (London: Weidenfeld & Nicolson, 1983), 296.

10. The list is quoted in Rose, *King George V*, 295.

11. *Times* (London), June 1, 1927, 16.

12. *Observer* (London), September 18, 1927.

13. *Sandringham: A Guide to the Grounds and Museum* (Norwich, UK: Jarrold & Sons, 1976) 1.

14. Windsor, *A King's Story*, 32.

15. www.sandringhamestate.co.uk/house-museum-and-gardens/history, accessed November 18, 2015.

16. Nikolaus Pevsner and Bill Wilson, *The Buildings of England, Norfolk 2: North-West and South* (London: Penguin Books, 2000), 627. Humbert retained a conservatory by S. S. Teulon, which had been added to the eighteenth-century house in 1852; it was turned into a billiard room, and a bowling alley was built on beside it.

17. Alan Powers, "Edis, Sir Robert William (1839–1927)", *Oxford Dictionary of National Biography*, (Oxford University Press, 2004), www.oxforddnb.com.ezproxy .londonlibrary.co.uk/view/article/63284, accessed November 4, 2015.

18. J. Pope-Hennessy, *Queen Mary* (London: Allen & Unwin, 1959), 342.

19. Windsor, *A King's Story*, 74.

20. Rose, *King George V*, 97.

21. Sir Frederick Ponsonby, *Recollections of Three Reigns* (London: Eyre & Spottiswoode, 1951), 279.

22. Both in Rose, *King George V*, 291.

23. John Matson, chapter 12, in *Sandringham Days: The Domestic Life of the Royal Family in Norfolk, 1862–1952* (Stroud, UK: The History Press, 2012).

24. Ibid.

25. Transcript at www.bl.uk/onlinegallery/onlineex/voiceshist/georgev, accessed November 18, 2015.

CHAPTER 5: **Reinstatement**

1. Philip Tilden, *True Remembrances: The Memoirs of an Architect* (London: Country Life, 1954), 11.

2. Ibid., 13.

3. *Country Life*, December 4, 1942, 1082.

4. *Country Life*, May 4, 1918, 424.

5. Sir Martin Conway, "Allington Castle, Kent," *Country Life*, March 31, 1928, 438.

6. Amicia de Moubray, *Twentieth Century Castles in Britain* (London: Frances Lincoln, 2013), 80.

7. Sir Martin Conway, *Episodes in a Varied Life* (London: Country Life, 1932), 101.

8. Ibid., 99.

9. Tilden, *True Remembrances*, 126.

10. Anonymous, *Handbook for Travellers in Kent* (London: John Murray, 1892), 24.

11. Clive Aslet, *The Last Country Houses* (New Haven, CT, and London: Yale University Press, 1982), 190.

12. A Visitor (William Waldorf Astor), "Hever Restored," *The Pall Mall Magazine*, January 1907, 15.

13. Aslet, *Last Country Houses*, 196.

14. Tilden, *True Remembrances*, 114.

15. de Moubray, *Twentieth Century Castles*, 15.

16. Adrian Tinniswood, *Historic Houses of the National Trust* (London: The National Trust, 1991), 39.

17. de Moubray, *Twentieth Century Castles*, 16.

18. Tilden, *True Remembrances*, 114.

19. de Moubray, *Twentieth Century Castles*, 21.

20. Conway, *Episodes in a Varied Life*, 102, 103.

21. de Moubray, *Twentieth Century Castles*, 146.

22. Ibid., 148.

23. Tilden, *True Remembrances*, 164.

24. Christopher Hussey, *Country Life*, December 4, 1942, 1085.

25. E. V. Lucas, "A Wanderer's Notebook," *Sunday Times* (London), July 19, 1931, 10.

26. *Times* (London), May 17, 1921, 1.

27. H. H., "The Rev. F. Meyrick-Jones," *Times* (London), December 20, 1950, 8.

28. Ibid.

29. S. John Elyard, *Some Old Wiltshire Homes* (London: C. J. Clark, 1894), 15.

30. *Country Life*, May 17, 1924, 783.

31. Ibid., 776.

32. Ibid.

33. Ibid., 780.

34. "Mr. E. G. Lister," (obituary), *Times*, July 13, 1956, 14.

35. "Howbridge Hall," *Country Life*, March 8, 1924, 379.

36. Conway, *Episodes in a Varied Life*, 103–104.

37. *Times* (London), January 6, 1912, 7.

38. *Times* (London), September 7, 1921, 4.

39. *Times* (London), June 14, 1923, 15.

40. *Times* (London), May 19, 1919, 8.

41. *Times* (London), September 13, 1921, 13.

chapter 6: **A New Culture**

1. Peter Stansky, *Sassoon: The Worlds of Philip and Sybil* (New Haven, CT, and London: Yale University Press, 2003), 6.

2. Stansky, *Sassoon*, 148; Henry Channon, *Chips: The Diaries of Sir Henry Channon,* ed. R. R. James (London: Weidenfeld & Nicolson, 1967), 202.

3. Stansky, *Sassoon*, 48.

4. Ibid., 46–47.

5. Philip Tilden, *True Remembrances: The Memoirs of an Architect* (London: Country Life, 1954), 42.

6. *Country Life*, May 19, 1923, 681, 682; May 26, 1923, 722.

7. Channon, *Chips*, 73.

8. Ibid., 7.

9. Stansky, *Sassoon*, 153.

10. *Country Life*, May 26, 1923, 718.

11. Virginia Woolf, *The Letters of Virginia Woolf*, eds. Nigel Nicolson and Joanne Trautmann (New York: Mariner Books, 1981), vol. 4, 47.

12. Harold Nicolson, *Diaries and Letters: 1930–1939*, ed. Nigel Nicolson (London: Collins, 1966), 76.

13. Robert Boothby, *I Fight to Live* (London: Victor Gollancz, 1947), 48.

14. Channon, *Chips*, 7, 24.

15. Ibid., 202.

16. *Country Life*, January 10, 1931, 43.

17. *Country Life*, January 10, 1931, 40; *Times* (London), February 17, 1916, 16.

18. *Country Life*, January 10, 1931, 44.

19. Hugh Cecil and Mirabel Cecil, *In Search of Rex Whistler: His Life and Work* (London: Frances Lincoln, 2012), 85.

20. Robert Boothby, *Boothby: Recollections of a Rebel* (London: Hutchinson, 1978), 72.

21. *Country Life*, May 10, 1930, 691.

22. *Country Life*, September 19, 1931, 302.

23. *Country Life*, May 10, 1930, 691.

24. "Is Modern Architecture on the Right Track?," *Listener*, July 26, 1933, 123.

25. *Times* (London), July 8, 1937, 30.

26. Adrian Tinniswood, *The Art Deco House* (London: Mitchell Beazley, 2002), 123.

CHAPTER 7: **Lutyens**

1. "Queen's Dolls' House," *Times* (London), July 29, 1924, xxi.

2. Clayre Percy and Jane Ridley, eds., *The Letters of Edwin Lutyens to His Wife Lady Emily* (London: Collins, 1985), 199.

3. Adrian Tinniswood, *Historic Houses of the National Trust* (London: National Trust, 1991), 272.

4. Percy and Ridley, *The Letters of Edwin Lutyens*, 396.

5. Nikolaus Pevsner, *The Buildings of England: Yorkshire, The West Riding* (London: Penguin Books, 2001), 220.

6. *Times* (London), November 4, 1933, 2.

7. Robert Lutyens, *Six Great Architects* (London: Hamilton, 1959), 182.

8. Ibid., 182.

9. Lutyens to Lady Emily, quoted in Percy and Ridley, *The Letters of Edwin Lutyens*, 397.

10. Gavin Stamp, *Edwin Lutyens Country Houses* (London: Aurum, 2012), 176.

11. "Death of Sir E. Lutyens," *Manchester Guardian*, January 3, 1944, 3.

CHAPTER 8: **Making Plans**

1. A. Welby Pugin, *The True Principles of Pointed or Christian Architecture* (London: John Weale, 1841), 61.

2. George Gilbert Scott, *Remarks on Secular and Domestic Architecture* (London: John Murray, 1857), 149.

3. Hermann Muthesius, *The English House* (Oxford, UK: BSP Professional Books, 1987), 203.

4. Ibid., 205.

5. Mark Girouard, *Life in the English Country House: A Social and Architectural History* (New Haven, CT, and London: Yale University Press, 1978), 310.

6. Harold Nicolson, *Diaries and Letters: 1930–1939*, ed. Nigel Nicolson (London: Collins, 1966), 112.

7. "Modernising Old Country Houses," *Country Life*, June 12, 1920, 841.

8. "Allington Castle," *Country Life*, May 4, 1918, 428.

9. *Country Life*, February 4, 1939, 116.

10. Ibid.

11. Ibid., 118.

12. Ibid., 120.

13. *Country Life*, February 13, 1937, 172.

14. Randall Phillips, "Heath Lodge," *Country Life*, October 25, 1919, 534.

15. *Country Life*, February 13, 1937, 176.

16. Janet Smith, *Liquid Assets: The Lidos and Open Air Swimming Pools of Britain* (London: English Heritage, 2005), 20.

17. Oliver Hill, "The Modern Movement," *Architectural Design and Construction*, September 1, 1931, 461.

18. *Country Life*, February 25, 1939, xxxvii.

19. *Times* (London), May 13, 1938, 22.

20. Evelyn Waugh, *Decline and Fall* (London: Penguin Books, 1986), 128.

21. Ruth Binney, chapter 1, in *Wise Words and Country House Ways* (Newton Abbot, UK: David & Charles, 2012).

22. *Times* (London), February 24, 1921, 5.

23. "Electricity in the Country House: XIX—The Installation at Kimbolton Castle," *Country Life*, February 4, 1939, xxxii.

24. Ibid.

25. Ibid., xxxiii.

26. "Historic Monuments and Buildings Illuminated by Flood-Lighting," *Illustrated London News*, September 5, 1931, 346.

27. Ibid.

28. *Times* (London), September 2, 1931, 12.

29. *British Journal of Ophthalmology* 15 (November 1931): 654.

30. *Times* (London), May 8, 1935, 15.

31. Henry Channon, *Chips: The Diaries of Sir Henry Channon*, ed. R. R. James (London: Weidenfeld & Nicolson, 1967), 205.

32. "Country House Flood-Lighting," *Country Life*, April 3, 1937, 348.

CHAPTER 9: **Home Decorating**

1. Richard B. Fisher, *Syrie Maugham* (London: Duckworth, 1978), 18.

2. This paragraph draws heavily on "Appendix 4: Charles Carrick Allom (1865–1947) and White, Allom & Co.," in Diana Brooks, *Thomas Allom* (London: Heinz Gallery, 1998).

3. Woolf to Gwen Raverat, May 1, 1925, in William Pryor, ed., *Virginia Woolf and the Raverats* (Bath, UK: Clear Books, 2003), 181.

4. Harold Nicolson, *Diaries and Letters: 1930–1939*, ed. Nigel Nicolson (London: Collins, 1966), 264.

5. Sibyl Colefax Ltd. business card, MS Eng. C.3184, fol. 18., Bodleian Library, University of Oxford, UK.

6. Cecil Beaton, *The Glass of Fashion* (London: Weidenfeld & Nicolson, 1954), 210.

7. Kirsty McLeod, *A Passion for Friendship: Sibyl Colefax and Her Circle* (London: Michael Joseph, 1991), 145.

8. A. D. F. Hamlin, *A History of Ornament Ancient and Medieval*, vol. 1 (London: Batsford, 1916), x.

9. H. Avray Tipping, "Old Buckhurst," *Country Life*, October 25, 1919, 525.

10. McLeod, *A Passion for Friendship*, 49.

11. Alec Waugh, *The Best Wine Last* (London: W. H. Allen, 1978), 57.

12. "We Salute . . . ," *Vogue*, November 1, 1932, 34.

13. *Sunday Times*, January 20, 1929, 13; July 22, 1928, 13.

14. Marchese Malacrida, "Modernist Tendencies in Decoration," *Vogue*, October 13, 1928, 98.

15. Ibid., 122.

16. Ibid.

17. F. H. W. Shepard, ed., "Upper Brook Street: North Side," in *Survey of London: Volume 40; The Grosvenor Estate in Mayfair, Part 2 (The Buildings)* (London: London County Council, 1980), 200–210.

18. "The Marchese Malacrida's Apartment," *Vogue*, November 23, 1929, 70.

19. Christopher Hibbert et al., *The London Encyclopaedia* (London: Macmillan, 2008), 271.

20. Clive Aslet, "An Interview with the Late Paul Paget," *The Thirties Society Journal* 6 (1987): 20.

21. Christopher Hussey, "Eltham Hall," *Country Life*, May 29, 1937, 594.

22. Adam de Hegedus, "A Memorial in Letters," *Observer* (London), January 12, 1936.

23. Clive Aslet, "An Interview with the Late Paul Paget," *The Thirties Society Journal* 6 (1987): 20.

CHAPTER 10: **The New Georgians**

1. C. Bruyn Andrews, ed., *The Torrington Diaries*, vol. 3 (London: Methuen Library Reprints, 1970), 314–315.

2. Stephen Calloway, *Twentieth Century Decoration* (London: Weidenfeld & Nicolson, 1988), 240.

3. Martin Wood, *Nancy Lancaster: English Country House Style* (London: Frances Lincoln, 2005), 41.

4. Ibid., 57.

5. *Times* (London), July 5, 1933, 28.

6. Wood, *Nancy Lancaster*, 57.

7. Henry Channon, *Chips: The Diaries of Sir Henry Channon*, ed. R. R. James (London: Weidenfeld & Nicolson, 1967), 39.

8. Thomas Hardy, *Late Lyrics and Earlier* (New York: Macmillan, 1922), v.

9. *Guardian* (London), February 6, 1926, 10.

10. *Times* (London), March 5, 1929, 19.

11. *Times* (London), March 18, 1929, 12.

12. *Times* (London), March 4, 1930, 12.

13. *Country Life*, February 18, 1930, 264.

14. *Times* (London), March 26, 1930, 14.

15. *Times* (London), February 23, 1931, 15.

16. *Times* (London), May 27, 1937, 12.

17. Ronald Tree, *When the Moon Was High* (London: Macmillan, 1975), 43.

18. Wood, *Nancy Lancaster*, 60.

19. Philip Tilden, *True Remembrances: The Memoirs of an Architect* (London: Country Life, 1954), 162.

20. Loelia Lindsay, *Grace and Favour: The Memoirs of Loelia, Duchess of Westminster* (London: Weidenfeld & Nicolson, 1961), 199.

CHAPTER 11: **The Princess Bride and Her Brothers**

1. Quoted in Kenneth Rose, *King George V* (London: Weidenfeld & Nicolson, 1983), 311.

2. Evelyn Graham, *Princess Mary, Viscountess Lascelles: An Intimate and Authoritative Life-Story* (London: Hutchinson, 1929), 243.

3. Ibid., 212.

4. Ibid., 213.

5. *Manchester Guardian*, October 27, 1931, 8.

6. Nikolaus Pevsner and Bridget Cherry, *The Buildings of England: London 1: The City of London* (London: Penguin Books, 1985), 182.

7. Edward Windsor, *A King's Story: The Memoirs of the Duke of Windsor* (London: Cassell and Company, 1951), 239.

8. *Manchester Guardian*, January 3, 1936, 8.

9. *Manchester Guardian*, April 18, 1938, 8.

10. *Times* (London), July 26, 1939, 3.

11. *Times* (London), June 6, 1939, 28.

12. Windsor, *A King's Story*, 333.

13. Sarah Bradford, *George VI* (London: Weidenfeld & Nicolson, 1989), 105.

14. Bradford, *George VI*, 110.

15. *Manchester Guardian*, April 27, 1923, 9.

16. Ibid.

17. Bradford, *George VI*, 114.

18. Ibid.

19. Ibid., 114–115.

20. Ibid., 129.

21. *Country Life*, November 2, 1929, 616.

22. Ibid., 618.

23. Windsor, *A King's Story*, 235.

24. *Country Life*, November 19, 1959, 899.

25. Windsor, *A King's Story*, 236.

26. Ibid., 235.

27. Ibid., 237.

28. Ibid.

29. Diana Cooper, "The Light of Common Day," in *Diana Cooper: Autobiography* (London: Faber Finds, 2014), Kindle edition, chap. 8; first published 1958 by Rupert Hart-Davis (London).

30. Philip Tilden, *True Remembrances: The Memoirs of an Architect* (London: Country Life, 1954), 99.

31. Roger Wilkes, "A Dainty Dish to Set Before the Prince," *Telegraph* (London),

January 9, 2002, www.telegraph.co.uk/property/3297140/A-dainty-dish-to-set
-before-the-Prince.html, accessed November 18, 2015.

32. Gloria Vanderbilt and Thelma Lady Furness, *Double Exposure: A Twin Autobi-ography* (New York: David McKay, 1958), 282.

33. Ibid., 283–284.

34. Ibid., 306.

35. Michael Bloch, ed., *Wallis and Edward: Letters 1931–1937* (London: Weidenfeld & Nicolson, 1986), 294.

36. *Cairns Post*, December 15, 1936, 5.

37. Windsor, *A King's Story*, 380.

38. Ibid., 401.

39. Harold Nicolson, *Diaries and Letters 1930–1939*, ed. Nigel Nicolson (London: Collins, 1966), 282–283.

40. Ibid., 412.

CHAPTER 12: **My New-Found-Land, My Kingdom**

1. Consuelo Vanderbilt Balsan, *The Glitter and the Gold* (Maidstone, UK: George Mann, 1973), 37.

2. Ibid., 40.

3. Quoted in Richard W. Davis, "We Are All Americans Now," *Proceedings of the American Philosophical Society* 135, no. 2 (June 1991): 148.

4. Balsan, *The Glitter and the Gold*, 44.

5. Ibid., 41.

6. *New York Times*, April 19, 1893.

7. Davis, "We Are All Americans Now," 158.

8. Ibid.

9. *Times* (London), June 24, 1921, 13.

10. *Manchester Guardian*, June 14, 1923, 6.

11. Hugo Vickers, "Gladys, Duchess of Marlborough: The Aristocrat with Atti-tude," *Telegraph* (London), February 7, 2011, www.telegraph.co.uk/culture/art/art
-features/8303256/Gladys-Duchess-of-Marlborough-the-aristocrat-with-attitude
.html, accessed November 18, 2015.

12. Amicia de Moubray, *Twentieth Century Castles in Britain* (London: Frances Lincoln, 2013), 103.

13. Edward Windsor, *A King's Story: The Memoirs of the Duke of Windsor* (London: Cassell and Company, 1951), 237.

14. John Harris, *Moving Rooms: The Trade in Architectural Salvages* (New Haven, CT, and London: Yale University Press, 2007), 255–256.

15. *Manchester Guardian*, January 27, 1926, 12; February 24, 1926, 8.

16. *Basildon Park* (Swindon, UK: National Trust, 2004), 2. This George Ferdi-nando may or may not have been the same George Ferdinando who was jailed for twelve months in Dublin in 1894 for a stockbroker fraud.

17. www.waldorfnewyork.com/events/venues-and-floor-plans/third-floor.html, accessed November 18, 2015.

18. *Manchester Guardian*, December 30, 1920, 6.

19. Harris, *Moving Rooms*, 61.

20. Philip Tilden, *True Remembrances: The Memoirs of an Architect* (London: Country Life, 1954), 53.

21. Ibid., 57.

22. de Moubray, *Twentieth Century Castles in Britain*, 134.

23. Tilden, *True Remembrances*, 58.

24. Ibid., 54.

25. Ibid., 56.

26. de Moubray, *Twentieth Century Castles in Britain*, 134.

27. Tilden, *True Remembrances*, 59.

28. http://query.nytimes.com/gst/abstract.html?res=9C06E5DB133AEF3ABC 4E52DFBE66838E639EDE, accessed November 18, 2015.

29. R. T. W. Denning and John B. Hilling, *The Story of St. Donat's Castle and Atlantic College* (Cambridge, UK: D. Brown and Sons, 1983), 69.

30. Marion Davies, *The Annotated Marion*, ed. Taylor Coffman (San Luis Obispo, CA: Coffman Books, 2013), e-book, chap. 7, www.coffmanbooks.com/TAMpdfs /TAMChapter07-v4.pdf, accessed November 19, 2015.

31. *Observer* (London), May 12, 1929, 17.

32. *Times* (London), May 10, 1929, 13.

33. Ibid.

34. A. R. Powys, secretary to the Society for the Protection of Ancient Buildings, in *Times* (London), October 4, 1930, 6.

35. Mary L. Levkoff, *Hearst: The Collector* (New York: Abrams, 2008), 94.

36. Ibid.

37. Denning and Hilling, *Story of St. Donat's Castle and Atlantic College*, 75.

38. Ibid.

39. *Manchester Guardian*, August 3, 1934, 8.

40. Mark Purcell, William Hale, and David Pearson, *Treasures from Lord Fairhaven's Library* (Swindon, UK: National Trust, 2013), 16.

41. *New York Times*, September 19, 1907.

42. Purcell, Hale, and Pearson, *Treasures from Lord Fairhaven's Library*, 21.

43. *Times* (London), January 31, 1929, 14.

44. *Times* (London), June 15, 1923, 28.

45. *Edinburgh Gazette*, January 17, 1933, www.thegazette.co.uk/Edinburgh/issue /14931/page/59/data.pdf, accessed November 18, 2015.

46. Purcell, Hale, and Pearson, *Treasures from Lord Fairhaven's Library*, 8.

47. James Lees-Milne, *Ancestral Voices* (London: Faber & Faber, 1987), 238–239.

48. Robin Fedden, *Anglesey Abbey* (London: National Trust, 1990; first published 1972), 31.

49. A point that is well made by Purcell, Hale, and Pearson in their excellent *Treasures from Lord Fairhaven's Library at Anglesey Abbey*, a book that I have pillaged ruthlessly in my remarks on Fairhaven and Anglesey Abbey.

CHAPTER 13: **A Queer Streak**

1. Mark Amory, *Lord Berners: The Last Eccentric* (London: Faber Finds, 2012), Kindle edition, chap. 6; first published 1999 by Random House (London).

2. Cecil Beaton, *Ashcombe: The Story of a Fifteen-Year Lease* (Stanbridge, Wimborne Minster, Dorset, UK: Dovecote Press, 2014), 44.

3. Ibid., 69.

4. Ibid., 55.

5. Ibid.

6. Ibid., 72.

7. Cecil Beaton, "Suggestions for Fancy Dress," *Vogue*, December 15, 1937, 116.

8. Beaton, *Ashcombe*, 72.

9. Ibid., 74.

10. "Its ultimate fate is unknown," says Matthew Parris, in the account of the affair he included in *Great Parliamentary Scandals* (London: Robson Books, 1995).

11. Paula Byrne, *Mad World: Evelyn Waugh and the Secrets of Brideshead* (London: HarperPress, 2009), 131.

12. Christobel Aberconway, *A Wiser Woman?* (London: Hutchinson, 1966), 127.

13. *Times* (London), March 31, 1931, 17.

14. Byrne, *Mad World*, 144.

15. *Manchester Guardian*, May 15, 1931, 10.

16. Byrne, *Mad World*, 149.

17. Noel Coward, *Present Indicative* (London: Heinemann, 1937), 283.

18. Ibid., 284.

19. *Observer* (London), October 18, 1931, 15.

20. Coward, *Present Indicative*, 309.

21. Amory, *Lord Berners*, chap. 10.

22. Ibid., chap. 11.

23. *Sunday Times* (London), August 11, 1935, 16.

24. *Sunday Times* (London), August 7, 1938, 16.

25. Obituary of Zita James, *Daily Telegraph*, February 23, 2006, www.telegraph.co.uk/news/obituaries/1511193/Zita-James.html, accessed November 18, 2015.

CHAPTER 14: **Field Sports**

1. Duke of Portland, *Men, Women, and Things: Memories of the Duke of Portland* (London: Faber & Faber, 1937).

2. The figure comes from John Martin, "British Game Shooting in Transition, 1900–1945," *Agricultural History*, Spring 2011, 204–224. For what follows I have drawn heavily on Martin's article.

3. A. H. D. Acland et al., *The Land: The Report of the Land Enquiry Committee*, vol. 1, 3rd ed. (London: Hodder & Stoughton, 1913), 260.

4. Julian Tennyson, *Rough Shooting for the Owner-Keeper* (London: A. & C. Black, 1938), 2.

5. Ibid., 31.

6. A Member of the Aristocracy (anonymous author), *Manners and Rules of Good Society* (London: Frederick Warne, 1916), 217.

7. Loelia Lindsay, *Grace and Favour: The Memoirs of Loelia, Duchess of Westminster* (London: Weidenfeld & Nicolson, 1961), 210.

8. Ibid.

9. Member, *Manners and Rules of Good Society*, 223.

10. Cecil Beaton, *Ashcombe: The Story of a Fifteen-Year Lease* (Stanbridge, Wimborne Minster, Dorset, UK: Dovecote Press, 2014), 46.

11. Ibid., 47.

12. *Manchester Guardian*, May 28, 1931, 9.

13. George V to the Prince of Wales, March 30, 1924, in Edward Windsor, *A King's Story* (London: Cassell and Company, 1951), 196.

14. *Ludington Daily News* (MI), January 22, 1936, 6.

15. *Times* (London), December 29, 1934, 19.

16. George Malcolm Thomson, *Lord Castlerosse: His Life and Times* (London: Weidenfeld & Nicolson, 1973), 150.

17. Ibid., 152.

CHAPTER 15: **In Which We Serve**

1. Arthur Martin, *The Small House: Its Architecture and Surroundings* (London: A. Rivers, 1906), 82.

2. Selina Todd, "Domestic Service and Class Relations in Britain 1900–1950," *Past and Present*, no. 203 (May 2009), 195.

3. Frank Victor Dawes, *Not in Front of the Servants* (London: Hutchinson, 1984), 159.

4. Rosina Harrison, ed., *Gentlemen's Gentlemen: My Friends in Service* (London: Arlington Books, 1976), 39.

5. *Times* (London), March 17, 1919, 7.

6. Dawes, *Not in Front of the Servants*, 152–153.

7. *Times* (London), March 18, 1919, 7.

8. P. Thomson and T. Lummis, *Family Life and Work Experience Before 1918, 1870–1973*, interview 388, http://discover.ukdataservice.ac.uk/QualiBank/Document /?id=q-a023053e-6d67-4763-a857-206646a9519.

9. Ibid.

10. Ibid.

11. Geoffrey Tyack, "Service on the Cliveden Estate Between the Wars," *Oral History* 5, no. 1 (Spring 1977): 67.

12. The domestic side of life at Cliveden is particularly well documented. The 1970s saw the appearance of the autobiography of Rosina Harrison, who was in service with the Astors for thirty-five years from 1928, followed by a valuable oral history of the indoor and outdoor staff between the wars by Geoffrey Tyack. In what follows, I have drawn on both sources.

13. Rosina Harrison, *Rose: My Life in Service* (London: Book Club Associates, 1975), 48.

14. Tyack, "Service on the Cliveden Estate," 82.

15. Ibid., 68.

16. Harrison, *Rose*, 163–164.

17. Lee quoted in Harrison, *Rose*, 118.

18. Harrison, *Rose*, 126.

19. Ibid., 121.

20. Ibid., 124.

21. Tyack, "Service on the Cliveden Estate," 71.

22. Harrison, *Rose*, 151.

23. Ibid., 105.

24. Ibid., 64.

25. Ibid., 210.

26. Ibid., 85.

27. Ibid., 86.

28. Ibid., 95.

29. Hilda Newman, *Diamonds at Dinner: My Life as a Lady's Maid in a 1930s Stately Home*, with Tim Tate (London: John Blake, 2013), Kindle edition, chap. 8.

30. Harrison, *Rose*, 137.

31. Tyack, "Service on the Cliveden Estate," 69.

32. Harrison, *Rose*, 115.

33. Ibid., 119.

34. Merlin Waterson, *The Country House Remembered: Recollections of Life Between the Wars* (London: Routledge & Kegan Paul, 1985), 172.

35. Harrison, *Rose*, 120–121.

36. Ibid., 131.

37. Tyack, "Service on the Cliveden Estate," 81.

CHAPTER 16: **The Political House**

1. A. J. A. Morris, *C. P. Trevelyan 1870–1958: Portrait of a Radical* (Belfast, Ireland: Blackstaff Press, 1977), 172.

2. Ibid., 173.

3. Ibid., 192.

4. *Times* (London), August 4, 1936, 10.

5. Ibid., 11.

6. Peter Stansky, *Sassoon: The Worlds of Philip and Sybil* (New Haven, CT: Yale University Press, 2003), 87.

7. Ibid., 92.

8. Ibid.

9. *Hansard*, February 8, 1922.

10. Oswald Mosley, *My Life* (London: Black House Publishing, 2012), Kindle edition, chap. 7; first published 1968 by Thomas Nelson and Sons (London).

11. *Times* (London), May 15, 1920, 14.

12. *Manchester Guardian*, April 25, 1921, 7. The film was *Shoulder Arms*, Chaplin's 1918 war comedy.

13. Stansky, *Sassoon*, 118.

14. Philip Tilden, *True Remembrances: The Memoirs of an Architect* (London: Country Life, 1954), 77.

15. Ibid., 75.

16. Ibid., 81.

17. Frances Stevenson, *Lloyd George: A Diary by Frances Stevenson*, ed. A. J. P. Taylor (New York: Harper & Row, 1971), 284.

18. Churchill to John Leaning & Sons Ltd. (his firm of chartered surveyors), September 4, 1926; quoted in Stefan Buczacki, *Churchill and Chartwell* (London: Frances Lincoln, 2007), 141.

19. Tilden to Clarice Fisher, Churchill's secretary, March 17, 1927; in Buczacki, *Churchill and Chartwell*, 151.

20. Norma Major, *Chequers: The Prime Minister's Country House and Its History* (London: HarperCollins, 1996), 70, 111.

21. *Times* (London), October 5, 1917, 3.

22. Ibid.

23. Ibid.

24. Ibid.

25. Major, *Chequers*, 99.

26. Ibid., 104.

27. Ibid., 166.

28. *Manchester Guardian*, October 20, 1923, 10.

29. Baldwin Papers 123/58, August 19, 1937; quoted in Andrew Roberts, *The Holy Fox: The Life of Lord Halifax* (London: Head of Zeus, 2014), Kindle edition, chap. 7; first published 1991 by Weidenfeld and Nicolson (London).

30. Ibid.

31. *Manchester Guardian*, December 31, 1938, 11.

32. *Times* (London), May 5, 1938, 17.

33. Harold Nicolson, *Diaries and Letters: 1930–1939*, ed. Nigel Nicolson (London: Collins, 1966), 266.

34. Ibid.

35. Norman Rose, *The Cliveden Set: Portrait of an Exclusive Fraternity* (London: Vintage Digital, 2011), Kindle edition, chap. 8; first published 2000 by Jonathan Cape (London).

36. *Manchester Guardian*, March 28, 1938, 9.

37. Reported in *Western Daily Press* (Bristol), December 17, 1938, 7.

38. *Manchester Guardian*, May 23, 1939, 8.

39. Rose, *The Cliveden Set*, chap. 8.

40. Rosina Harrison, *Rose: My Life in Service* (London: Book Club Associates, 1975), 244.

41. Nicolson, *Diaries and Letters: 1930–1939*, 396.

42. Rose, *The Cliveden Set*, chap. 9.

43. http://hansard.millbanksystems.com/lords/1939/apr/13/the-international-situation#S5LV0112P0_19390413_HOL_15, accessed November 18, 2015.

chapter 17: **The Old Order Doomed**

1. *Times* (London), May 26, 1939, 11.

2. *Times* (London), May 25, 1939, 17.

3. *Table Talk* (Melbourne), August 10, 1939, 10.

4. *Lancashire Evening Post*, July 15, 1939, 4.

5. *Bucks Herald* (Aylesbury), July 21, 1939, 3.

6. *Dundee Courier*, August 8, 1939, 7.

7. *Hull Daily Mail* (Yorkshire), August 26, 1939, 5.

8. *Country Life*, July 22, 1939, 56.

9. *Country Life*, March 4, 1939, xxxiii.

10. "Some Things You Should Know If War Should Come," Civil Defence Public Information Leaflet No. 1, Lord Privy Seal's Office (July 1939).

11. Ibid.

12. *Country Life*, September 30, 1939, 325.

13. Roy Strong, *Country Life, 1897–1997: The English Arcadia* (London: Country Life, 1996), 130.

14. *Times* (London), July 20, 1934, 9.

15. *Times* (London), February 26, 1936, 9.

16. *Observer* (London), July 11, 1937, 32.

17. *Manchester Guardian*, November 19, 1937, 12.

18. *Observer* (London), July 11, 1937, 32.

19. John Martin Robinson, *Requisitioned: The British Country House in the Second World War* (London: Aurum Press, 2014), 120.

20. Strong, *Country Life, 1897–1997*, 134.

21. Ibid., 128.

22. Mark Amory, *Lord Berners: The Last Eccentric* (London: Faber Finds, 2012), Kindle edition, chap. 16; first published 1999 by Random House (London).

23. *Western Daily Press* (Bristol), October 22, 1934, 7.

24. *Manchester Guardian*, June 15, 1935, 14.

25. *Gloucester Citizen*, June 17, 1940, 7.

INDEX

Helen Rogers

Adrian Tinniswood is a Senior Research Fellow at the University of Buckingham and the author of many books, including *The Rainborowes* (Basic) and *The Verneys*, which was shortlisted for the BBC Samuel Johnson Prize for Nonfiction. His book *His Invention So Fertile* was a *New York Times* Essential Summer Reading selection and was named one of the *Times's* Notable Books of 2002. Tinniswood has worked with heritage institutions including the National Trust and the Heritage Lottery Fund, and has lectured at English and American universities, including Bristol, Oxford, Nebraska-Lincoln, and UC Berkeley. In 2013 he was awarded an OBE by the queen for services to heritage.